In Search of the Simple Life

In

Search

David E. Shi

PEREGRINE SMITH BOOKS

GIBBS M. SMITH, INC.

SALT LAKE CITY, UTAH

of the

Simple

Life

AMERICAN VOICES,

PAST AND PRESENT

Published by Gibbs M. Smith, Inc.
P.O. Box 667, Layton, Utah 84041

Printed and bound in the United States of America

90 89 88 87 86 5 4 3 2 1

First Edition

Painting on the jacket: *Independence
(Squire Jack Porter)* by Frank Mayer,
courtesy the National Museum of American Art

Book design by M. Clane Graves

Library of Congress Cataloging-in-Publication Data

In search of the simple life.

Bibliography: p.
1. Simplicity—Religious aspects—Christianity—
Addresses, essays, lectures. 2. Simplicity—Moral and
ethical aspects—Addresses, essays, lectures. I.
Shi, David E.
BV4647.S48I5   1986   248.4   85–26174
ISBN 0-87905-217-1

Acknowledgments of permission to use copyrighted
materials will be found at the end of this book.

For my mother and father

Contents

To know the chief rival attitudes toward life as the history of thinking has developed them, and to have heard some of the reasons they can give for themselves ought to be considered an essential part of liberal education.

—*William James*

Introduction

Simplicity, simplicity, simplicity!" This was Henry David Thoreau's repeated message to those of his countrymen caught up in the spiral of compulsive getting and spending. It was good advice. And it has become even more relevant with the passage of time. Americans still lead lives of "quiet desperation." Underneath the glamor and glitter of affluent life is the disturbing fact that the three most frequently prescribed drugs are an ulcer medication, a hypertension reliever, and a tranquilizer. Many people yearn for a means of escape from the excesses of consumerism and careerism. To cite but one example: a California company selling books recorded on cassette tapes for people to listen to as they commute to and from work reports that one of the most popular selections is Thoreau's *Walden*. Though the Concord poet and saunterer would no doubt cringe at the thought of Los Angeles commuters rushing to work through smog-shrouded streets, he might take solace in the fact that Americans in the late twentieth century are still attracted by his philosophy of living.

Indeed, the concept of simpler living has always been a prominent aspect of American thought. Long before Thoreau began professing simplicity's virtues, commentators had been stressing the dangers of luxury and the virtues of an ethic of plain living and high thinking. From the colonial period to the present, moralists and intellectuals, some well-known, others unfamiliar, have rejected the sumptuous life in favor of some version of the simple life. These idealists—John Winthrop, John Woolman, Samuel Adams, John and Abigail Adams, Thomas Jefferson, Ralph Waldo Emerson, Thoreau, John Burroughs, Lewis Mumford, Scott and Helen Nearing, Wendell Berry, and many others—have viewed America primarily as a spiritual commonwealth and a republic of virtue rather than as a cornucopia of worldly delights and entrepreneurial opportunities. In doing so they have sustained an elevated vision of the good life that has proved both enduring and elusive.

This anthology is intended to illuminate the rich heritage of the simple life by presenting journal entries, correspondence, essays, sermons, poems, prints, paintings, and photographs dealing with the subject from the seventeenth century to the present. These original materials convey the variety, color, and persistence of the ideal over the years. Selections are organized chronologically according to certain broad themes and trends. Chapter introductions and headnotes provide background and context, but the selections themselves offer the clearest and most compelling insights into the complex history of the simple life in the American experience.

As the following readings indicate, the simple life is not simple—either to define or to live. There is no universal formula or convenient checklist that specifies what is simple and what is not. The meaning of simple living can never be precisely stated because it is not a single idea. Rather it is an imprecise label used to refer to one or more of the following attitudes, ideas, and beliefs: a concern for family nurture and community cohesion; a hostility toward luxury and a suspicion of riches; a belief that the primary reward of work should be well-being rather than money; a desire for maximum personal self-reliance and creative leisure; a nostalgia for the supposed simplicities of the past and an anxiety about the technological and bureaucratic complexities of the present and future; a taste for the plain and functional, especially in the home environment; a reverence for nature and a preference for country living; and a sense of both religious and ecological responsibility for the proper use of the world's resources. What unifies this cluster of attitudes is the conscious desire to purge life of some of its complexities and superfluities in order to pursue 'higher' values—faith, family, civic duty, artistic creativity, and social service.

Of course such a vision of the good life is not unique to the American scene. Simplicity is an old and universal ethic, perhaps primordially old. Most of the world's great religions and philosophies have advocated some form of simple living. The Greek and Roman moral philosophers preached the virtues of the golden mean, as did the Old Testament prophets—Amos, Hosea, and Jeremiah. As the author of Proverbs prayed, "Give me neither poverty nor wealth but only enough." And it was such a life of pious simplicity that Jesus led and preached. He repeatedly warned of the "deceitfulness of riches" and the corrupting effects of luxury. Experience had shown, he noted, that it was "easier for a camel to go through the head of a needle than for a rich man to enter into the kingdom of God." The way to avoid the dangers of covetousness and overindulgence was to exercise restraint and relish contentment.

So much for the ideal and its tradition. What does this ethic of plain living and high thinking entail in practice? This is where the concept becomes even more slippery. The nature and extent of simplicity vary greatly from individual to individual and from era to era. As a way station between too little and too much, the ethic encompasses a wide spectrum of motives and behavior, a spectrum bounded on one end by religious asceticism and on the other by refined gentility. In between there is much room for individual expression.

Over the years people have differed dramatically in their methods and motives for promoting such values. Simplicity is an ideal that cuts across the conventional ideological spectrum. Some proponents have been quite conservative, even reactionary, in appealing to traditional values and ways of life; others have been liberal or radical in their assault on corporate capitalism and its ethos of compulsive consumerism. Federalists, Jeffersonians, Whigs, Democrats, Transcendentalists, Republicans, Libertarians, and Socialists are among the political perspectives represented here. Many Americans have been led to seek simplicity out of a deep sense of religious commitment. Others have been provoked by more secular but still potent concerns. In addition, class biases, individual personality traits, and historical circumstances have also combined to produce many differing versions of simple living in the American experience. Consequently, there is no simple life as such that can be universally prescribed or adopted, only an array of different patterns of living that in their own context are considered "simpler" than other ways of life.

It is a mistake, therefore, to associate simple living solely with rustic serenity or mortifying self-denial, as is so often the case in the popular mind. Although most proponents of the ideal have celebrated an unassuming, self-sustaining country life, such pastoral contentment has not been the only path to simplicity. The suburban or urban dweller whose spending is guided by carefully considered choices may also be leading a simple life. Nor is simplicity merely a joyless program of denial. While preaching self-restraint and conscientious consumption, the simple life does not mandate a primitive or monastic regimen. The essence of simplicity is not in renunciation but in discrimination. It requires learning to distinguish between the necessary and superfluous, between the useful and wasteful, beautiful and vulgar. Wisdom, the philosopher William James once remarked, is knowing what to overlook. Indeed, the key to mastering the fine art of simple living is discovering the difference between personal trappings and personal traps.

And each individual must learn that lesson on his own. The exemplars of simple living presented here offer insights and experiences, not models to be slavishly followed. As Thoreau stressed in *Walden*, "I would not have anyone adopt *my* mode of living on my account. . . . I would have each one be very careful to find out and pursue *his own* way." Simplicity requires an individual commitment and an individual program. In this sense it is ultimately a state of mind, a well-ordered inner harmony among the material, sensual, and ideal, rather than a particular standard of living. It preaches contentment and self-control and promises spontaneity and freedom.

If the simple life is difficult to define, it is even more

difficult to live. As these selections reveal, the history of the simple life has been a festival of irony. American culture, of course, has always been animated by contradictory impulses. The United States is at once the most materialistic and idealistic country in the world. We have been a nation of dreamers and schemers. And the ideal of enlightened restraint has always been linked in an awkward dialectical embrace with the growth of abundance and complexity. People have both celebrated and questioned the effects of unparalleled prosperity. The nation's phenomenal economic and social expansion has in one sense provoked the desire for simpler living. Only those who have too much can aspire to live on less. Only those surrounded by bigness can decide that smaller is more beautiful.

Yet if America's abundance has made simplicity possible, it has also helped prevent it from being widely embraced. The hedonistic values of the consumer culture have become so deeply embedded in the popular imagination and in the social structure that it has become increasingly difficult to sustain a simpler way of life in the midst of such prosperity. Initially espoused as a societal ethic, for all to accept and practice, simplicity has in fact only been practiced by a distinct minority. Americans have found it devilishly hard to locate and maintain that elusive middle way between poverty and luxury.

This is not surprising. Since the colonial era, advocates of simple living have been professing a way of life at odds with an American environment full of bountiful resources, entrepreneurial opportunities, and increasingly powerful institutions that combine to exalt the glories of self-indulgence and war against contentment. In the face of such alluring and potent forces, the ideal of enlightened restraint has been generally disregarded by the public at large—and by historians. We have become a people increasingly dependent on plenty, frenetic in our pursuit of wealth, conspicuous in our consumption, notorious for our wastefulness, and often ruthless in our individualism.

In the process we have lost sight of many traditional values. As the distinguished sociologist Daniel Bell stressed in *The Cultural Contradictions of Capitalism* (1976), the modern consumer culture threatens to overwhelm individual self-expression. "By the 1950s," he argued, American "culture was no longer concerned with how to work and achieve." Instead it "had become primarily hedonistic, concerned with play, fun, display, and pleasure—and, typical of things in America, in a compulsive way." Bell feared that a society employing consumption to achieve "self-realization" or "self-gratification" was in danger of self-destruction. Two years later, historian and social critic Christopher Lasch made the same point even more forcefully in his surprise best-seller, *The Culture of Narcissism.* Like a modern Jeremiah, he relentlessly catalogued the sins and conceits of modern American life— excessive egoism, smothering bureaucracy, dehumanizing technology, pervasive envy, greed, and self-display. And he charged that modern mass advertising was largely to blame for such social ills. By manipulating public desires, it creates a consumer who is "perpetually unsatisfied, restless, anxious, and bored." Advertising "upholds consumption as the answer to the age-old discontents of loneliness, sickness, weariness, lack of sexual satisfaction; at the same time it creates new forms of discontent peculiar to the modern age."

There is much truth to such charges. The capitalist system and its pervasive medium—advertising—do wield great power. Every time we read a newspaper or magazine, turn on the television or radio, or glance at billboards, we are confronted with the alluring propaganda of consumption. Yet Madison Avenue has not simply foisted compulsive acquisitiveness upon an unknowing and unwilling public. Long before the emergence of mass marketing and sophisticated advertising, Americans expressed their eagerness to embrace material standards of value and behavior. As several of the following readings indicate, moralists were lamenting the misplaced priorities and personal weaknesses of their countrymen as early as the seventeenth century, long before commercial capitalism became the dominant social force. Thus it is too facile to argue that corporate capitalism has defeated simple living by *imposing* upon Americans a consumer culture mentality; people from the first days of settlement have expressed their own desire for such a way of life. The relationship between the economic order and popular behavior has been more reciprocal than most contemporary social critics recognize. In this sense modern advertising reflects as well as shapes societal values and consumer preferences. Human nature, it seems, tends to incline people to want more and more and to be impatient with less. Recent reports of "excessive consumerism" in Russia and the People's Republic of China reveal that even in socialist countries the public can be preoccupied with the cult of more and more.

So it is not surprising that simple living has always been a minority ethic. Both our natural selves and our economic system militate against such enlightened restraint. The modern consumer culture has displayed tremendous absorptive capacities, and it has frequently co-opted sincere challenges to its materialistic ethos. The "hippie" phenomenon of the 1960s, for example, was eventually transformed into a retailing bonanza. Entrepreneurs and marketing specialists were also quick to exploit the interest in ecological concerns and simpler living in the 1970s. "Come to Metropolitan and simplify your life," crowed one commercial for an insurance company. Hence, the history of the simple life in the United States has frequently been the tale of repeated frustrations and compromises.

In some cases these defeats have been self-inflicted. Proponents of simplicity have often been naively sentimental about the quality of life in olden times, narrowly anti-urban in outlook, and disdainful of the liberating and enlightening effects of prosperity and technology. Any virtue pressed too far can become counterproductive. Some simplifiers have reverted to a primitive and sometimes fanatical survivalism in order to live out their version of the good life; others have displayed a self-righteous, prickly individualism that has alienated potential supporters and impeded attempts at collective social or political action. And a few have been faddish or silly in their simplicity. Showy plainness is the red spider in the rose of simple living.

Yet the following readings reveal that the history of the simple life is a history of victories as well as defeats. There have been many successful and inspiring practitioners of simple living. Most have sustained their ideal on an individual basis. The few successful collective expressions of simple living, such as those practiced by the Amish or Hutterites, have usually been distinctive for their intense spiritual commitment and rigid framework of regulations and enforcement procedures. But whatever method employed, Americans have displayed since the seventeenth century the will and wisdom required to preserve their version of simplicity in the face of contrary forces. As a guide for individual living and as a myth for dreaming, simplicity has thus displayed remarkable resiliency. No sooner is it declared an anachronism than it undergoes a revival of interest. During periods of war, depression, or social crisis, its merits have been successfully invoked by politicians, ministers, and reformers to help revitalize public virtue, self-restraint, and mutual aid. In this way simplicity has exerted a powerful influence on the complex patterns of American culture.

The concept of the simple life, however ambiguous, however fitfully realized, has survived in part because it speaks to an idealistic strain inherent in human nature. There is indeed something obvious yet ennobling in its attempt to elevate aspirations beyond the material and the mundane. Who has not occasionally yearned for simplicity, for a reduction in the pace and complexity of everyday life and material encumbrances? In the American experience the simple life has remained particularly enticing because it reminds us of what so many of the original settlers and "founding fathers" hoped America would become—a nation of practical dreamers devoted to spiritual, civic, and ideal purposes, a "city upon a hill" serving as a beacon of piety, enlightenment, and moderation to the rest of the world.

Today, simplicity remains what it has always been: an animating vision of moral purpose. It offers us the recovery of personal autonomy and meaning through the stripping away of faulty desires and extraneous activities and possessions. But as is the case with all noble visions, most people prefer to view it from a distance. Yet even though the ideal does not move the millions, it still seizes and nourishes sensitive imaginations. Properly interpreted, a modern version of the simple life informed by its historical tradition can be a socially constructive and personally satisfying path to happiness.

Happiness. Americans have always considered its pursuit to be their inalienable right. Indeed it should be. But how few of us have carefully considered the meaning of that elusive concept. One purpose of this anthology is to provoke readers to reflect upon their vision of happiness. For those already committed to the ideal of simple living, who still believe that less can mean more, the following selections will reveal that you are in good company. There has indeed been an inspiring tradition of plain living and high thinking in the American experience. For those living in a press of anxieties, straining desperately, hectically, often miserably after more money, more things, and more status, only to wonder in troubled moments how to get off such a treadmill, these past and present spokesmen for simplicity may provide the answer. And finally, for those who genuinely prefer the cult of more and more, whose sense of well-being is truly increased by ostentation and luxury, and who are impatient with transcendent ideals and the demands of self-reliant living, this material will challenge your beliefs.

VOLUNTARY SIMPLICITY
Richard Gregg

Voluntary simplicity involves both inner and outer condition. It means singleness of purpose, sincerity and honesty within, as well as avoidance of exterior clutter, of many possessions irrelevant to the chief purpose of life. It means an ordering and guiding of our energy and our desires, a partial restraint in some directions in order to secure greater abundance of life in other directions. It involves a deliberate organization of life for a purpose. . . . Of course, as different people have different purposes in life, what is relevant to the purpose of one person might not be relevant to the purpose of another. Yet it is easy to see that our individual lives and community life would be much changed if every one organized and graded and simplified his purposes so that one purpose would easily dominate all the others, and if each person then re-organized his outer life in accordance with this new arrangement of purposes,—discarding possessions and activities irrelevant to the main purpose. The degree of simplification is a matter for each individual to settle for himself.

Richard Gregg, *The Value of Voluntary Simplicity* (Wallingford, Pa.: Pendle Hill, 1936), p. 2.

Pious Simplicity

1

A variety of motives spurred the settlers who migrated to America in the seventeenth and eighteenth centuries. Some risked the Atlantic passage in order to make a fortune, or at least better their economic condition. Others were intent primarily upon escaping religious persecution and establishing communities of piety and virtue. Many, no doubt, had both economic and spiritual motives. Certainly this was the case with the Pilgrims who arrived at Plymouth in 1620, and the more numerous Puritans who began streaming into Massachusetts Bay in the 1630s and after. But the New England "saints" insisted that religion was their guiding motive. Those who signed the Mayflower Compact affirmed that the voyage was undertaken primarily "for the glory of God and advancement of the Christian faith."

These religious dissenters brought with them to the New World a delicately balanced social ethic stressing hard work, self-control, plain living, civic virtue, social harmony, and spiritual devotion. They were intent upon establishing what Governor John Winthrop called a New Eden of "increasing knowledge, power, goodness and truth." Theirs would be a model society in which simplicity of worship, dress, manners, and speech would be practiced and enforced. The Puritans were to walk the narrow tightrope between poverty and luxury. People were encouraged to work hard and be frugal, and at the same time resist the temptations of riches and the sin of covetousness. This "middle way" was the core of the Puritan ethic.

To ensure the success of their Bible Commonwealth, Winthrop and the other magistrates initially regulated prices and wages and established sumptuary laws prescribing appropriate attire for a godly community. Within a few years, however, they found themselves waging a losing battle against the combined effects of rapid population growth, religious pluralism, and a selfish materialism. Their fragile synthesis of hard work, social deference, spiritual devotion, and plain living did not hold. Promoting simplicity and piety among an increasingly diverse people proved impossible, and by the 1660s, pulpits in Massachusetts began to resound with lamentations bemoaning the degeneracy of the colony. New sumptuary laws were passed, but they too were soon disregarded by a populace unwilling to accept restraints upon their social behavior.

The simple Puritans were becoming grasping Yankees. Or so it seemed to disgruntled traditionalists. Not even the fiery revivals of the Great Awakening (1730–1750) could reverse the tide of individualism and materialism. The Puritans thus found themselves caught in the ideological bind inherent in the Protestant work ethic. Their emphasis on industry and frugality inevitably brought prosperity and the temptations of luxury and indolence. Boston merchants grew wealthy, and they chafed at restrictions on their right to display their prosperity. Likewise, many of the industrious laboring folk felt oppressed by restrictions on their upward social mobility. The Puritan leaders, much to their dismay, never learned how to limit social excesses without stifling economic enterprise. By the nineteenth century the British literary traveler Anthony Trollope could wryly note that Boston still "calls itself a Puritan city, but it has divested its Puritans of austerity. . . . The Puritans of Boston are single in their tastes and expense. Champagne and canvas-back ducks I found to be the provisions most in vogue among those who desired to adhere to the manners of their forefathers."

In the 1680s, as the New England Puritans were struggling to maintain their original social vision, another group of religious dissenters left England and began establishing their own "holy experiment" in the Delaware Valley. Though the Society of Friends differed vehemently with the Puritans over several key theological matters, they shared a common allegiance to the ideal of simple living. Indeed, the Quakers were even more explicit in advocating plain living and spiritual devotion. George Fox, the founder of the sect, told his followers that "you must always outstrip and exceed the world, in virtue, in purity, in chastity, in godliness, and in holiness; and in modesty, civility, and in righteousness, and in love."

Encouraged and facilitated by their proprietor, William Penn, these Quaker colonists quickly established thriving settlements and farms in West Jersey and Pennsylvania. And soon they too began to experience the tension between piety and prosperity that was plaguing the Puritans. Pennsylvania's economic opportunities and religious toleration attracted increasing numbers of German and Scots-Irish settlers. By 1750 Quakers were a distinct minority in Pennsylvania, even though they still maintained tenuous political control. But this was of little comfort to those Friends anxious about the growing worldliness of their fellow Quakers. During the mid-eighteenth century the same pleas for revival and regeneration that had echoed through Puritan meetinghouses began to be heard in Quaker meetings.

The Friends, however, were able to revitalize their original social ideals to a much greater degree than had the Puritans. The reformers succeeded in part because they were willing to give up political control of the colony in order to preserve their community ethic. Equally important to their success was the saintly leadership provided by Quaker reformers such as John Woolman. He became an inspiring symbol of piety and plainness and thereby helped provoke a dramatic revival during the second half of the eighteenth century. Quaker meetings during the 1770s and after adopted stringent disciplinary procedures in an attempt to reform or purge those Friends who flagrantly violated traditional principles.

Yet the reforming Friends paid a price for their sincerity of purpose. They increasingly became a "quiet and peculiar" people set apart from the larger society. Moreover, disputes over theological and social issues continued to fragment the sect. Living a simple life of piety and pacifism proved too taxing or too dull for many Friends, and they either grew spiritually indifferent or opted for more fashionable Protestant churches.

That neither the Puritans nor the Quakers were able to translate their original ideal of pious simplicity into an enduring *societal* ethic testifies to the difficulty of sustaining such a self-limiting ideal in the face of growing social diversity and alluring economic and social opportunities. Never again would Christian simplicity be comprehensively enforced by the state. Yet the dream of America as a spiritual "city upon a hill" and a beacon of pious simplicity did not die. Even as their countrymen rushed to seize the main chance and parade their new wealth, many American idealists during the eighteenth century and after would adhere to the command to love the world with weaned affections.

John Winthrop's Journal

The Puritans' efforts to strike a well-ordered balance between the priorities of the spirit and the needs of the flesh produced both joy and frustration. No one was more aware of such difficulties and exhilarations than John Winthrop (1588–1649), the first governor of Massachusetts Bay. Born into a prominent family in Suffolk, England, he led the life of a young country gentleman, having attended Cambridge and practiced law in London before succeeding his father as lord of Groton manor. He remembered that as a youth he was "very wild, and dissolute, and as years came on my lusts grew stronger." But at some point as a young man, perhaps during a serious illness, he underwent an intense conversion experience and became a Puritan. Thereafter, for the next several years, he struggled to learn how to "love the world with moderation and God without." As his journal entries between 1606 and 1616 indicate, it was not easy to practice the Puritan ethic. But he persisted and eventually discovered a "middle way" between complete renunciation of the world and its delights and complete indulgence.

In my youth I was very lewdly disposed, inclining unto and attempting (so far as my years enabled me) all kind of wickedness, except swearing and scorning religion, which I had no temptation unto in regard of my education. About ten years of age, I had some notions of God, for in some great frighting or danger, I have prayed unto God, and have found manifest answer; the remembrance whereof many years after made me think that God did love me, but it made me no whit the better. . . .

The 20 of April 1606, I made a new Covenant with the Lord which was this:

Of my part, that I would reform these sins by his grace: pride, covetousness, love of this world, vanity of mind, unthankfulness, sloth, both in his service and in my calling, not preparing myself with reverence and uprightness to come to his word: Of the Lord's part that he would give me a new heart, joy in his spirit, that he would dwell with me, that he would strengthen me against the world, the flesh, and the Devil, that he would forgive my sins and increase my faith.

God give me grace to perform my promise and I doubt not but he will perform his. God make it fruitful. Amen.

Feb. [1611]. Getting my self to take too much delight in a vain thing which I went about without the warrant of faith, I was by it by degrees drawn to make shipwreck of a good conscience and the love of my father, so as my heart began to grow hardened and inclining to a reprobate mind; prayer and other duties began to grow irksome, my confidence failed me, my Comfort left me, yet I longed after reconciliation, but could not obtain it; I earnestly sought to repent but could not get an heart unto it, I grew weary of myself, unprofitable to others, and God knows whether ever I shall recover that estate which I lost;—O that this might be a warning to me to take good heed how I grieve the good spirit of my God and wound my conscience, and that as the penning of this is in many tears, so the reading of it when occasion shall may be a strong motive unto sobriety. . . .

May 23, 1613. When my condition was much straightened, partly through my long sickness, partly through want of freedom, partly through lack of outward things, I prayed often to the Lord for deliverance, referring the means to himself, and with all I promised to put forth myself to much fruit when the Lord should enlarge me. . . . I do resolve first to give myself, my life, my wit, my health, my wealth to the service of my God and Saviour, who by giving himself for me, and to me, deserves whatsoever I am or can be, to be at his Commandment, and for his glory:

2. I will live where he appoints me.

3. I will faithfully endeavor to discharge that calling which he shall appoint me unto.

4. I will carefully avoid vain and needless expenses that I may be the more liberal to good uses.

5. My property, and bounty, must go forth abroad, yet I must ever be careful that it begin at home.

6. I will so dispose of my family affairs as my morning prayers and evening exercises be not omitted.

7. I will have a special care of the good education of my children.

8. I will banish profanities from my family.

9. I will diligently observe the Lords Sabbath both for the avoiding and preventing [of] worldly business, and also for the religious spending of such times as are free from public exercises, viz. the morning, noon, and evening.

10. I will endeavor to have the morning free for private prayer, meditation and reading.

11. I will flee Idleness, and much worldly business.

12. I will often pray and confer privately with my wife. . . .

1616. I find by often and evident experience, that when I hold under the flesh by temperate diet, and not suffering the mind or outward senses to have every thing that they desire, and wean it from the love of the world, I ever then pray without weariness, or ordinary wandering of heart, and am far more fit and cheerful to the duties of my calling and other duties, performing them with more alacrity and comfort than at other times.

Not long after falling into a light ague, I took occasion thereby to favor myself more than I needed, and Satan made use of this opportunity by reason of the weakness of my head to fill my heart, first with wandering thoughts, so drawing me from good meditations, and then enticing me to delight in worldly thoughts, which at last my heart did embrace so eagerly, as I could not for my life get my mind from them, but they interrupted my prayers, broke my sleep, abated the wanted relish of heavenly things, took away my appetite from the word, made the duties of my calling tedious,

John Winthrop.

and filled me with much discomfort, so as I thought upon that saying, All is vanity, and vexation of spirit.

I see therefore I must keep a better watch over my heart, and keep my thoughts close to good things, and not suffer a vain or worldly thought to enter, etc.: lest it draw the heart to delight in it. . . .

When I had some time abstained from such worldly delights as my heart most desired, I grew very melancholic and uncomfortable, for I had been more careful to refrain from an outward conversation in the world, than to keep the love of the world out of my heart, or to uphold my conversation in heaven; which caused that my comfort in God failing, and I not daring to meddle with any earthly delights, I grew into a great dullness and discontent: which being at last perceived, I examined my heart, and finding it needful to recreate my mind with some outward recreation, I yielded unto it, and by a moderate exercise herein was much refreshed; but here grew the mischief: I perceiving that God and mine own conscience did allow me so to do in my need, I afterwards took occasion, from the benefit of Christian liberty, to pretend need of recreation when there was none, and so by degrees I ensnared my heart so far in worldly delights, as I cooled the graces of the spirit by them: Whereby I perceive that in all outward comforts, although God allow us the use of the things themselves, yet it must be in sobriety, and our hearts must be kept free, for he is jealous of our love, and will not endure any pretenses in it.

Massachusetts Historical Society, *Winthrop Papers*, 5 vols. (Boston: Plimpton Press, 1929), 1:154, 162, 166, 168, 197-98, 200-02. [I have taken the liberty of modernizing the spelling of this selection.]

A Modell of Christian Charity

John Winthrop

By 1629 John Winthrop was forty years of age, had a large family, and found himself struggling to manage a floundering English estate that could not support his seven sons. Equally unsettling was the government's growing religious intolerance and the general decline in spirituality and sobriety among his English countrymen. Such conditions led him to encourage the idea of a Puritan migration to the New World. He was named governor and embarked on March 22, 1630, on the *Arbella*, with three of his sons. The rest of the family would join him later. During the Atlantic crossing Winthrop delivered a lay sermon entitled "A Modell of Christian Charity," which has become justly famous as a representative statement of the original Puritan social ethic. It is an inspiring and forceful description of what he and other early leaders hoped the Massachusetts Bay Colony would become—a cohesive, deferential community of simple and pious souls dedicated to the public good and the life of the spirit.

Thus stands the cause between God and us. We are entered into covenant with Him for this work, we have taken out a commission, the Lord hath given us leave to draw our own articles, we have professed to enterprise these actions upon these and these ends, we have hereupon besought Him of favor and blessing. Now if the Lord shall please to hear us, and bring us in peace to the place we desire, then hath He ratified this covenant and sealed our commission, [and] will expect a strict performance of the articles contained in it, but if we shall neglect the observations of these articles which are the ends we have propounded, and dissembling with our God, shall fall to embrace this present world and prosecute our carnal intentions, seeking great things for ourselves and our posterity, the Lord will surely break out in wrath against us, be revenged of such a perjured people, and make us know the price of the breach of such a covenant.

Now the only way to avoid this shipwreck and to provide for our posterity is to follow the counsel of Micah, to do justly, to love mercy, to walk humbly with our God. For this end we must be knit together in this work as one man, we must entertain each other in brotherly affection, we must be willing to abridge ourselves of our superfluities for the supply of others' necessities, we must uphold a familiar commerce together in all meekness, gentleness, patience, and liberality, we must delight in each other, make others' conditions our own, rejoice together, mourn together, labor and suffer together, always having before our eyes our commission and community in the work, our community as members of the same body. So shall we keep the unity of the spirit in the bond of peace. The Lord will be our God and delight to dwell among us as His own people, and will command a blessing upon us in all our ways, so that we shall see much more of His wisdom, power, goodness, and truth than formerly we have been acquainted with. We shall find that the God of Israel is among us, when ten of us shall be able to resist a thousand of our enemies, when He shall make us a praise and glory, that men shall say of succeeding plantations, the Lord make it like that of New England. For we must consider that we shall be as a city upon a hill, the eyes of all people are upon us. So that if we shall deal falsely with our God in this work we have

George Henry Broughton, *Pilgrims Going to Church.*

Restored Plymouth.

undertaken and so cause Him to withdraw His present help from us, we shall be made a story and a byword through the world, we shall open the mouths of enemies to speak evil of the ways of God and all professors for God's sake, we shall shame the faces of many of God's worthy servants, and cause their prayers to be turned into curses upon us till we be consumed out of the good land whither we are going. . . .

Perry Miller, ed., *The American Puritans* (Garden City, New York: Doubleday, 1956), pp. 81–83.

JOHN WINTHROP TO MARGARET WINTHROP (1630)

I praise God, we have many occasions of comfort here, and do hope, that our days of affliction will soon have an end, and that the Lord will do us more good in the end then we could have expected, that will abundantly recompense for all the troubles we have endured. Yet we may not look at great things here. It is enough that we shall have heaven, though we should pass through hell to it. We here enjoy God and Jesus Christ. Is not this enough? What would we have more? I thank God, I like so well to be here, as I do not repent my coming; and if I were to come again, I would not have altered my course, though I had foreseen all these afflictions.

Robert C. Winthrop, *Life and Letters of John Winthrop*, 2 vols. (Boston: Little, Brown, 1869), 2:48–49.

Sumptuary Laws

Massachusetts General Court

The Puritan magistrates and ministers of Massachusetts Bay quickly discovered that not all of their number were willing to adhere to the pious simplicity they preached. In 1634 the General Court, concerned about the growing evidence of high living, passed the first of a series of sumptuary laws designed to specify what simple living actually entailed in terms of appropriate dress. But as the following selections reveal, the public continued to resist such restraints on their behavior. Perhaps most disturbing to later Puritan political and social leaders was the desire of the lower ranks to engage in costly display beyond their means and inappropriate to their social standing. In 1651 the Court issued a new sumptuary decree that prohibited only those persons of little means from wearing sumptuous attire. It said little about the wealthy indulging themselves. This double standard reflects the way in which simplicity as a principle could be used as an instrument of social control. Ostentation came to be seen by many of the elite as a danger to the virtue of others but not to themselves, and the simple life in this sense, both then and later, ran the risk of becoming an ethic that one group wishes (or enforces) on another.

1634

The Court, taking into consideration the great, superfluous, & unnecessary expenses occasioned by reason of some new & immodest fashions, as also the wearing of silver, gold, & silk laces, girdles, hatbands, etc., hath therefore ordered that no person, either man or woman, shall hereafter make or buy any apparel, either woolen, silk, or linen, with any lace on it, silver, gold, silk, or thread, under the penalty of forfeiture of such clothes.

1639

Whereas there is much complaint of the excessive wearing of lace, & other superfluities tending to little use or benefit, but to the nourishing of pride & exhausting of men's estates, & also of evil examples to others, it is therefore ordered by this Court, & decreed, that henceforward no person whatsoever shall presume to buy or sell, within this jurisdiction, any manner of lace, to be worn or used within our limits.

1651

Although several declarations & orders have been made by this Court against excess in apparel, both of men & women, which hath not yet taken that effect which were to be desired, but on the contrary we cannot but to our grief take notice that intolerable excess & bravery hath crept in upon us, & especially amongst people of mean condition, to the dishonor of God, the scandal of our profession, the corruption of estates, & altogether unsuitable to our poverty; & although we acknowledge it to be a matter of much difficulty, in regard to the blindness of men's minds & the stubbornness of their wills, to set down exact rules to confine all sorts of persons, yet we cannot but account it our duty to commend unto all sort of persons a sober & moderate use of those blessings which, beyond our expectation, the Lord hath been pleased to afford unto us in this wilderness, & also to declare our utter detestation & dislike that men or women of mean condition,

Interior of Pilgrim home.

educations & callings should take upon the garb of gentlemen, by the wearing of gold or silver lace, or buttons, or points at their knees, to walk in great boots; or women of the same rank to wear silk or tiffany hoods or scarves, which though allowable to persons of greater estates, or more liberal education, yet we cannot but judge it intolerable in persons of such like condition. . . . No person . . . whose visible estates shall not exceed the true and indifferent value of 200 pounds shall wear any gold or silver lace, or gold or silver buttons, or any bone lace above 2 shillings per yard, or silk hoods or scarves, upon the penalty of 10 shillings for every such offense.

Nathaniel B. Shurtleff, ed., *Records of the Governor and Company of the Massachusetts Bay in New England*, 5 vols. (Boston: W. White, 1854):1:126, 274; 3:243; 4:41.

NEW ENGLAND PLEADED WITH (1674)
Urian Oakes

Consider what will be the latter end of what Worldliness that is among us. Would not that great *Apostle Paul*, if he were here to tell you *even weeping*, that many of you mind *earthly things*? Is not this an *Epidemical* disease of New-England? Hence *general calling* neglected, the work of Religion goes on heavily, the strength and Spirits of men are *exhausted*, or laid out on other things, and they have no heart to work, to family dutys, which are neglected, or slubbered and polted over shamefully. . . . And are there not sad complaints of this in *New-England*? and are they altogether without cause? may not any man that observes what Griping, and Squeezing, and Grinding the faces of the poor, and Greediness there is among us, fear it? Hence a private Selfish spirit; that works of Charity and Beneficence, and of Publick concernment are neglected to the damage of the *publick* and the *disgrace* of *Religion*. Hence no progress in a Course of Piety, no getting onward in the Journey to Heaven; You have men now, where they were *twenty* years ago: for they are sunk and stuck fast in the mire and clay of the present world, & cannot stir: there is much *thorny ground* in this Country, and the *Seed of the Word* is *choaked*, and the springing of any good in their Souls is checked and hindered by the *cares of the World, deceitfulness of Riches* and *lusts of other things*. There is so much rooting in the Earth, that there is little growing upward, Heavenward, I mean.

Urian Oakes, *New England Pleaded With* (Boston, 1674), p. 27.

An Essay for Reviving Religion

Samuel Wigglesworth

Puritan ministers began lamenting the seeming decline of their "city upon a hill" from its original ideal almost immediately after arriving in Massachusetts Bay. By the 1730s such concerns helped to provoke a series of excited revivals. The causes of this Great Awakening were many and complex, but a central concern of the revivalists was to combat the raging materialism that had infected the populace. Samuel Wigglesworth, the first Hollis Professor of Divinity at Harvard, reflected this theme in the annual "election" sermon he delivered in 1733. And many people heeded his and other ministers' appeals for a renewal of spiritual fervor and worldly moderation. Jonathan Edwards, the towering leader of the Awakening, observed in his *Thoughts on the Revival* that New Englanders were abandoning "those things of which they were extremely fond, and in which they had placed the happiness of their lives." But the redemptive effects of the revivals soon waned, and the pious simple life promoted by the ministers continued its retreat in the face of the burgeoning economic and social growth of the colonies.

It is a Truth, that we have a *goodly exterior Form of Religion*; Our *Doctrine, Worship* and *Sacraments* are *Orthodox, Scriptural* and *Divine*. There is an external Honour paid to the *Sabbath*; and a professed Veneration for Christ's *Ambassadors* for the sake of their Lord. We set up and maintain the *Publick Worship* of God, and the Voice of the Multitude saying, *Let us go into the House of the Lord*, is yet heard in our Land.

Moreover *Practical Religion* is not quite extirpated among us, and there are, it is to be hoped, a considerable number of serious and vigorous Christians in our Churches, whose *Piety* is acknowledged and respected by their Neighbours, whilst Living; and their *Memories* preserved for it when deceased. Whilst on the other hand, the *prophane and wicked Person* is generally abhor'd; and the more deformed Vices seek the retreats of Darkness to hide their detestable heads.

And yet with what sorrow must we speak, that these things are but the *Remains* of what we *Once* might show; the shadow of past and vanish'd Glory! ...

If the *Fear of the Lord* be to *Hate Evil*, as *Prov.* 8.13. Then it is to be feared that our *Religion runs low*, and but little of this Fear is in us: Inasmuch as we find our selves stained with so many most odious Vices, especially *Uncleanness, Drunkenness, Theft, Covetousness, Violence, Malice, Strife*, and others: Which tho', as 'twas said before, they be look'd upon with dishonour, yet multitudes are found who are not ashamed to commit them; and where such *Iniquities abound*, may we not infer that *the Love of many waxeth cold*?

Again, How *Weak is the Testimony that is born by our Good Men against those Transgressions*! Ought not holy Ones when they *Behold the Transgressor, to be grieved*! Will they not hate the things which God hates, and express a suitable indignation at the presumption of the Wicked, and the affronts which they put upon the Majesty of Heaven? *Reproving*, and bringing them to *Punishment*? If therefore our *Professors of Religion* think *Open Prophaneness* unworthy of their Wrath: If our *Ministers of Religion* are sparing to bear their publick Testimony against it; and when also the *Ministers of Justice* are too Complaisant to the Sons of Wickedness, to Execute the wholesome Laws of the

Province upon them; unto how low an ebb is our Goodness come! . . .

Nor is it less evident that many of us who have given our *Consent to Religion*; are for *Curtailing* and *Abridging* it as much as we can: contenting ourselves with the *lowest degrees* of it, and carefully avoiding all its most *Arduous, Mortifying Duties*, such as *Mortification* of our *Beloved Lusts, Self-Denial, Weaning ourselves from the world, Bestowing our Riches on Works of Piety*, and *Overcoming Evil with Good*: As if we were resolved not to *Wrestle with Flesh and Blood*, and to make *Christ's Yoke lighter* than Himself hath done? Many Men are upon Enquiry, *What strict Duty requires of them*, How often they must *Pray*, How often going to *Meeting* will serve the turn; and if they can satisfy their *Conscience*, they care not how seldom: How far *Christian Liberty* may be *extended*, and whither they may not take this or that *Gratification consistently with Religion*? How *sunk* and *debas'd a Temper* is this! And yet 'tis too evidently our own to be deny'd. . . .

I shall only now add, That the *Powerful Love of the World, and Exhorbitant Reach after Riches*, which is become the reigning Temper in Persons of all Ranks in our Land, is alone enough to awaken our concerns for abandon'd, slighted and forgotten Religion. 'Tis this that takes up our Time, seizes our Affections, and governs our Views: Straitens our Hands: respecting Works of Charity, and pusheth us into the most wicked Schemes and Methods. This *Worldly Spirit* has in a great measure thrust out Religion, and given it a *Wound* which will prove *Deadly* unless infinite Mercy prevent. . . .

Samuel Wigglesworth, *An Essay for Reviving Religion. A Sermon Delivered . . . May 30th. MDCCXXXIII. Being the Anniversary for the Election* . . . (Boston, 1733), pp. 22–26.

PIETY AND PROSPERITY

John Wesley

The Methodist leader John Wesley perceptively recognized the paradox of the Protestant work ethic in the early eighteenth century.

I fear that wherever riches have increased, the essence of religion has decreased in the same proportion. Therefore, I do not see how it is possible, in the nature of things, for any revival of true religion to continue long. For religion must of necessity produce both industry and frugality, and these cannot but produce riches. But as riches increase, so will pride, anger, and love of the world in all its branches.

Max Weber, *The Protestant Ethic and the Spirit of Capitalism* (New York: Scribners, 1930), p. 175.

Some Fruits of Solitude

William Penn

Though he spent only a little over four years in America, William Penn exerted a powerful influence on the development of Quakerism in the New World. Like John Winthrop, he served as an inspirational guide to the first Friends who settled in Pennsylvania, Delaware and Jersey. And he was greatly disappointed as he saw evidence of the decline of Quaker plainness as the colonies grew and prospered. To remind the Friends in America and England of the practical meaning of pious simplicity, he distilled his view of Quaker social philosophy into a series of maxims entitled *Some Fruits of Solitude*, published in 1693. In doing so he not only drew upon traditional Christian sources but also upon the ethical writings of numerous classical philosophers— Aristotle, Epictetus, Horace, and others. *Fruits of Solitude* reflects most of the values and attitudes associated with the ideal of simple living then and since—Christian devotion, social concern, country living, and honest work.

LUXURY

28. Such is now become our delicacy, that we will not eat ordinary meat, nor drink small, palled liquor; we must have the best, and best-cooked, for our bodies, while our souls feed on empty or corrupted things.

29. In short, man is spending all upon a bare house, and hath little or no furniture to recommend it; which is preferring the cabinet before the jewel, a lease of seven years before an inheritance. So absurd a thing is man, after all his proud pretences to wit and understanding.

FRUGALITY AND BOUNTY

50. Frugality is good, if liberal.,y be joined with it. The first, is leaving-off superfluous expenses; the last, bestowing them to the benefit of others that need. The first without the last, begins covetousness; the last without the first, begins prodigality: both together make an excellent temper. Happy the place where that is found.

51. Were it universal, we should be cured of two extremes, want and excess: and the one would supply the other, and so bring both nearer to a mean; the just degree of earthly happiness.

52. It is a reproach to religion and government, to suffer so much poverty and excess.

53. Were the superfluities of a nation valued, and made a perpetual tax or benevolence, there would be more alms-houses than poor; schools than scholars; and enough to spare for government besides.

54. Hospitality is good, if the poorer sort are the subjects of our bounty; else too near a superfluity.

INDUSTRY

57. Love labour: for if thou dost not want it for food, thou mayest for physic. It is wholesome for thy body, and good for thy mind. It prevents the fruits of idleness, which many times comes of nothing to do, and leads too many to do what is worse than nothing.

58. A garden, a laboratory, a work-house, improvements and breeding, are pleasant and profitable diversions to the idle and ingenious: for here they miss ill company, and converse with nature and art; whose varieties are equally grateful and instructing; and preserve a good constitution of body and mind.

TEMPERANCE

59. To this a spare diet contributes much. Eat therefore to live, and do not live to eat. That is like a man, but this below a beast.

60. Have wholesome, but not costly food; and be rather cleanly than dainty, in ordering it.

61. The receipts of cookery are swelled to a volume; but a good stomach excels them all; to which nothing contributes more, than industry and temperance.

62. It is a cruel folly, to offer up to ostentation so many lives of creatures, as make up the state of our treats; as it is a prodigal one, to spend more in sauce than in meat.

APPAREL

73. Excess in apparel is another costly folly: the very trimming of the vain world would clothe all the naked one.

74. Choose thy clothes by thine own eyes, not another's. The more plain and simple they are, the better: neither unshapely, nor fantastical; and for use and decency, and not for pride.

75. If thou are clean and warm, it is sufficient; for more doth but rob the poor, and please the wanton.

76. It is said of the true church, "The king's daughter is all glorious with-in:" let our care, therefore, be of our minds, more than of our bodies, if we would be of her communion.

77. We are told, with truth, that, "Meekness and modesty are the rich and charming attire of the soul:" and the plainer the dress, the more distinctly, and with greater lustre, their beauty shines.

A COUNTRY LIFE

220. The country life is to be preferred; for there we see the works of God; but in cities, little else but the works of men: and the one makes a better subject for our contemplation than the other.

221. As puppets are to men, and babes to children, so is man's workmanship to God's. We are the picture, He the reality.

222. God's works declare his power, wisdom, and goodness: but man's works, for the most part, his pride, folly, and excess. The one is for use, the other, chiefly, for ostentation and lust.

223. The country is both the philosopher's garden and library, in which he reads and contemplates the power, wisdom, and goodness of God.

224. It is his food, as well as study; and gives him life, as well as learning.

225. A sweet and natural retreat from noise and talk; and allows opportunity for reflection, and gives the best subjects for it.

226. In short, it is an original; and the knowledge and improvement of it, man's oldest business and trade, and the best he can be of.

TEMPORAL HAPPINESS

237. Do good with what thou hast, or it will do thee no good.

238. Seek not to be rich, but happy. The one lies in bags, the other in content; which wealth can never give.

239. We are apt to call things by wrong names. We will have prosperity to be happiness, and adversity to be misery; though

that is the school of wisdom, and oftentimes the way to eternal happiness.

240. If thou wouldst be happy, bring thy mind to thy condition, and have an indifferency for more than what is sufficient.

241. Have but little to do, and do it thyself: and do to others as thou wouldst have them do to thee: so, thou canst not fail of temporal felicity.

242. The generality are the worse for their plenty. The voluptuous consumes it, the miser hides it: it is the good man that uses it, and to good purposes. But such are hardly found among the prosperous.

243. Be rather bountiful, than expensive.

244. Neither make nor go to feasts; but let the laborious poor bless thee at home in their solitary cottages.

245. Neither voluntarily want what thou hast in possession; nor so spend it, as to involve thyself in want unavoidable.

246. Be not tempted to presume by success: for many that have got largely, have lost all, by coveting to get more.

247. To hazard much to get much, has more of avarice than wisdom.

248. It is great prudence, both to bound and use prosperity.

249. Too few know when they have enough; and fewer know how to employ it.

The Select Works of William Penn, 3 vols. (London: W. Phillips, 1825), 3:357, 359-61, 371-73.

QUAKER SUMPTUARY LAWS

If any men wear longlapp'd sleeves, or Coats folded at the sides, Superfluous buttons, Broad ribbons about the hat, or gaudy, flower'd or strip'd Stuffs, or any sort of perriwigs unless necessitated, and if any are necessitated, that then it be as near in Colour as may be to their own and in other respects resembling as much as may be, a sufficient natural head of hair without the vain customs being long behind or mounting on the forehead. Also, if any women that profess the Truth wear or suffer their children to wear their Gowns not plain or open at the breast with gaudy Stomachers, needless rolls at the Sleeves or with their Mantuas or Bonnets with gaudy colours, or cut their hair and leave it out on the brow, or dress their heads high, or to wear hoods with long lapps, or long Scarfs open before, or their Capps or pinners plaited or gathered on the brow or double hemm'd or pinch'd. . . . It being not agreeable to that Shame-fac'dness, plainness and modesty which people professing Godliness with good works ought to be found in.

Philadelphia Discipline (1704), in J. William Frost, *The Quaker Family in Colonial America: A Portrait of the Society of Friends* (New York: St. Martins, 1973), p. 194.

John Woolman's Journal

Among the leaders of the mid-eighteenth-century Quaker reform movement, none was more inspiring than John Woolman (1720–1772). In fact, he may be the noblest exemplar of pious simplicity ever produced in America. It was easy enough for a William Penn and other affluent Friends to tell the lower ranks to be contented with a simple way of life, but to command the sustained respect of commoners required a saintly willingness to share some of their austerities. Woolman displayed such an applied empathy, and in doing so he became a figure both believed and beloved. In his humble yet effective way, Woolman served as both an apostle of simple living and an early crusader against slavery, urging those around him to abandon their worship both of worldly treasure and leisurely ease and redirect their attention to the service of God and all of humanity. His *Journal* is one of the finest examples of the genre. As Samuel Taylor Coleridge stressed in 1797, "I should almost despair of that man who could peruse the life of John Woolman without an amelioration of heart."

I have often felt a motion of love to leave some hints in writing of my experience of the goodness of God, and now, in the thirty-sixth year of my age, I begin this work. I was born in Northampton, in Burlington County in West Jersey, A.D. 1720, and before I was seven years old I began to be acquainted with the operations of divine love. Through the care of my parents, I was taught to read near as soon as I was capable of it, and as I went to school one Seventh Day, I remember, while my companions went to play by the way, I went forward out of sight; and sitting down, I read the twenty-second chapter of the Revelations: "He showed me a river of water, clear as crystal, proceeding out of the throne of God and the Lamb, etc." And in reading it my mind was drawn to seek after that pure habitation which I then believed God had prepared for his servants. The place where I sat and the sweetness that attended my mind remains fresh in my memory. . . .

Another thing remarkable in my childhood was that once, going to a neighbor's house, I saw on the way a robin sitting on her nest;

and as I came near she went off, but having young ones, flew about and with many cries expressed her concern for them. I stood and threw stones at her, till one striking her, she fell down dead. At first I was pleased with the exploit, but after a few minutes was seized with horror, as having in sportive way killed an innocent creature while she was careful for her young. I beheld her lying dead and thought that those young ones for which she was so careful must now perish for want of their dam to nourish them; and after some painful considerations on the subject, I climbed up the tree, took all the young birds and killed them, supposing that better than to leave them to pine away and die miserably, and believed in this case that Scripture proverb was fulfilled, "The tender mercies of the wicked are cruel" [Prov. 12:10]. I then went on my errand, but for some hours could think of little else but the cruelties I had committed, and was much troubled.

Thus he whose tender mercies are over all his works hath placed a principle in the human mind which incites to exercise goodness toward every living creature; and this being singly attended to, people become tender-hearted and sympathizing, but being frequently and totally rejected, the mind shuts itself up in a contrary disposition. . . .

Having now been several years with my employer, and he doing less at merchandise than heretofore, I was thoughtful of some other way of business, perceiving merchandise to be attended with much cumber in the way of trading in these parts. My mind through the power of Truth was in a good degree weaned from the desire of outward greatness, and I was learning to be content with real conveniences that were not costly, so that a way of life free from much entanglements appeared best for me, though the income was small. I had several offers of business that appeared profitable, but did not see my way clear to accept of them, as believing the business proposed would be attended with more outward care and cumber that was required of me to engage in. I saw that a humble man with the blessing of the Lord might live on a little, and that where the heart was set on greatness, success in business did not satisfy the craving, but that in common with an increase of wealth the desire of wealth increased. There was a care on my mind to so pass my time as to things outward that nothing might hinder me from the most steady attention to the voice of the True Shepherd.

My employer, though now a retailer of goods, was by trade a tailor and kept a servant man at that business; and I began to think about learning the trade, expecting that if I should settle, I might by this trade and a little retailing of goods get a living in a plain way without the load of great business. I mentioned it to my employer and we soon agreed on terms, and then when I had leisure from the affairs of merchandise, I worked with his man. I believed the hand of Providence pointed out this business for me and was taught to be content with it, though I felt at times a disposition that would have sought for something greater. But through the revelation of Jesus Christ, I had seen the happiness of humility, and there was an earnest desire in me to enter deep into it; and at times this desire arose to a degree of fervent supplication, wherein my soul was so environed with heavenly light and consolation that things were made easy to me which had been otherwise. . . .

Until the year 1756 I continued to retail goods, besides following my trade as a tailor, about which time I grew uneasy on account of my business growing too cumbersome. I began with selling trimmings for garments and from thence proceeded to sell clothes and linens, and at length having got a considerable shop of goods, my trade increased every year and the road to large business appeared open; but I felt a stop in my mind.

Through the mercies of the Almighty I had in a good degree learned to be content with a plain way of living. I had but a small family, that on serious consideration I believed Truth did not require me to engage in much cumbrous affairs. It had been my general practice to buy and sell things really useful. Things that served chiefly to please the vain mind in people I was not easy to trade in, seldom did it, and whenever I did I found it weakened me as a Christian.

The increase of business became my burden, for though my natural inclination was toward merchandise, yet I believed Truth required me to live more free from outward cumbers, and there was now a strife in my mind between the two; and in this exercise my prayers were put up to the Lord, who graciously heard me and gave me a heart resigned to his holy will. Then I lessened my outward business, and as I had opportunity told my customers of my intentions that they might consider what shop to turn to, and so in a while wholly laid down merchandise, following my trade as a tailor, myself only, having no apprentice. I also had a nursery of apple trees, in which I employed some of my time—hoeing, grafting, trimming, and inoculating.

In merchandise it is the custom where I lived to sell chiefly on credit, and poor people often get in debt, and when payment is expected, not having where-with to pay, their creditors often sue for it at law. Having often observed occurrences of this kind, I found it good for me to advise poor people to take such goods as were most useful and not costly.

After abandoning merchandising Woolman began traveling throughout the colonies, encouraging Friends to abide by their traditional religious and social practices. In Newport he chastised Quaker slaveholders and encouraged the wives of whalers to live modestly so as not to tempt their husbands to take unnecessary risks. Along the Pennsylvania frontier he urged white traders to resist taking advantage of Indians. And in the Carolinas, as revealed in the following letter he included in his *Journal*, he appealed to Friends to moderate their acquisitive desires and to end slaveowning.

TO FRIENDS AT THEIR MONTHLY MEETING AT NEW GARDEN AND CANE CREEK IN NORTH CAROLINA

Dear Friends,

It having pleased the Lord to draw me forth on a visit to some parts of Virginia and Carolina, you have often been in my mind, and though my way is not clear to come in person to visit you, yet I feel it in my heart to communicate a few things as they arise in the love of Truth. First, my dear Friends, dwell in humility and take heed that no views of outward gain get too deep hold of you, that so your eyes being single to the Lord you may be preserved in the way of safety.

Where people let loose their minds after the love of outward things and are more engaged in pursuing the profits and seeking the friendships of this world than to be inwardly acquainted with the way of true peace, such walk in a vain shadow while the true comfort of life is wanting. Their examples are often hurtful to others, and their treasures thus collected do many times prove dangerous snares to their children.

But where people are sincerely devoted to follow Christ and dwell under the influence of his Holy Spirit, their stability and firmness through a divine blessing is at times like dew on the tender plants round about them, and the weightiness of their spirits secretly works on the minds of others; and in this condition, through the spreading influence of divine love they feel a care over the flock and way is opened for maintaining good order in the Society. And though we meet with opposition from another spirit, yet as there is a dwelling in meekness, feeling our spirits subject and moving only in the gentle, peaceable wisdom, the inward reward of quietness will be greater than all our difficulties. Where the pure life is kept to and meetings of discipline are held in the authority of it, we find by experience that they are comfortable and tend to the health of the body. . . .

And now, dear Friends and brethren, as you are improving a wilderness and may be numbered amongst the first planters in one part of a province, I beseech you in the love of Jesus Christ to wisely consider the force of your examples and think how much your successors may be thereby affected. It is a help in a country, yea, a great favour and a blessing, when customs first settled are agreeable to sound wisdom; so when they are otherwise the effect of them is grievous, and children feel themselves encompassed with difficulties prepared for them by their predecessors.

As a moderate care and exercise under the direction of sound wisdom is useful both to mind and body, so by this means in general the real wants of life are easily attained, our gracious Father having so proportioned one to the other that keeping in the true medium we may pass on quietly. Where slaves are purchased to do our labour, numerous difficulties attend it. To rational creatures bondage is uneasy and frequently occasions sourness and discontent in them, which affects the family and such who claim the mastery over them, and thus people and their children are many times encompassed with vexations which arise from their applying to wrong methods to get a living.

I have been informed that there are a large number of Friends in your parts who have no slaves, and in tender and most affectionate love I now beseech you to keep clear from purchasing any. Look, my dear Friends, to divine providence, and follow in simplicity that exercise of body, that plainness and frugality, which true wisdom leads to; so may you be preserved from those dangers which attend such who are aiming at outward ease and greatness.

Treasures, though small, attained on a true principle of virtue are sweet in the possession, and while we walk in the light of the Lord there is true comfort and satisfaction. Here neither the murmurs of an oppressed people, nor throbbing, uneasy conscience, nor anxious thoughts about the event of things hinder the enjoyment of it.

When we look toward the end of life and think on the division of our substance among our successors, if we know that it was collected in the fear of the Lord, in honesty, in equity, and in uprightness of heart before him, we may consider it as his gift to us and with a single eye to his blessing bestow it on those we leave behind us. Such is the happiness in the plain ways of true virtue. "The work of righteousness is peace, and the effect of righteousness is quietness and assurance forever" [Is. 32:17]. . . .

In 1771 Woolman decided to make a missionary journey to Great Britain. He had learned of the considerable social misery caused there by the enclosure movement, and he decided to do what he could to help ameliorate the plight of the poor and oppressed. As he boarded the ship, however, he noticed that the cabins were decorated with "carved work and imagery" and "some superfluity of workmanship," and he could not in good conscience pay extra for such ornamentation. So he decided to travel in the steerage, where for six weeks he shared the hardships of the sailors, "their exposure, their soaking clothes, their miserable accommodations, their wet garments often trodden underfoot." The ship landed in June 1772. Woolman eventually made his way to Yorkshire. There he contracted the much feared smallpox, then so common, that had earlier claimed his sister and cousin. As the disease progressed, Woolman calmly accepted his fate. "This trial is made easier than I could have thought," he reflected, "by my Will being wholly taken away, for if I was anxious to the Event, it would be harder but I am not, and my mind enjoys a perfect calm." A few days later he died, "without Sigh, Groan or Struggle."

I have felt great distress of mind since I came on this island [Great Britain], on account of the members of our Society being mixed with the world in various sorts of business and traffic carried on in impure channels. Great is the trade to Africa for slaves! And in loading these ships abundance of people are employed in the factories, amongst whom are many of our Society!

Friends in early times refused on a religious principle to make or trade in superfluities, of which we have many large testimonies on record, but for want of faithfulness some gave way, even some whose examples were of note in Society, and from thence others took more liberty. Members of our Society worked in superfluities and bought and sold them, and thus dimness of sight came over many. At length Friends got into the use of some superfluities in dress and in the furniture of their houses, and this hath spread from less to more, till superfluity of some kinds is common amongst us.

In this declining state many look at the example one of another and too much neglect the pure feeling of Truth. Of late years a deep exercise hath attended my mind that Friends may dig deep, may carefully cast forth the loose matter and get down to the rock, the sure foundation, and there hearken to that divine voice which gives a clear and certain sound; and I have felt in that which doth not deceive that if Friends who have known the Truth keep in that tenderness of heart where all views of outward gain are given up, and their trust is only on the Lord, he will graciously lead some to be patterns of deep self-denial in things relating to trade and handicraft labour, and that some who have plenty of the treasures of this world will example in a plain frugal life and pay wages to such whom they may hire, more liberally than is now customary in some places. . . .

A deviation amongst us as a Society from that simplicity that there is in Christ becoming so general, and the trade from this island to Africa for slaves, and other trades carried on through oppressive channels, and abundance of the inhabitants being employed in factories to support a trade in which there is unrighteousness, and some growing outwardly great by gain of this sort: the weight of this degeneracy hath lain so heavy upon me, the depth of this revolt been so evident, and desires in my heart been so ardent for a reformation, so ardent that we might inhabit that holy mountain on which they neither hurt nor destroy! and may not only stand clear from oppressing our fellow creatures, but may be so disentangled from connections in interest with known oppressors, that in us may be fulfilled that prophecy: "Thou shalt be far from oppression" [Is. 54:14]. Under the weight of this exercise the sight of innocent birds in the branches and sheep in the pastures, who act according to the will of their Creator, hath at times tended to mitigate my trouble.

Phillips P. Moulton, ed., *The Journal and Major Essays of John Woolman* (New York: Oxford University Press, 1971), pp. 23, 24-25, 35-36, 53-54, 67-69, 184-85.

THE QUAKER OF THE OLDEN TIME

John Greenleaf Whittier

> The Quaker of the olden time!
> How calm and firm and true,
> Unspotted by its wrong and crime,
> He walked the dark earth through.
> The lust of power, the love of gain,
> The thousand lures of sin
> Around him, had no power to stain
> The purity within.
>
> With that deep insight which detects
> All great things in the small,
> And knows how each man's life affects
> The spiritual life of all,
> He walked by faith and not by sight,
> By love and not by law
> The presence of the wrong or right
> He rather felt than saw.

The Complete Poetical Works of John Greenleaf Whittier
(Boston: Houghton Mifflin, 1848), p. 351.

Peculiar Customs at Nantucket

J. Hector St. John de Crèvecoeur

The efforts of Quaker reformers such as John Woolman produced much fruit. Many American Friends did rekindle their piety and plainness during the Revolutionary era and after. We have evidence of such in the form of two of J. Hector St. John de Crèvecoeur's famous *Letters from an American Farmer*. Crèvecoeur (1735–1813), the son of a minor French aristocrat, migrated to New France to fight with Montcalm in 1758. Thereafter he rambled through the

American colonies from Nantucket to Charleston, South
Carolina, before he settled on a farm in Orange County,
New York. While in Nantucket he was particularly struck
by the distinctive attire and manners of the Quakers.

The manners of *the Friends* are entirely founded on that
simplicity which is their boast, and their most distinguished
characteristic; and those manners have acquired the authority of
laws. Here they are strongly attached to plainness of dress, as well
as to that of language; insomuch that though some part of it may
be ungrammatical, yet should any person who was born and
brought up here, attempt to speak more correctly, he would be
looked upon as a fop or an innovator. On the other hand, should a
stranger come here and adopt their idiom in all its purity (as they
deem it) this accomplishment would immediately procure him the
most cordial reception; and they would cherish him like an ancient
member of their society. So many impositions have they suffered
on this account, that they begin now indeed to grow more cautious.
They are so tenacious of their ancient habits of industry and
frugality, that if any of them were to be seen with a long coat made
of English cloth, on any other than the *first-day* (Sunday) he would
be greatly ridiculed and censured; he would be looked upon as a
careless spendthrift, whom it would be unsafe to trust, and in vain
to relieve. A few years ago two *single-horse chairs* were imported
from Boston, to the great offence of these prudent citizens;
nothing appeared to them more culpable than the use of such
gaudy painted vehicles, in contempt of the more useful and more
simple *single-horse carts* of their fathers. This piece of extravagant
and unknown luxury, almost caused a schism, and set every
tongue a-going; some predicted the approaching ruin of those
families that had imported them; others feared the dangers of example; never since the foundation of the town had there happened
any thing which so much alarmed this primitive community. One
of the possessors of these profane chairs, filled with repentance,
wisely sent it back to the continent; the other, more obstinate and
perverse, in defiance to all remonstrances, persisted in the use of
his chair until by degrees they became more reconciled to it;
though I observed that the wealthiest and the most respectable
people still go to meeting or to their farms in a *single-horse cart*
with a decent awning fixed over it: indeed, if you consider their
sandy soil, and the badness of their roads, these appear to be the
best contrived vehicles for this island. . . .

A Visit with John Bartram

J. Hector St. John de Crèvecoeur

As he made his way south from New England, Crèvecoeur stopped in Philadelphia, where he visited the
prominent Quaker naturalist, John Bartram. Crèvecoeur
found him to be a pure example of enlightened, yet pious
simplicity.

Thus I spent my time with this enlightened botanist—this
worthy citizen; who united all the simplicity of rustic manners to
the most useful learning. Various and extensive were the
conversations that filled the measure of my visit. I accompanied
him to his fields, to his barn, to his bank, to his garden, to his
study, and at last to the meeting of the society on the Sunday
following. It was at the town of Chester, whither the whole family
went in two wagons; Mr. Bertram [sic] and I on horse back. When I
entered the house where the friends were assembled, who might be
about two hundred men and women, the involuntary impulse of
ancient custom made me pull off my hat; but soon recovering
myself, I sat with it on, at the end of a bench. The meetinghouse
was a square building devoid of any ornament whatever; the
whiteness of the walls, the conveniency of seats, that of a large
stove, which in cold weather keeps the whole house warm, were the
only essential things which I observed. Neither pulpit nor desk,
fount nor altar, tabernacle nor organ, were there to be seen; it is
merely a spacious room, in which these good people meet every
Sunday. . . .

How simple their precepts, how unadorned their religious
system: how few the ceremonies through which they pass during
the course of their lives! At their deaths they are interred by the
fraternity, without pomp, without prayers; thinking it then too
late to alter the course of God's eternal decrees: and as you well
know, without either monument nor tomb-stone. Thus after having
lived under the mildest government, after having been guided by
the mildest doctrine, they die just as peaceably as those who being
educated in more pompous religions, pass through a variety of
sacraments, subscribe to complicated creeds, and enjoy the
benefits of a church establishment. These good people flatter
themselves, with following the doctrines of Jesus Christ, in that
simplicity with which they were delivered: an happier system
could not have been devised for the use of mankind. It appears to
be entirely free from those ornaments and political additions which

Friends Meetinghouse, New Garden, North Carolina.

each country and each government, hath fashioned after its own manners.

At the door of this meetinghouse, I had been invited to spend some days at the houses of some respectable farmers in the neighborhood. The reception I met with everywhere insensibly led me to spend two months among these good people; and I must say they were the golden days of my riper years. I never shall forget the gratitude I owe them for the innumerable kindnesses they heaped on me. . . .

J. Hector St. John de Crèvecoeur, *Letters from an American Farmer* (1782; New York: Peter Smith, 1968), pp. 149–50, 199–201.

Simplicity and Spirituality
Rufus Jones

Since the eighteenth century, the Quakers have continued to struggle with the implications of their traditional commitment to simplicity. It has not been easy. Debates about how to define and encourage plainness among the Friends have occasionally divided meetings and alienated

members. Rufus Jones (1863–1948) was a widely revered
Quaker philosopher, historian, and reformer who tried
repeatedly to promote a reasonable approach to the issue.
In this statement he made in 1897 as editor of *The
American Friend*, he articulated the tension that had
developed within the Friends about the meaning of simplicity. His thoughts are as illuminating now as they were
at the turn of the century.

Two writers have recently called attention to the increasing
tendency to make a display, and to lose spirituality and simplicity
by adopting the attractive methods of a worldly society. This same
tendency has more than once sapped the vitality of the Church,
and any pronounced tendency to exalt external display and to
draw crowds by a show of magnificence instead of by genuine
spiritual power, is an unmistakable evidence that degeneration has
set in.

Nearly every community of Friends has some representative
whose memory goes back to the time when the proposition to paint
the meeting-house seats, or to carpet the floor, or to put in large
window-panes seemed almost sacrilege to some members of the
meeting, and every change from the stoic simplicity of the fathers'
time has been looked upon as a dangerous step. Now there are here,
as in almost every case, two extremes, either of which is to be
avoided. There is no reason why a place of worship should not be
comfortable, and even attractive, in an unostentatious way.
Unpainted pine board seats are no more conducive to spirituality
than are cushioned oak ones, nor does the size of the window-pane
determine the orthodoxy of the worshipers, but the moment the
line of comfort and pure taste is passed, and a display of
superfluous ornament or of extravagance appears, it is a wrong use
of money, and it is an exaltation of the lower things of life over the
higher. The proportion and perspective are wrong, and a penalty
always follows such a course. . . .

There is almost as much need in our day of a powerful testimony
for simplicity in life and in worship as there was when Friends first
made their splendid stand against the fashions and elaborate
formalities of a corrupt age.

Plainness in speech and apparel, simplicity in life and worship,
singleness of heart to gain the blessings of Christ's kingdom,
hunger for righteousness and joy in spiritual living mark the best

type of men and women, and our church can do the world an unparalleled service by exemplifying such lives.

Rufus Jones, "Simplicity and Spirituality," *The American Friend* 4 (29 April 1897), pp. 1–2.

QUAKER SIMPLICITY

Our testimony respecting simplicity is wrongly understood if it is interpreted as mere self-discipline or self-mortification. It does not require any rigid rule as to the outward things of life; but it is the outcome of the necessity which the disciple instinctively feels of subordinating everything to principle. In all times Christians have been constrained to free themselves from luxurious and self-indulgent ways of living. . . . In life, as in art, whatever does not help hinders. In all kinds of effort, whether moral, intellectual, or physical, the first condition of vigour is the resolute surrender of that which is not essential.

Christian Discipline of the Society of Friends (Philadelphia, 1911).

Pietistic Simplicity

2

In the process of restoring the simplicity of their faith and way of living, the Quaker reformers increasingly turned away from much of their earlier involvement in the larger society. Perhaps this was the only way to maintain a traditional form of pious simplicity in a rapidly changing American society. Certainly that was the guiding assumption of the many pietistic sects that settled in America in the eighteenth century and after. The so-called "plain people"—Mennonites, Amish, Dunkers (German Baptist Brethren), Brethren in Christ, Moravians, Schwenckfelders, and later Hutterites—shared a strong commitment to communal values and a strict nonconformity to the ways of the world. So too did the Shakers, a religious group with different origins and beliefs but similar social principles.

Most of these small religious sects grew out of the Anabaptist tradition. During the sixteenth century Anabaptism represented the radical wing of the Protestant Reformation, and its adherents were vigorously persecuted by both Lutherans and Catholics. People then and later regarded their practices as odd and even dangerous to the social and religious order. The Anabaptists fervently believed that religion was primarily a felt experience rather than a dry body of doctrine. They were Christians of the heart and openly gave vent to their spiritual emotions. Convinced that the apocalypse was near at hand, the Anabaptists believed that God would first gather and separate his own people from the unregenerate majority. They would follow the "narrow gate" of pure faith while the rest of the world continued along its destructive path.

Thus perceiving themselves as the chosen ones, the Anabaptists disavowed the established churches and creeds. They instead stressed a literal interpretation of the Bible and sought to revive the Apostolic Church of Jerusalem. They looked back to the early days of Christianity in the first century and were determined to restore the simplicity and purity of that era. This led them to stress adult rather than infant baptism and to revive long-abandoned Christian practices such as foot-washing. It also encouraged them to promote the "innocence" and self-sufficiency of rural life in opposition to urban and commercial corruption.

Like the later Puritans and Quakers, the Anabaptists argued that the Catholics overemphasized the role of sacraments, the priesthood, and dogma. They believed in people and not in institutions, in ideals and not in possessions. And they took as their guide the Sermon on the Mount. The Anabaptists insisted that the true church was a visible community of disciplined saints separated from the nonbelieving world. As the Schleitheim Confession of 1527 decreed: "A separation shall be made from the evil and from the wickedness which the devil planted in the world; in this manner, simply, that we shall not have fellowship with them and not run with them in the multitude of their abominations." Inherently sinful people could become good if they followed Christ's example and lived a meek, caring life and remained "unspotted from the world."

But they could not do so on their own. The faithful needed the regulating influence of others to help sustain their piety and purity. They must "fence themselves in" by obeying rules and by maintaining communal solidarity. So they gathered together among themselves, withdrew as far as possible from civil and social involvement, refused to bear arms or swear oaths, and tried to nurture a communal life stressing Christian devotion, charity, pacifism, and simplicity. They succeeded remarkably well. One of the earliest accounts of the Swiss Brethren, written in 1525, testified to their distinctive way of life: "They shun costly clothing, they shun expensive food and drink, clothe themselves with coarse cloth, cover their heads with broad felt hats. Their entire manner of life is completely humble." Even their harshest critics recognized their self-evident piety. In 1582 a Catholic theologian published a tract entitled *Against the Terrible Errors of the Anabaptists,* in which he observed: "Among the existing heretical sects there is none which in appearance leads a more modest or pious life than the Anabaptists. As concerns their outward public life they are irreproachable. No lying, deception, swearing, strife, harsh language, no intemperate eating and drinking, no outward personal display, is found among them. . . ."

Throughout the sixteenth century the Anabaptists suffered repeated abuses at the hands of political and religious authorities in Europe. So it is not surprising that emigration to America became an enticing option. Once in the New World these various "people of the Book" established small, isolated, traditional, self-sustaining, homogeneous rural communities. Through mutual aid, intensive agriculture, thrift, and industry, their settlements prospered. Yet, unlike the Puritans, most were able to make such economic success serve rather than subvert their piety and simplicity. Pride, worldliness, materialism, pretentious display, and complexity were the evils to be avoided, and it was universally agreed that this could be best accomplished in the countryside, away from the corrupting effects of commerce and cosmopolitan ways.

Some of the pietistic communities required communal ownership; others allowed private property but restricted individualism. Some verged on asceticism, practicing celibacy and renunciation; others allowed cohabitation and a comfortable sufficiency. But all insisted upon maintaining the priorities of faith and community, and this resulted in an array of strictly-enforced regulations governing social behavior. As far as plain living was concerned, these nonconformists required conformity. Indeed, they took for granted the connection between piety and plain living. Hence they left few documents explaining their rationale for simplicity. Instead they expressed their values through their practices and their precise guidelines. Such patriarchal rules were intended to reinforce community order as well as to accentuate the doctrine of separation from the world. Often they provoked more dissension than consent. Legislating simplicity, as the Puritans and Quakers learned, is not easy.

The Mennonites were the first and largest of the plain sects to settle in the New World. They derived their name from the martyred Dutch Anabaptist leader Menno Simons (1496–1561), who had tried to rid early Anabaptism of some of its fanatical excesses. William Penn visited the Palatinate region in Europe in the 1670s and was strongly impressed by the Mennonites' knowledge of husbandry and their obvious spiritual intensity. He recognized the similarities between these Swiss-German pietists and the Quakers. Both rejected the prevailing world of rigid social classes and artificial complexity; both stressed simplicity and pacifism and believed in an "inner light" inherent in each individual. "They are very near the Truth," Penn wrote to a friend.

Eager to people his new colony in America with such industrious yet pious settlers, Penn offered the Mennonites a tract of land at generous terms, and in 1683 the first group of German Mennonites arrived in Pennsylvania. They founded Germantown, just north of Philadelphia, and soon prospered. Some were weavers and artisans, but most were farmers who quickly found the fertile soil of the Lancaster Plain to their liking. Other colonists from the Lower Rhine area followed and began establishing settlements in rural Lancaster County. Mennonites eventually migrated southward into Maryland, Virginia, and the Carolinas and westward into Ohio, Illinois, Iowa, and Indiana. Initially the Mennonites participated with the Quakers in Pennsylvania governmental life, but as the complexities and compromises of colonial affairs increased, they withdrew, leaving such matters to the Friends and later the Scots-Irish and Anglicans.

Early on, the Mennonites experienced disputes and even divisions within their sect, both in Europe and America. The most notable of these schisms involved the Amish, and it grew out of the doctrine of *Meidung* or shunning. In 1693 Jacob Ammann, a Dutch Mennonite preacher, began to insist upon the strict practice of avoiding excommunicated members. He based this insistence on St. Paul's instruction for Christians "not to keep company" with an unfaithful member. Most Mennonites felt that strict shunning was too severe, so Ammann and his followers broke off and formed their own sect. The Amish first arrived in America in 1727, settling in Pennsylvania's Berks and Lancaster counties. As their numbers grew, however, they began drifting further westward in groups, or "colonies." Other Amish continued to come directly from Europe throughout the nineteenth century.

The German Baptist Brethren, popularly known as Dunkers, represented another of the major sects associated with the "plain people." They differed from the Mennonites primarily in their practice of baptising by complete immersion in a flowing stream. The Dunkers began arriving in Pennsylvania in the 1720s. Like the Mennonites and reform Quakers they were ardent opponents of slavery and insistent pacifists. This led to much harassment of the sect during the Revolutionary war, and many of the German Brethren moved west to escape local persecution. They were usually excellent farmers—thrifty, diligent, and efficient.

A distinctive aspect of the history of pietism in America was the creation by some of the Dunkers of a communal form of pious simplicity. Led by Conrad Beissel (1691–1768), a charismatic exile from the Palatinate who had arrived in Germantown in 1720, a group of mystical Brethren in the 1730s formed Ephrata, a community along the Cocalico River that for over fifty years successfully practiced a communal economy and an almost monastic regimen. Austere plainness was the rule at Ephrata. The residents wore white habits modeled after the Capuchins, slept on benches, and used all wooden eating utensils. The day was divided into periods of labor, meditation, worship, and sleep. Ephrata soon flourished in its spiritual vision. The Cloister became famous for the humility and charity practiced by its residents. One visitor remarked that God "will always have a visible people on earth, and these are his people at present, above any other in the world."

The Moravians, though technically not considered one of the "plain sects" because of their loyalty to much of Lutheran theology and their rejection of the Pietists' insistence on a wrenching conversion experience, nevertheless brought with them to the New World a similar desire to establish a self-sustaining community of piety. In the early eighteenth century a group of Moravians had taken refuge from Catholic persecution on the Saxony estate of the young, pietistic nobleman, Count Nicholas Ludwig Zinzendorf. Their communal settlement at Herrnhut (as they called it) flourished, and soon they began migrating to America in order to evangelize the Indians. The Moravians established thriving settlements in Pennsylvania, and later in North Carolina.

The Shakers also differed from the plain sects. They were English rather than German, Swiss, or Dutch, and they arrived in America somewhat later than the other pietistic groups. The Shakers also differed on several key theological issues such as celibacy and modes of worship. But they, too, professed the same basic social ethic stressing simplicity, communalism, pacifism, and piety.

The Shakers, officially known as the United Society of Believers in Christ's Second Coming, were organized by Mother Ann Lee (1736–84). Her early life was a series of repeated tribulations that eventually led to a remarkable conversion experience. The daughter of a struggling blacksmith, she was sent to work at an early age in a cotton factory. She thus never went to school and was illiterate. In 1758 she joined a group known as the Shaking Quakers who were distinctive for their millennialist emphasis and emotional worship services. Ann Lee married four years later and subsequently gave birth to four children, all of whom died in infancy. During this period of trial and stress, she experienced numerous visions which convinced her that sexual relations were at the root of most social evils and that Christ's Second Coming would be in the form of a woman. She eventually decided that she was that woman. Animated by such illuminations, Ann Lee began speaking in tongues and preaching her prophetic beliefs to others. On several occasions the civil authorities arrested her.

So in 1774 Ann Lee and her small band of dedicated followers left for America. Near Albany, New York, they eventually established a Shaker community, living, working, and worshipping together, though practicing sexual abstinence. Mother Ann and the Elders repeatedly told their flock that they must be industrious, frugal, and humble. She urged them to "put your hands to work, and give your hearts to God." They heeded her advice. The Shakers' fervent piety and unique social organization quickly attracted much attention and many converts. By 1794 there were twelve Shaker communities scattered throughout the northern states. During the early nineteenth century they expanded into Kentucky, Ohio, and Indiana.

Despite persistent efforts, not all of these sects have successfully maintained their original ethic through two centuries. The Moravians quickly abandoned communal living and largely accepted the modern world and its institutions. Many Mennonites and Brethren no longer practice plainness of dress or advocate a rigid separation from the larger society and its consumer culture. Rising incomes, dispersed communities, generational conflicts, and the powerful lure of the urban marketplace and cosmopolitan living have all combined to erode much of their original otherworldly commitment. Yet many of these "plain people" have managed to retain much of their initial ethic. Old Order Mennonites, Brethren, and Amish, as well as the Hutterites and the few surviving Shakers, have remained remarkably insulated from the advance of modernity and its temptations and complexities. That their

Farmhouse, Lancaster, Pennsylvania, 1965.

pietistic version of pious simplicity has endured so long testifies to the strength of their spiritual commitment and social tradition as well as to the rigidity of their social discipline.

Early Mennonites

Morgan Edwards

There were and still are many different types of Mennonites originating from many different parts of Europe, thus making it difficult to generalize about their customs. But most of the first settlers were determined to be withdrawn from the mainstream of American life. They wanted to create a fellowship of saints "without spot or wrinkle." And they remained largely rural for several generations.

Mennonites used geographic isolation and their native languages to reinforce their traditional social and religious identity. The Mennonites frequently dressed in gray or black. The men, usually clean-shaven, wore flat broad-brimmed hats and coats without lapels. The women wore small, neat bonnets and dresses with long sleeves and tight necks. Mennonite meetinghouses were also typically plain. Walls and benches were whitewashed, no organ or instrumental music was played, and there was no separate choir.

Like the Quakers, the Mennonites have experienced numerous internal convulsions and changes since the eighteenth century. Schisms over such issues as pacifism, education, and dress have fragmented communities and congregations. Moreover, the larger social and economic developments have also intruded upon Mennonite other-worldliness. Parents have found it increasingly difficult to transmit their own piety and social ethic to their children. More and more Mennonites over the years have moved off the land into urban and suburban environments. And many have succumbed to the lure of affluence. Still, a large number of so-called "Old Order" Mennonites have successfully resisted the inroads of secularism and conformity. They continue to practice the old customs of speech, dress, worship, and work in ways not unlike the following account of their eighteenth-century ancestors written by a Philadelphia Baptist minister and historian.

The Mennonites do not, like the Dunkers, hold the doctrine of *general salvation*; yet, like them, they will neither swear nor fight, nor bear any civil office, nor go to law, nor take interest for the money they lend (though many break through this last). Some of them yet wear their beards; nor are the ancient rites of *washing feet*, &c wholly out of use among them. They, like the Dunkers, use great plainness of speech and dress. This last is so capital a point with them that some have been expelled from their societies for having buckles to their shoes and pocket holes to their coats. Their church government, like that of all Baptists, is wholly democratical or republican. Their ministers they choose by balloting. . . . They do not pay them; nor do their ministers assert their right to a livelihood from the gospel. . . . The epithets which these people give themselves in their writings are *Harmless Christians, Revengeless Christians, Weaponless Christians* &c; and as such are they considered by rulers of the province and by those of other states. Remarkable on this subject are the words of the Dutch ambassador (van Beuning) to monsieur de Turenne: "The Mennonites are good people and the most commodious to a state of any in the world; partly, because they do not aspire to places of dignity; partly because they edify the community by the simplicity of their manners and application to arts and industry; and partly because we fear no rebellion from a sect who make it an article of their faith never to bear arms." The said industry and frugality they carried with them to Pennsylvania. . . .

Morgan Edwards, *Materials Towards a History of Baptists in Pennsylvania* (Philadelphia: Joseph Crukshank, 1770), pp. 94–95.

MENNONITE SIMPLICITY
Attitude Toward Possessions

We understand the Scriptures to teach that the end of life for the Christian is not the amassing of wealth but Christian service and evangelism. Our Lord gave stern warnings on the dangers of money-seeking and avarice. Furthermore, whatever may come to us through honest toil and effort is not ours, to be used selfishly, but is God's, and we are but His stewards. Therefore we invoke His sanctifying power to deliver us from the materialistic age in which we are living, and to enable us to first give our own selves to the Lord. And we call upon all members of the church to practice lives of self-denial and frugality, to live simply rather than in luxury, and to use the things of this world in the full realization that we do not really belong to this world, but are strangers and pilgrims on the earth. . . .

"Declaration of Commitment in Respect to Christian Separation and Nonconformity to the World," Mennonite General Conference, 27 August 1955.

Amish Ordinances

The Amish have been distinguished from Mennonites by their stricter interpretation and enforcement of the principle of nonconformity to the world. They were so wary of institutionalized religion that they refused to build churches, preferring to meet in homes or barns. Today, as reflected in the following Ohio *Ordnung* of 1950, a list of social regulations, their descendants remain determined to

Amish men, Lancaster, Pennsylvania, 1966.

maintain their old ways of life. Most "Old Order" Amish still prefer horse-drawn buggies to cars, worship in homes rather than meetinghouses, retain their German dialect and customs, shun wayward brethren, and educate their own children. Their love and care for the land has become legendary, as has their emphasis on mutual aid and individual industry and integrity. When a barn burns down neighbors descend by the dozens to help the owner rebuild and to provide new livestock and equipment. Amish farmers use their prosperity simply; they earn and save enough money so as to provide new lands for their descendants. And they do *earn* their money. Few Americans work so hard or so well as the Amish—or find such satisfaction in toil. The agrarian myth, with its emphasis on the joys of rural self-sufficiency and community, is a reality for them.

Since it is the duty of the church, especially in this day and age to decide what is fitting and proper and also what is not fitting and proper for a Christian to do, (in points that are not clearly stated in the Bible), we have considered it needful to publish this booklet listing some rules and ordinances of a Christian Church.

No ornamental, bright, showy form-fitting, immodest or silk-like clothing of any kind. Colors such as bright red, orange, yellow and pink not allowed. Amish form of clothing to be followed as a general rule. Costly Sunday clothes to be discouraged. Dresses not shorter than halfway between knees and floor, nor over eight inches from floor. Longer advisable. Clothing in every way modest, serviceable and as simple as scripturally possible. Only outside pockets allowed are one on work *oberhem* or *vomas* and pockets on large overcoats. Dress shoes, if any, to be plain and black only. No high heels and pomp slippers. Dress socks, if any, to be black except white for foot hygiene for both sexes. A plain, unshowy suspender without buckles.

Hat to be black with no less than 3-inch brim and not extremely high in crown. No stylish impressions in any hat. No pressed trousers. No sweaters.

Prayer covering to be simple, and made to fit head. Should cover all the hair as nearly as possible and is to be worn wherever possible. Pleating of caps to be discouraged. No silk ribbons. Young children to dress according to the Word as well as parents. No pink or fancy baby blankets or caps.

Women to wear shawls, bonnets, and capes in public. Aprons to be worn at all times. No adorning of hair among either sex such as parting of hair among men and curling or waving among women.

A full beard should be worn among men and boys before baptism if possible. No shingled hair. Length at least halfway below top of ears.

No decorations of any kind in buildings inside or out. No fancy yard fences. Linoleum, oilcloth, shelf and wall paper to be plain and unshowy. Overstuffed furniture or any luxury items forbidden. No doilies or napkins. No large mirrors, fancy glassware, statues or wall pictures for decorations.

No embroidery work of any kind. Curtains either dark green rollers or black cloth. No boughten dolls.

No bottle gas or high line electrical appliances.

Stoves should be black if bought new.

Weddings should be simple and without decorations. Names not attached to gifts.

No ornaments on buggies or harness.

Tractors to be used only for such things that can hardly be done with horses. Only either stationary engines or tractors with steel tires allowed. No air-filled rubber tires.

Farming and related occupations to be encouraged. Working in cities or factories not permissible. Boys and girls working out away from home for world people forbidden except in emergencies.

Worldly amusements [such] as radios, card playing, party games, movies, fairs, etc., forbidden. Reading, singing, tract distribution, Bible games, relief work, giving of tithes, etc., are encouraged.

Musical instruments or different voice singing not permissible. No dirty, silly talking or sex teasing of children.

Usury forbidden in most instances. No government benefit payments or partnership in harmful associations. No insurance. No photographs.

No buying or selling of anything on Sunday. It should be kept according to the principles of the Sabbath. Worship of some kind every Sunday.

Women should spend time in doing good or reading God's Word instead of taking care of canaries, goldfish or house flowers. . . .

Because of a great falling away from sound doctrine, we do not care to fellowship, that is hold communion, with any churches that allow or uphold any unfruitful works of darkness such as worldliness, fashionable attire, bed-courtship, habitual smoking or drinking, old wives fables, non-assurance of salvation, anti-missionary zeal or anything contrary to sound doctrine. . . .

ORDNUNG REASONS

Webster's definition of luxury is the free indulgence in food and liquor, dress or equipage. Living in luxury is condemned. . . . Is it not to be feared that having costly modern machinery, furniture, auto, electricity, etc., would come into that class?

To have all these things a person usually has to invest much money that might well be used otherwise. It can also cause people to go into debt deeper. Those with tractors usually farm more land, sometimes taking it away from poor people.

Following certain rules regarding suspenders, window curtains, clothing, etc., does not mean that any church having any different rules regarding these items is necessarily wrong. We believe it is the right and the duty of our church to observe any restrictions that would help to keep its members from being tempted so much

Amish barn raising.

to buy or wear fashionable clothes or to be found in places of worldly amusements, etc.

Take, for example, window curtains. We have no doubt that the two kinds mentioned are sufficient and also scriptural and do not give an appearance of decorations. But that is not saying that churches having other curtains are wrong provided they are plain. But any lace, fancy or showy curtain is wrong anywhere.

As to buckle suspenders, we do not believe they violate any scripture if they can be had strictly plain. But as plain ones are oftimes hard to get and oftimes those that are bought are not plain, we believe it would be better to use the others.

Ordnung of a Christian Church, Pike County, Ohio, 1950, in John A. Hostetler, *Amish Society* (Baltimore: Johns Hopkins Press, 1963), pp. 59–61.

PIOUS BENEVOLENCE

The following tribute to the selflessness of the Dunkers
of Ephrata Cloister was written in 1777 by an American
officer who was wounded in the Battle of Brandywine
Creek.

I came upon this people by accident, but I left them with regret. I have
found out, however, that appearances may be delusive, and that where we
expected to meet with a cold reservedness, we may sometimes be surprised by exhibitions of the most charming affability and disinterested
benevolence. They all acted the part of the Good Samaritan to me, for
which I hope to be ever grateful; and while experiencing the benefits of
their kindnesses and attentions, witnessing the sympathies and emotions
expressed in their countenances, and listening to the words of hope and
pity with which they consoled their poor sufferers, is it strange that, under
such circumstances, their uncouth garments appeared more beautiful in
my eyes than ever did the richest robes of fashion, and their cowls more
becoming than head-dresses adorned with diamonds, and flowers, and
feathers? Until I entered the walls of Ephrata, I had no idea of pure and
practical Christianity. Not that I was ignorant of the forms, or even the
doctrines of religion. I knew it in theory before; I saw it in practice then.

Eugene Doll, *The Ephrata Cloister* (Ephrata, Pa.: Ephrata Cloister Associates, 1958–83), p. 31.

Brethren Annual Conference Report

For several generations the Brethren (Dunkers) retained
their original sense of piety and social purpose. But during
the nineteenth century, disputes over theological and social
issues caused numerous debates between liberals and
conservatives, and several schisms resulted. By the early
twentieth century, the Church of the Brethren had become
the official name for one of the largest of the sects. And
except among some of the older and conservative Pennsylvania communities, Brethren during the twentieth century
have more readily and swiftly than the Amish abandoned
much of their otherworldliness. Brethren over the years
have tried to preserve their identity and unity while at the
same time integrating themselves with the larger world.

They have not practiced shunning, and they have been more willing to accept urban life. As accommodation to the world grew more pronounced, the Brethren's Annual Conference struggled to revive and enforce traditional ways of dress and behavior. Rules about appearance became more specific and rigid as time passed. Between 1909 and 1911 the Conference undertook an exhaustive study of the issue of dress and simplicity which resulted in the comprehensive statement reprinted below. But like the earlier Puritans and Quakers, the twentieth-century Brethren allowed such rules to go unenforced. There have been no further attempts by the Conference to *legislate* simplicity. And today the Brethren are no longer a "separate and simple" people to the same degree as the Mennonites or Amish.

Pursuant to the following instructions "To take the whole matter under advisement and to make a restatement" we proceeded as follows:

I. We examined prayerfully the scriptural grounds of Christian attire and found that Jesus and the apostles taught honesty and simplicity of life and modesty in dress and manners. . . .

II. Investigation shows that the early church fathers and our own church fathers taught strongly and uniformly against pride and superfluity in dress, and constantly in favor of gospel plainness.

III. The Minutes of Conference show that the Church of the Brethren has, throughout her history, stood firmly against the fashions of the age, and extravagance in all manner of living, and on the other hand has taught faithfully the principles of simplicity of life and personal appearance. And, furthermore the Conference has, from time to time, adopted means and methods with the view of maintaining gospel simplicity in dress in the church body.

Now, since the gospel teaches plain and modest dress and since this is taught in the form of an obligation, without rules and methods of application further than to exclude plaiting of hair, the wearing of gold, pearls and costly raiment, and believing that a form that agrees with the spirit of the teaching is helpful in maintaining the principles of plainness and simplicity in dress and adornment in the general church body, "it seemed good to us" to submit the following restatement:

1. That the brethren wear plain clothing. That the coat with the standing collar be worn, especially by the ministers and deacons.

2. That the brethren wear their hair and beard in a plain and sanitary manner. That the mustache alone is forbidden.

3. That the sisters attire themselves in plainly made garments, free from ornaments and unnecessary appendages. That plain bonnets and hoods be the headdress, and the hair be worn in becoming Christian manner.

4. That the veil be worn in time of prayer and prophesying. The plain cap is regarded as meeting the requirement of scriptural teaching on the subject.

5. That gold for ornament and jewelry of all kinds shall not be worn.

6. That no brother be installed into office as minister or deacon who will not pledge himself to observe and teach the order of dress.

7. That no brother or sister serve as delegate to District or Annual Meeting, nor be appointed on committees to enforce discipline, who does not observe the order of dress.

8. That it be the duty of the official body of the church to teach faithfully and intelligently the simple, Christian life in dress; and bishops, who are the shepherds of the churches, are required to teach and to see that the simple life in general is taught and observed in their respective charges.

9. That those who do not fully conform to the methods herein set forth, but who manifest no inclination to follow the unbecoming fashions, and whose life and conduct is becoming a follower of Christ, be dealt with in love and forbearance; and that every effort be made to save all to the church until they see the beauty of making a larger sacrifice for Christ and the church. But if, after every effort has been made, they, in an arbitrary spirit, refuse to conform to said methods, and follow the foolish fashions of the world, they may be dealt with as disorderly members: and in dealing with such cases, both the salvation of the soul and the purity of the church should be kept in view.

10. That all are urged and implored, in the bonds of brotherly love and Christian fellowship, to teach and exemplify the order of the church in dress as a suitable expression of "the hidden man of the heart, in the incorruptible apparel of a meek and quiet spirit, which is in sight of God of great price."

Brethren Annual Conference, *Report* (1911), pp. 5-6.

Brotherly Agreement

In 1740 a group of Moravians settled in Pennsylvania on the Barony of Nazareth, owned by George Whitefield, the famous British evangelist. The Moravians erected a log house at Nazareth and later bought 500 acres where the Monocacy creek flows into the Lehigh. There, in 1741, they established another settlement under Count Zinzendorf's leadership. He named it Bethlehem, and he modeled it after its sister community in Saxony, Herrnhut.

At both Nazareth and Bethlehem, the Moravians developed a plan of communal organization called the "General Economy." Settlers were allowed to retain their private property, but their time and labor were placed at the disposal of the community. The "Economy" was supervised by a Board of Directors, headed by Bishop Augustus Spangenberg (1704–92), which soon established some thirty or so industries and handicrafts in addition to farming. Committees were organized to manage the various activities. In exchange for their labors, the residents were provided shelter and the necessities of life. No wages were paid. The church owned all the land and buildings as well as tools. The whole community was separated by age, sex, and marital status into groups called choirs. By living, working, and worshipping together in such small groups, it was assumed, spirituality and communal harmony would be more easily maintained. Infants were raised in nurseries managed by widows and single women. Dress was regulated as in the other pietistic communities of Pennsylvania at the time. Perhaps most importantly, Bethlehem was a closed community. Non-Moravians initially were not allowed to settle, and anyone opposed to the system was free to leave.

Under such guidelines Bethlehem and Nazareth prospered. By 1750 the settlements were virtually self-supporting. And soon thereafter Spangenberg set up similar communities at Bethabara and Salem in North Carolina. Visitors flocked to visit the Moravian villages there and in Pennsylvania, and they marveled at the industry and piety of the residents.

Yet the zeal and enthusiasm of the early years quickly faded. Young men increasingly left the Moravian communities in order to pursue more lucrative economic opportunities in the larger society. In addition, the very prosperity of the settlements led some to question whether the original communal ethic was still necessary. Ostentation began to creep into Bethlehem social life. As Zinzendorf lamented: "Our ethic was that of Mary Magdalene and we had not yet learnt how to play the role of Martha and deal with the outside world." In 1762 the General Economy structure was abandoned by common consent. Like the earlier Pilgrims of Plymouth, the Moravians tired of collective endeavor and exclusivity. At Bethlehem the various industries were sold to individuals, but many of the farms, the general store, and the inn remained under the control of the church. Yet during the nineteenth century Bethlehem lost its rural, homogeneous, and theocratic character and became a bustling, pluralistic, industrial city. At the same time, the Moravians increasingly deemphasized plain living. Simplicity for them has come to mean primarily the sincerity of one's relationship to Christ rather than the choice of hooks versus buttons. This stress on internal rather than external simplicity has remained a distinctive trademark of the Moravian faith during the twentieth century. Their motto, "In essentials unity, in nonessentials liberty, and in all things, love," expresses quite clearly their belief that it is up to the individual to decide upon an appropriate manner of Christian living.

It is not to be forgotten at any time that Bethlehem and Nazareth and the remaining communities thereto belonging were established, and developed in the manner in which they now appear, for no other purpose except that the Saviour's work not only in Pennsylvania but in all America, as well, particularly, in the English Provinces, may thereby be given the hand of assistance. The purpose of the said Economy, if one is to speak plainly, has in view, of course, that we conduct ourselves unitedly in an honorable manner and well pleasing to God, that we rear our children according to His will and guard our young people, sisters as well as brethren, until they are trained so as to be of use to Him, that we care for our poor and weak, aged and infirm and faithfully minister to them, that we regulate, also, our wedded state so that we may doubly care for that which belongs to the Lord. But something further is intended therewith; we have, indeed, agreed with one another that we would each, according to the gift and skill the Lord has granted him, be faithful and industrious so that we may be helpful when and where the Saviour may need us. . . .

As no one among us can say with truth that he was forced by men to go into the said Economy, or remain in it, since, on the contrary, we have agreed to it ourselves, not without previously understanding the matter, not in haste, but with good cause and conviction. . . . We declare, therefore, not only in general but, also, in particular, each one for himself, that we do not for this time nor for the future pretend to any wage or have reason to pretend to any. We were received into the said Economy with no idea of having, taking, or seeking wage, the Economy having dedicated itself to the service of the Saviour, and with no promise that wage or pay should be given; we, on the contrary, regard it a mark of grace that we are here and may labor according to the above stated intention. . . .

Einige Zur Bethlehemschen und Nazarethschen Gemeinschaftlichen Bruder Oconomie gehorige Momenta in "Diarium Bethlehem" (August 1754), Bethlehem Archives. Translated by Dr. W. N. Schwarze.

BETHLEHEM'S DECLINE

In 1765 a group of workers in Bethlehem remarked:

(1) Our Saviour observes, that we have left our primitive simplicity. (2) That much conformity to worldly values has gradually insinuated itself into the conduct of our Congregation. (3) That in the way of our trade and business profit is made a main matter and that in consideration thereof the congregation principles are neglected. (4) That we study more now to get money and profit, than how to save our souls.

Gilliam L. Golin, *Moravians in Two Worlds: A Study in Changing Communities* (New York: Columbia University Press, 1967), p. 197.

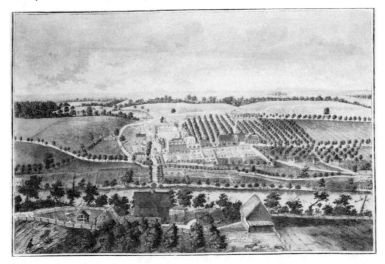

View of eighteenth-century Bethlehem, Pennsylvania.

MORAVIAN HYMN

G. Arnold

> O BLEST condition, happy living,
> Which true simplicity imparts,
> When we to God ourselves are giving,
> And Jesus' mind rules in our hearts:
> This lays our souls in deep prostration,
> And fervent prayer before the throne,
> Casts down each vain imagination,
> Till every thought is Christ's alone.
>
> That which is by the world esteemed,
> A single mind counts vanity;
> What's innocence by others deemed,
> Is shunn'd by true simplicity:

Because the love to things terrestrial
　　We must deny thro' Jesus' grace,
And, to obtain the prize celestial,
　　Cast off whate'er impedes our race.

The simple heart no care perplexes,
　　That robs the world of all content:
Envy nor strife his spirit vexes,
　　Who lives in that calm element;
He cherishes his hidden treasure,
　　Unruffled by the worldling's spite:
If others ask to share this pleasure.
　　Simplicity tastes true delight.

O Jesus, God of my salvation,
　　Thy single mind impart to me;
Root out the world's infatuation,
　　However keen the pain may be:
Thrice happy they who tread unwearied
　　The path of true simplicity;
They as wise virgins are prepared
　　To meet the Bridegroom cheerfully.

Shaker Simplicity

Because of their stringent social code and their emphasis
on celibacy, the Shakers have declined in numbers over the
years, finding it increasingly difficult to gain new converts
to their austere way of life. Today they are a mere remnant
of their former days, but they nevertheless sustain the
Christian humility and simplicity that have become their
trademark.

These Shaker communities have become justly famous
for their remarkable simplicity. As Father Joseph Meachem

stressed in the 1790s: "All work done on things made in the Church for their own use ought to be faithfully and well done, but plain and without superfluity. All things ought to be made according to their order and use; and all things kept decent and in good order." The settlements were almost always prosperous, the buildings were plain, clean, and functional, the furniture was gracefully austere, and concerns of the spirit pervaded the community. "Temperate" labor was sanctified, property was held in common, and mutual aid was expected. Shaker speech and dress bore the imprint of plainness. Though their life was minutely regulated by their "millennial laws," with duties individually assigned, the sexes separated, and conformity required, the Shakers seemed to observers to lead a genuinely joyous existence.

If brethren desire any garments or fixtures to garments, as pockets, etc. etc. or new articles of manufacture, that come in the sisters line of business, which are not common to the brethren in general, they must apply to the Elders.

2. Silk hat bands, may not be worn, save on fur hats, for nice use.

3. Dark colored hat bands may not be worn, on summer hats.

4. All should remember that these are not the true heirs of the Kingdom of Heaven, who multiply to themselves, needless treasures of this world's goods.

CONCERNING SUPERFLUITIES NOT OWNED

Fancy articles of any kind, or articles which are superfluously finished, trimmed or ornamented, are not suitable for Believers, and may not be used or purchased; among which are the following; also some other articles which are deemed improper, to be in the Church, and may not be brought in, except by special liberty of the Ministry.

2. Silver pencils, silver tooth picks, gold pencils, or pens, silver spoons, silver thimbles, (but thimbles may be lined with silver,) gold or silver watches, brass knobs or handles of any size or kind. Three bladed knives, knife handles with writing or picturing on them, bone or horn handled knives, except for pocket knives, bone or horn spools, superfluous whips, marbled tin ware, superfluous

Interior of Shaker building.

paper boxes of any kind, gay silk handkerchiefs, green veils, bought dark colored cotton handkerchiefs, for sisters use:— Checked handkerchiefs made by the world, may not be bought for sisters use, except head handkerchiefs. Lace for cap borders, superfluous suspenders of any kind. Writing desks may not be used by common members, unless they have much public writing to do. But writing desks may be used as far as it is thought proper by the Lead.

3. The following articles are also deemed improper, viz. Superfluously finished, or flowery painted clocks. Bureaus, and looking glasses, also superfluously painted or fancy shaped sleighs, or carriages, superfluously trimmed Harness, and many other articles too numerous to mention.

4. The forementioned things are at present, utterly forbidden, but if the Ministry see fit to bring in any among the forementioned articles, which are not superfluously wrought, the order prohibiting the use of such article or articles is thereby repealed.

5. Believers may not in any case or circumstances, manufacture for sale, any article or articles, which are superfluously wrought, and which would have a tendency to feed the pride and vanity of man, or such as would not be admissible to use among themselves, on account of their superfluity.

Father Joseph Meacham and Mother Lucy Wright, *Millennial Laws* (New Lebanon, 1821), pp. 3–12.

'TIS THE GIFT TO BE SIMPLE

Shaker Hymn

'Tis the Gift to be Simple, 'Tis the Gift to be Free,
  'Tis the Gift to come down where we ought to be.
And when we find ourselves in the place just right,
  'Twill be in the valley of Love and Delight!

When true Simplicity is gained
  To bow and to bend we shan't be ashamed.
To turn, turn will be our delight,
  'Till by turning, turning we come 'round right!

The Shakers

Thomas Low Nichols

Visitors to Shaker communities were numerous during the nineteenth century. Though many were critical of the celibate practices of the Shakers, virtually all were impressed by their living testimony to their faith and their social ethic. During the mid-nineteenth century, Thomas Low Nichols (1815–1901), a health reformer, visited the Shaker community at Lebanon, Ohio. Part of his account is excerpted below.

In Cincinnati, Ohio, I met one day with a Shaking Quaker. He wore a broad-brimmed hat, and shad-bellied coat of a bluish-gray homespun cloth, with his hair cropped short before and falling into the neck behind. He was mild in manner, simple in conversation, and his communications were "yea" and "nay." He conversed freely on the doctrines and polity of the society, and gave me a friendly invitation to visit the Shaker village of Lebanon, twenty miles distant.

The wisdom of the ruling elders could scarcely have selected a finer spot for the domain of a community. The land in the Miami valley is of a wonderful fertility, and the whole region is a rich and well-cultivated country; still the domain of the Shakers was marked by striking peculiarities. The fences were higher and stronger than those on the adjacent farms; the woods were cleared of underbrush; the tillage was of extraordinary neatness; the horses, cattle, and sheep were of the breeds, and in the best condition.

In the Shaker village are not taverns or shops, but large, plainly-built dwelling-houses, barns, work-shops, and an edifice for meetings and religious exercises. Simple utility is the only rule of architecture. There is not, in the whole village, any line of ornament. The brown paint is used only to protect the woodwork of the buildings. I did not see so much as an ornamental shrub or flower in the whole domain.

One house is set apart for the entertainment of strangers, who receive attention, food, and lodging as long as they choose to remain. The brethren and sisters who are appointed to fulfil the duties of hospitality, neither demand nor refuse payment.

The women, old and young, ugly and pretty, dress in the same neat but unfashionable attire. There are not bright colours; no ruffles or flounces or frills; no embroidery or laces; no ribbons or ornaments of any kind. The hair is combed smoothly back under a plain cap; a three-cornered kerchief of sober brown covers the bosom, and the narrow gored skirt had no room for crinoline.

The rooms and furniture are as plain and homely as the external architecture. There is not a moulding nor any coloured paper; not a picture nor print adorns the walls, nor is there a vase or statue. The only books are a few of their own religious treatises, collections of hymns, and works of education, science, and utility.

But there is everywhere the perfection of order and neatness. The floors shine like mirrors. Every visible thing is bright and clean. There is a place for everything, and everything is in its place.

Shaker boys taking a break from farm chores.

This order and neatness is carried out in the workshops, the farmyards, everywhere.

A community of two or three hundred industrious persons, all engaged in agriculture and useful manufactures, paying no rents, having no costly vices, producing for themselves all the necessaries of life, and selling their surplus produce, cannot fail to grow rich. I found this community living in comfort and abundance, surrounded with a great wealth of houses and lands, flocks and herds, and, as I was told, with large sums invested in the best securities. Men, women, and children all work. There are no idlers, and no time is lost. As the honesty of the Shakers is proverbial, they have the command of the best markets for their wooden wares, agricultural implements, brooms, garden seeds, preserved fruits and vegetables, and the surplus of their cloth, leather, &c. There is nothing, therefore, to hinder them from accumulating property to an immense extent; as can easily be done by any honest community in any country.

Thomas Low Nichols, *Forty Years of American Life, 1821-1861* (1864; New York: Stackpole, 1937), pp. 234–38.

SHAKER SAYINGS

Be temperate, and not go to excess in any calling or duty. Wisdom doth not mark her ways by intemperance; but with prudence she claims the virtue of temperance; and the thankful heart shall be blessed of Wisdom.

Love meekness; for this is a strong virtue. Pride will make no tarry with meekness; but flee away to a high minded zeal.

Simplicity should have a place in thy heart and soul: this beautifies the child of God.

Simplicity is needful in conversation; it forbids high flown words, and guides the tongue in wisdom, to speak in simple language.

Simplicity scorneth pride, and is far from mincing steps and stiffened joints. Selfishness is baneful to charity; it belongs to the sons of darkness, and not to the children of gospel light.

The Youth's Guide in Zion, and Holy Mother's Promises (Canterbury, N.H., 1842), p. 16.

Republican Simplicity

3

Even though the pietistic sects stressed that the truly simple and good life could be achieved only by withdrawing from the larger society and its corruptions, many eighteenth-century idealists refused to abandon the vision of America as a distinctively virtuous society. Thus, even though collective spiritual ideals continued to give way to the forces of pluralism, secularism, and materialism during the eighteenth century, the utopianism inherent in the original Protestant social ethic retained much of its potency. Many of America's "Founding Fathers" integrated its premises into the ideology of classical republicanism that they developed in opposition to British tyranny.

This Revolutionary-era republicanism entailed a comprehensive moral vision that drew not only upon the heritage of Protestant simplicity but also upon the rich tradition of enlightened simplicity in classical Greek and Roman thought. Prominent colonial patriots such as John and Sam Adams, John Dickinson, Benjamin Rush, Thomas Jefferson, and Richard Henry Lee steeped themselves in the pastoral poetry of Hesiod, Horace, and Virgil, as well as in the ethical writings of Socrates, Aristotle, Cicero, Seneca, Epictetus, and Epicurus. And by the 1760s they were repeatedly drawing upon such classical sources in developing a theory of social change that stressed the insidious effects of unchecked luxury and selfishness on any republican society. The original republic of Rome had fallen, they believed, when it had grown avaricious and imperial. The lure of foreign plunder had transformed a virtuous society of sturdy, independent yeomen into a ruthless, tyrannical, and corrupt empire engaged in a program of plunder and sensual indulgence. As the political crisis with England deepened, the American republican theorists used such ancient analogies to contrast the pervasive luxury, immorality, and avarice of the British ruling class with an idealized image of an agrarian American republic in the classical tradition. Like the early Roman republic, their dream for America entailed a cohesive nation inhabited primarily by hard-working, plain-living citizen-farmers led by an enlightened natural aristocracy of virtue and talent.

Increasingly after 1763, with the onset of new and especially onerous British regulatory decrees, these idealistic Revolutionaries interpreted the general corruption of American manners as the result not of their own failings but as a consequence of their continued attachment to a degenerate mother country led by greedy commercialists. To reduce the infectious effects of such an imperial association, these classical republican leaders pleaded with the public to boycott British luxuries and simplify their tastes and thereby become more self-sufficient. Doing so would not only force the British to repeal their hated ordinances but would also encourage a revival of self-reliance and virtuous simplicity among the American people. In this sense a major factor influencing the development of the Revolutionary movement was the desire on the part of civic and religious moralists to restore the purity and simplicity of American life by ridding the country of British corruption.

So much for their hopes. No sooner did the hostilities with Great Britain commence than many of these republican idealists recognized that their diagnosis of the disease infecting American character was superficial. The Revolution did indeed generate a surge of patriotic simplicity. Many citizens made great personal sacrifices in support of the American cause. But the conflict also unleashed a torrent of speculative activity, price-gouging, and hoarding. As the fiery patriot James Otis predicted, "When the pot boils the scum will rise." But neither he nor other idealists expected the Revolution to produce such an outpouring of selfishness among so many.

The failure of the Revolution in and of itself to generate a widespread reformation of manners and priorities suggests that the classical simplicity preached by republican leaders had not penetrated very deeply into the social consciousness. Most colonial Americans, of course, were not steeped in the classics, and many of those who supported the Revolution and fought with Washington did so not because they wanted to provoke a revival of plain living and high thinking but because they saw in political independence a means of personal liberation from a confining social structure that denied them upward mobility and political participation.

Thus, as had been the case with the first settlers, Revolutionary Americans differed sharply over the meaning of the "pursuit of happiness." At least that was the assessment of many disillusioned Revolutionary leaders. As John Adams observed, self-realization, not self-restraint, was the most popular outlook spawned by independence.

This revelation dismayed many of the old patriot idealists such as Sam Adams. But it did not surprise a new generation of public spokesmen who emerged in the aftermath of independence. Alexander Hamilton and a number of other rising political figures maintained that the classical republican simplicity promoted by aging Revolutionaries such as Sam Adams was an anachronism. He scoffed at their "whining laments" and their "deceitful dream of a golden age." National greatness, Hamilton insisted, lay not in limiting social and economic development to subsistence agriculture and small retailing but in encouraging an ever-expanding program of domestic manufacturing and international commerce. Thus he broke with the classical republican tradition which stressed that republics must remain small and predominantly agrarian in order to survive. Hamilton saw nothing wrong with the British model of economic development. After all, he repeatedly noted, the desire to accumulate money and live in luxury was the driving dynamic of human nature. Statesmen, he argued, must recognize this historical fact and should manage public policy so as to stimulate and facilitate rather than restrain private ambition. If this led to large fortunes and extravagant living among the elite, then so be it, for commercial and territorial expansion would also serve to elevate the standard of living for all.

Hamilton's bald realism, of course, won out in the shaping of public policy in the early national period. In the decades after independence, as the new nation experienced rapid territorial expansion and population growth, fewer and fewer Americans were attracted to the classical republican program of a self-limiting agrarianism. The commercial and speculative opportunities were too alluring, both in farming and in trade. By the mid-nineteenth century the age of steam was generating conceptions of the good life that the classical republican spokesmen had never envisioned. Yet idealists in the young nation continued to keep the old dream of republican simplicity alive. It was too deeply engrained in the American imagination to be totally discarded.

Letter from a Farmer

John Dickinson

John Dickinson (1732–1808) emerged as one of the most effective early spokesmen for republican simplicity and Revolutionary resistance. Born in Maryland, he was trained in the law and steeped in classical study. During the 1760s he campaigned against the British regulatory decrees and called on Americans to boycott British goods. His *Letters from a Farmer* displayed most of the assumptions of classical republicanism, even though his self-portrait was highly idealized. Soon after the *Letters* were published, a Boston town meeting sent Dickinson a commendation for his "Spartan, Roman, British Virtue, and Christian spirit joined."

My Dear Countrymen,

I am a farmer, settled after a variety of fortunes near the banks of the River Delaware in the province of Pennsylvania. I received a liberal education and have been engaged in the busy scenes of life; but am now convinced that a man may be as happy without bustle as with it. My farm is small; my servants are few and good; I have a little money at interest; I wish for no more; my employment in my own affairs is easy; and with a contented, grateful mind . . . I am completing the number of days allotted to me by divine goodness.

Being generally a master of my time, I spend a good deal of it in a library, which I think the most valuable part of my small estate; and being acquainted with two or three gentlemen of abilities and learning who honor me with their friendship, I have acquired, I believe, a greater share of knowledge in history and the laws and constitution of my country than is generally attained by men of my class, many of them not being so fortunate as I have been in the opportunities of getting information.

From infancy I was taught to love humanity and liberty. Inquiry and experience have since confirmed my reverence for the lessons then given me by convincing me more fully of their truth and excellence. Benevolence toward mankind excites wishes for their welfare, and such wishes endear the means of fulfilling them. These can be found in liberty only, and therefore her sacred cause ought to be espoused by every man, on every occasion, to the utmost of his power. As a charitable but poor person does not withhold his mite because he cannot relieve *all* the distresses of the miserable, so should not any honest man suppress his sentiments concerning freedom, however small their influence is likely to be. Perhaps he may "touch some wheel" that will have an effect greater than he could reasonably expect.

John Dickinson, *Letters from a Farmer in Pennsylvania* (Philadelphia: Hall and Sellers, 1768), pp. 1-2.

CLASSICAL SIMPLICITY

Observe moderation: proportion is best in all things.
— Hesiod, *Works and Days*, 1.694

Socrates: Here, then, is a discovery of new evils, I said, against which the guardians will have to watch, or they will creep into the city unobserved.

What evils?

Wealth, I said, and poverty; the one is the parent of luxury and indolence, and the other of meanness and viciousness, and both of discontent.

—Plato, *The Republic*, IV, 421b

Happiness, whether consisting in pleasure or virtue, or both, is more often found with those who are highly cultivated in their mind and in their character, and have only a moderate share of external goods, than among those who possess external goods to a useless extent but are deficient in higher qualities.

— Aristotle, *Politics*, X, 1323b

To accustom one's self, therefore, to simple and inexpensive habits is a great ingredient in the perfecting of health, and makes a man free from hesitation with respect to the necessary uses of life.

— Epicurus, *Diogenes Laertus*, X, 131

Beware of an inordinate desire for wealth. Nothing is so revealing of narrowness and littleness of soul than love of money. Conversely, there is nothing more honorable or noble than indifference to money, if one doesn't have any; or than genuine altruism and well-doing if one does have it.

— Cicero, *De Officiis*, I, 20

Whoever cultivates the golden mean avoids both the poverty of a hovel and the envy of a palace.

— Horace, *Odes*, I, 10

You ask what is the proper limit to a person's wealth? First, having what is essential, and second, having what is enough.

— Seneca, *Letters to Lucilius*, 2

Samuel Adams and Patriotic Simplicity

The most fervent spokesman for classical republican simplicity during the Revolutionary era was Samuel Adams (1722-1803). A Frenchman visiting Massachusetts in the 1770s observed that Adams "has the excess of republican virtues,—untainted probity, simplicity, modesty, and above all, firmness." The son of pious parents, Sam Adams inherited their intense spirituality and their conscious commitment to their Puritan ethical heritage. At Harvard he read widely in the classics, and his vocational interests quickly shifted from religion to politics. By the mid-eighteenth century Adams was managing the family brewery he inherited after his father's death and becoming increasingly active as a social and political activist. Like the earlier Puritan leaders, he was concerned that New Englanders were becoming preoccupied with material gain at the expense of their spiritual vitality and political rights. "Our Morals, our Constitution, and our Liberties," he argued, "must needs degenerate" under such conditions, and he repeatedly reminded Bostonians of the "dreadful example" of republican Rome's collapse from virtuous simplicity into luxurious corruption.

Throughout the 1760s Adams was in the forefront of the colonial resistance movement. He especially promoted the non-importation associations designed to encourage colonial frugality and reduce British imports. With the passage of the Port Bill and the other Coercive Acts of 1774, he saw the crisis coming to a climax. The colonists must either succumb to tyrannical intimidation or resurrect the spartan determination of their Puritan forebears. He was delighted to see that many colonial patriots were willing to endure the sacrifices required by the Revolutionary cause.

SAMUEL ADAMS TO WILLIAM CHECKLEY, 1 JUNE 1774

If Britain by her multiplied oppressions is now accelerating that Independency of the Colonies which she so much dreads, and which in process of time must take place, who will she have to blame but herself? We live in an important Period, & have a post to maintain, to desert which would be an unpardonable Crime, and would entail upon us the Curses of posterity. The infamous Tools of Power are holding up the picture of Want and Misery; but in vain do they think to intimidate us; the Virtue of our Ancestors inspires us—they were contented with Clams & Muscles [sic]. For my own part, I have been wont to converse with poverty; and however disagreeable a Companion she may be thought to be by the affluent & luxurious who never have been acquainted with her, I can live happily with her the remainder of my days, if I can thereby contribute to the Redemption of my Country.

SAMUEL ADAMS TO THOMAS YOUNG, 17 OCTOBER 1774

I have written to our Friends to provide themselves without Delay with Arms & Ammunition, get well instructed in the military Art, embody themselves & prepare a complete Set of

Rules that they may be ready in Case they are called to defend themselves against the violent Attacks of Despotism. . . . I think our Countrymen discover the Spirit of Rome or Sparta. I admire in them that Patience which you have often heard one say is characteristick of the Patriot.

As the Revolution began, Adams was optimistic that the conflict would continue to provoke a revival of austerity and public virtue among the colonists. But within a few months after Lexington and Concord, he and other republican idealists were shocked to learn that many Americans were refusing to make sacrifices on behalf of independence. In Boston, he discovered to his dismay, residents were resisting the price controls imposed by the government to minimize profiteering and speculation.

SAMUEL ADAMS TO JOHN SCOLLAY, 20 MARCH 1777

The Act for regulating Prices, you tell me[,] has made a great Convulsion especially in Boston. I am exceedingly sorry to hear that Dissensions should arise in a Community, remarkable for its Publick Spirit, and which has heretofore by the united Exertions of Individuals repeatedly done essential Services in Support of the Liberties of America. Is it indeed true, my Friend, that "Self Denial is a Virtue rarely to be seen among you"? How great a Change in a few years! The Self Denial of the Citizens of Boston, their Patience and long Suffering under the cruel Oppression of the Port bill[,] was astonishing both to their Friends and their Enemies. Their Firmness and Resolution in that severe Conflict, and the Cheerfulness with which they endured the Loss of all things, rather than the publick Liberty should Suffer by their submission, will be handed down to their Honour in the impartial History. God forbid that they should so soon forget their own generous Feelings for the Publick and for each other, as to set private Interest in Competition with that of the great Community.

SAMUEL ADAMS TO MRS. SAMUEL ADAMS, 24 NOVEMBER 1780

You are Witness that I have not raised a Fortune in the Service of my Country. I glory in being what the World calls, a poor Man.

From Schroeder, *Life and Times of Washington*

Samuel Adams.

If my Mind has ever been tinctured with Envy, the Rich and the Great have not been its objects. . . . I will trust in that all gracious Being, who, in his own good Way, has provided us with Food and

Raiment; and having spent the greater Part of my Life in Publick Cares, like the weary Traveller, fatigued with the Journey of the Day, I can rest with you in a Cottage.

Adams grew increasingly disgusted at the behavior of many of the patriot leaders during the Revolution. He especially resented the extravagance of John Hancock, who was elected the first governor of Massachusetts in 1780 and brought to that office an Old World preference for pomp and display. To the plain-living Adams it was scandalous for a public official in the new state government to engage in such arrogant ostentation.

SAMUEL ADAMS TO JOHN SCOLLAY,
30 DECEMBER 1780

Our Government [Massachusetts], I perceive, is organized on the Basis of the new Constitution. I am afraid there is more Pomp & Parade than is consistent with those sober Republican Principles, upon which the Framers of it thought they had founded it. Why should this new Era be introduced with Entertainments expensive & tending to dissipate the Minds of the People? Does it become us to lead the People to such publick Diversions as promote Superfluity of Dress & Ornament, when it is as much as they can bear to support the Expense of clothing a naked Army? Will Vanity & Levity ever be the Stability of Government, either in States, in Cities. . . . Our Bradfords, Winslows & Winthrops would have revolted at the Idea of opening Scenes of Dissipation & Folly; knowing them to be inconsistent with their great Design, in transplanting themselves into what they called this "Outside of the World." But I fear I shall say too much. I love the people of Boston. I once thought, that City would be the *Christian* Sparta. But Alas! Will men ever be free! They will be free no longer than while they remain virtuous.

That the Revolution failed to generate a renewed commitment to pious or republican simplicity was a sharp disappointment to Samuel Adams. After the conflict ended in 1783, a raging materialism seemed to pervade all ranks. British ships clogged Boston harbor, unloading luxury items that the patriots had virtuously gone without during the fighting. In addition, many among the young gentry of the city began practicing a self-indulgent and licentious way of life that directly contradicted the ideal of republican simplicity. Adams was especially irritated by the founding of the Sans Souci Club, an exclusive gathering place for the wealthy where dancing, card-playing, and extravagant spending were the rule. This incited him to write a series of scathing attacks in the Boston press. But they did little good. Sam Adams discovered only too late that his version of republicanism based on classical philosophy and Puritan ethics was not shared by the majority of his fellow citizens.

SAMUEL ADAMS, *MASSACHUSETTS CENTINEL*, 15 JANUARY 1785

If there ever was a period wherein reason was bewildered, and stupefied by dissipation and extravagance, it surely is the present. Did ever effeminacy with her languid train, receive a greater welcome in society than at this day? New amusements are invented—new dissipations are introduced, to lull and enervate those minds already too much softened, poisoned and contaminated by idle pleasures, and foolish gratifications. We are exchanging prudence, virtue and economy, for those glaring spectres luxury, prodigality and profligacy. We are prostituting all our glory as a people, for new modes of pleasure, ruinous in their expenses, injurious to virtue, and totally detrimental to the well being of society.

Did we consult the history of Athens and Rome, we should find that so long as they continued their frugality and simplicity of manners, they shone with superlative glory; but no sooner were effeminate refinements introduced amongst them, than they visibly fell from whatever was elevated and magnanimous, and became feeble and timid, dependent, slavish and false. . . . Say, my country. Why do you thus suffer all the intemperances of Great-Britain to be fostered in our bosom, in all their vile luxuriance?

Harry Alonzo Cushing, ed., *The Writings of Samuel Adams*, 4 vols. (New York: G. P. Putnam's Sons, 1908): 3:128, 163, 365; 4:226, 236-38.

FOURTH OF JULY ORATION 1778
David Ramsay

Republics are favorable to truth, sincerity, frugality, industry, and simplicity of manners.... It was the interest of Great Britain to encourage our dissipation and extravagance, for the two-fold purpose of increasing the sale of her manufactures, and of perpetuating our subordination. In vain we sought to check the growth of luxury, by sumptuary laws; every wholesome restraint of this kind was sure to meet with the royal negative. While the whole force of example was employed to induce us to copy the dissipated manners of the country from which we sprung. If, therefore, we had continued dependent, our frugality, industry, and simplicity of manners, would have been lost in an imitation of British extravagance, idleness, and false refinements.

David Ramsay, *Fourth of July Oration* (1778), in H. Niles, ed., *Principles and Acts of the Revolution in America* (Baltimore: W. O. Niles, 1822), p. 64.

John and Abigail Adams

Equally illustrative of the blending of the Puritan ethic and classical republicanism was Sam Adams's cousin, John Adams (1735-1826). The eldest son of Deacon John Adams, a farmer and cordwainer in the tiny rural village of Braintree, ten miles south of Boston, he entered Harvard intending to become a minister but soon changed his mind. His excited reading of the classics led him to become a free-thinker, and he soon abandoned his inherited theology. But he retained the strict personal regimen of his Puritan fore-fathers. Throughout his long and distinguished career, John Adams fought a running battle with his passions, determined to lead a classically balanced, temperate life devoted to study, public service, and family nurture.

Abigail Adams (1744-1818) shared her husband's commitment to republican simplicity. During his frequent absences from home, she was an efficient manager of the household. In the spring of 1776 Abigail wrote John that she hoped "in time to have the reputation of being as good a *Farmeress* as my partner has of being a good Statesman." She succeeded. As the Revolutionary crisis deepened, the

Adamses engaged in acts of patriotic frugality and simplicity. While serving in France during the conflict, John Adams frequently contrasted the luxuries and indolence of the European aristocracy to the republican manners of the Americans. Yet upon his return to the United States he joined Abigail, Sam Adams, and many other older patriots in bemoaning the collapse of patriotic simplicity.

For the rest of his life John Adams would grow increasingly frustrated by the inability of his countrymen to restrain their grasping materialism and selfish individualism. Like the earlier Puritans and ancient republicans, Adams discovered the difficulty of developing a societal ethic that encouraged hard work and initiative yet frowned on indulgence. In 1819 he asked Thomas Jefferson: "Will you tell me how to prevent riches from becoming the effects of temperance and industry? Will you tell me how to prevent riches from becoming luxury? Will you tell me how to prevent luxury from becoming effeminacy, intoxication, extravagance, Vice and folly?"

JOHN ADAMS,
DIARY, 28 APRIL 1756

Our proper Business in this Life is, not to accumulate large Fortunes, not to gain high Honours and important offices in the State, not to waste our Health and Spirits in pursuit of the Sciences, but constantly to improve our selves in Habits of Piety and Virtue. Consequently, the meanest Mechanick, who endeavours in proportion to his Ability, to promote the happiness of his fellow men, deserves better of Society, and should be held in higher Esteem than the Greatest Magistrate, who uses his power for his own Pleasures or Avarice or Ambition.

JOHN ADAMS,
DIARY, JANUARY 1759

Let Virtue address me—"Which, dear Youth, will you prefer? a Life of Effeminacy, Indolence and obscurity, or a Life of Industry, Temperance, and Honour? Take my Advice, rise and mount your Horse, by the Mornings dawn, and shake away amidst the great and beautiful scenes of Nature, that appear at that Time of the day, all the Crudities that are left in your stomach, and all the obstructions that are left in your Brains. Then return to your Study, and bend your whole soul to the Institutes of the Law, and the Reports of Cases, that have been adjudged by the Rules, in the Institutes. Let no trifling Diversion or amuzement or Company decoy you from your Books, i.e. let no Girl, no Gun, no Cards, no flutes, no Violins, no Dress, no Tobacco, no Laziness, decoy you from your Books."

JOHN ADAMS,
DIARY, 30 JANUARY 1768

To what Object, are my Views directed? What is the End and Purpose of my Studies, Journeys, Labours of all Kinds of Body and Mind, of Tongue and Pen? Am I grasping at Money, or Scheming for Power? Am I planning the Illustration of my Family or the Welfare of my Country? These are great Questions. In Truth, I am tossed about so much, from Post to Pillar, that I have not Leisure and Tranquillity enough, to consider distinctly my own Views, Objects and Feelings.—I am mostly intent at present, upon collecting a Library, and I find, that a great deal of Thought, and Care, as well as Money, are necessary to assemble an ample and well chosen assortment of Books.—But when this is done, it is only a means, an Instrument.

JOHN ADAMS,
DIARY, 30 JUNE 1772

It has been my Fate, to be acquainted, in my Way of Business, with a Number of very rich Men—Gardiner, Bowdoin, Pitts, Hancock, Rowe, Lee, Sargeant, Hooper, Doane. . . . But there is not one of all these, who derives more Pleasure from his Property than I do from mine. My little Farm, and Stock, and Cash, affords me as much Satisfaction, as all their immense Tracts, extensive Navigation, sumptuous Buildings, their vast Sums at Interest, and Stocks in Trade yield to them. The Pleasures of Property, arise from Acquisition more than Possession, from what is to come rather than from what is. These Men feel their Fortunes. They feel the Strength and Importance, which their Riches give them in the World. Their Courage and Spirits are buoyed up, their Imaginations are inflated by them. The rich are seldom remarkable for Modesty, Ingenuity, or Humanity. Their Wealth has rather a Tendency to make them penurious and selfish.

Birthplace of John Adams, Quincy, Massachusetts.

JOHN ADAMS,
DIARY, 1 JULY 1772

I have served my Country, and her professed Friends, at an immense Expense, to me, of Time, Peace, Health, Money, and Preferment, both of which last have courted my Acceptance, and been inexorably refused, least I should be laid under a Temptation to forsake the Sentiments of the Friends of this Country. . . . I will devote myself wholly to my private Business, my Office and my farm, and I hope to lay a Foundation for better Fortune to my Children, and an happier Life than has fallen to my Share.

JOHN ADAMS TO ABIGAIL ADAMS,
29 JUNE 1774

Let us therefore my dear Partner, from that Affection which we feel for our lovely Babes, apply ourselves by every Way, we can, to the Cultivation of our Farm. Let Frugality, And Industry, be our Virtues, if they are not of any others. And above all Cares of this Life let our ardent Anxiety be, to mould the Minds and Manners of our Children.

Home of John and Abigail Adams, Quincy, Massachusetts.

JOHN ADAMS TO ABIGAIL ADAMS,
20 SEPTEMBER 1774

Frugality, my Dear, Frugality, Economy, Parcimony must be our Refuge. I hope the Ladies are every day diminishing their ornaments, and the Gentlemen too.

Let us Eat Potatoes and drink Water. Let us wear Canvass, and undressed Sheepskins, rather than submit to the unrighteous, and ignominious Domination that is prepared for Us.

ABIGAIL ADAMS TO JOHN ADAMS,
16 OCTOBER 1774

If we expect to inherit the blessings of our Fathers, we should return a little more to their primitive Simplicity of Manners, and not sink into inglorious ease. We have too many high sounding words, and too few actions that correspond with them. I have spent one Sabbath in Town since you left me. I saw no difference in respect to ornaments, &c. &c. but in the Country you must look for that virtue, of which you find but small Glimmerings in the Metropolis. Indeed they have not the advantages, nor the resolution to encourage our own Manufactories which people in the country have. To the Mercantile part, tis considered as throwing away their own Bread; but they must retrench their expenses to be content with a small share of gain for they will find but few who will wear their Livery. As for me I will seek wool and flax and work willingly with my Hands, and indeed there is occasion for all our industry and economy.

JOHN ADAMS TO MERCY WARREN, 8 JANUARY 1776

Virtue and Simplicity of Manners are indispensably necessary in a Republic among all orders and Degrees of Men. But there is so much Rascallity, so much Venality and Corruption, so much Avarice and Ambition, such a Rage for Profit and Commerce among all Ranks and Degrees of Men even in America, that I sometimes doubt whether there is public Virtue enough to Support a Republic.

ABIGAIL ADAMS TO JOHN ADAMS, 17 APRIL 1777

I seek wool and flax and can work willingly with my Hands, and tho my Household are not cloathed with fine linnen nor scarlet, they are cloathed with what is perhaps full as Honorary, the plain and decent manufactory of my own family, and tho I do not abound, I am not in want. I have neither poverty nor Riches but food which is conveniant for me and a Heart to be thankfull and content that in such perilous times so large a share of the comforts of life are allotted to me.

JOHN ADAMS TO ABIGAIL ADAMS, 12 APRIL 1778, PASSI, FRANCE

The Delights of France are innumerable. The Politeness, the Elegance, the Softness, the Delicacy, is extreme.

In short, stern and hauty Republican as I am, I cannot help loving these People, for their earnest Desire, and Assiduity to please.

It would be futile to attempt Descriptions of this Country especially of Paris and Versailles. The public Buildings and Gardens, the Paintings, Sculpture, Architecture, Musick, &c. of these Cities have already filled many Volumes. The Richness, the Magnificence, and Splendor, is beyond all Description.

This Magnificence is not confined to public Buildings such as Churches, Hospitals, Schools &c., but extends to private Houses, to Furniture, Equipage, Dress, and especially to Entertainments. —But what is all this to me? I receive but little Pleasure in beholding all these Things, because I cannot but consider them as Bagatelles, introduced, by Time and Luxury in Exchange for the great Qualities and hardy manly Virtues of the human Heart. I cannot help suspecting that the more Elegance, the less Virtue in all Times and Countries.—Yet I fear that even my own dear Country wants the Power and Opportunity more than the Inclination, to be elegant, soft, and luxurious.

All the Luxury I desire in this World is the Company of my dearest Friend, and my Children, and such Friends as they delight in, which I have sanguine Hopes, I shall, after a few Years enjoy in Peace.

JOHN ADAMS TO ABIGAIL ADAMS, 17 JUNE 1780, PARIS

May Heaven permit you and me to enjoy the cool Evening of Life, in Tranquility, undisturbed by the Cares of Politicks or War—and above all with the sweetest of all Reflections, that neither Ambition, nor Vanity, nor Avarice, nor Malice, nor Envy, nor Revenge, nor Fear, nor any base Motive, or sordid Passion through the whole Course of this mighty Revolution, and the rapid impetuous Course of great and terrible Events that have attended it, have drawn Us aside from the Line of our Duty and the Dictates of our Consciences!—Let Us have Ambition enough to keep our Simplicity, our Frugality and our Integrity, and transmit these Virtues as the fairest Inheritances to our Children.

ABIGAIL ADAMS TO JOHN ADAMS, 9 DECEMBER 1781

Two years my dearest Friend have passed away since you left your Native land. Will you return e'er the close of another year? I will purchase you a retreat in the woods of Virmont [sic] and retire with you from the vexations, toils and hazards of publick Life. Do you not sometimes sigh for such a Seclusion—publick peace and domestick happiness,

> "an elegant Sufficiency, content
> Retirement, Rural quiet, Friendship, Books
> Ease and alternate Labour, usefull Life
> progressive Virtue and approveing Heaven."

May the time, the happy time soon arrive when we may realize these blessings so elegantly described by [James] Thomson, for tho many of your country Men talk in a different Style with regard to their intentions, and express their wishes to see you in a conspicuous point of view in your own State, I feel no ambition for a share of it. I know the voice of Fame to be a mere weathercock, unstable as Water and fleeting as a Shadow.

Lyman Butterfield, ed., *Diary and Autobiography of John Adams*, 2 vols. (Cambridge, Mass.: Harvard University Press, 1961): 1:23, 72, 337; 2:61, 62, 63; Lyman Butterfield, et al., eds., *The Book of Abigail and John: Selected Letters of the Adams Family, 1762-1784* (Cambridge, Mass.: Harvard University Press, 1975), pp. 58, 77, 80, 210, 222, 303-04.

Jeffersonian Simplicity

Though he drew his inspiration more from classical than Puritan sources, Thomas Jefferson (1743-1826) was equally committed to the ideal of patriotic simplicity. And he was much more optimistic than John Adams about its survival in the young nation. The Virginia statesman-philosopher and farmer practiced a refined and learned form of simplicity, one that stressed the superiority of rural living, enlightened study and reflection, and agricultural work. He initially assumed that the United States could remain insulated from the corrupting effects of Old World commercialism and industrialism. This would require an American willingness to forego European luxuries and superfluities. By practicing such restraint and contentment, Americans, he argued, could preserve their decentralized, agrarian-based republic. In the process they would maintain their private virtue as well. Jefferson succinctly expressed this agrarian ideal in Query XIX of his *Notes on the State of Virginia* (1781), written during the Revolution in response to a Frenchman's request for information about the region. It remains the most concise and compelling statement of agrarian simplicity in American literature.

NOTES ON THE STATE OF VIRGINIA

The political economists of Europe have established it as a principle that every State should endeavour to manufacture for itself; and this principle, like many others, we transfer to America, without calculating the difference of circumstance which should often produce a difference of result. In Europe the lands are either cultivated, or locked up against the cultivator. Manufacture must therefore be resorted to of necessity not of choice, to support the surplus of their people. But we have an immensity of land courting the industry of the husbandman. Is it best then that all our citizens should be employed in its improvement, or that one half should be called off from that to exercise manufactures and handicraft arts for the other? Those who labour in the earth are the chosen people of God, if he ever had a chosen people, whose breasts he has made his peculiar deposit for substantial and genuine virtue. It is the focus in which he keeps alive that sacred fire, which otherwise might escape from the face of the earth. Corruption of morals in the mass of cultivators is a phenomenon of which no age nor nation has furnished an example. It is the mark set on those, who not looking up to heaven, to their own soil and industry, as does the husbandman, for their subsistence, depend for it on the casualties and caprice of customers. Dependence begets subservience and venality, suffocates the germ of virtue, and prepares fit tools for the designs of ambition. This, the natural progress and consequence of the arts, has sometimes perhaps been retarded by accidental circumstances: but, generally speaking, the proportion which the aggregate of the other classes of citizens bears in any state to that of its husbandmen, is the proportion of its unsound to its healthy parts, and is a good enough barometer whereby to measure its degree of corruption. While we have land to labour then, let us never wish to see our citizens occupied at a workbench, or twirling a distaff. Carpenters, masons, smiths, are wanting in husbandry: but, for the general operations of manufacture, let our workshops remain in Europe. It is better to carry provisions and materials to workmen there, than bring them to the provisions and materials, and with them their manners and principles. The loss by the transportation of commodities across the Atlantic will be made up in happiness and permanence of government. The mobs of great cities add just so much to the support of pure government, as sores do to the strength of the human body. It is the manners and spirit of a people which preserve a republic in vigour. A degeneracy in these is a canker which soon eats to the heart of its laws and constitution.

"Notes on the State of Virginia," in Merrill Peterson, ed., *The Portable Jefferson* (New York: Viking, 1975), p. 217.

Like John Adams, Jefferson was greatly disheartened by the behavior of his countrymen in the aftermath of the Revolution. He worried especially about the mounting indebtedness incurred by Americans eager to buy foreign goods. This was ironic, for Jefferson himself would eventually verge on bankruptcy. His own financial difficulties resulted not so much from his taste for fine books and paintings as from his extended absences from Monticello and its affairs. Jefferson spent much of his time overseas, serving as the American minister to France. From that vantage he came to appreciate even more the ideal of republican simplicity in contrast to Old World ostentation. He also came to look back nostalgically at the patriotic simplicity of the Revolutionary era. By the early nineteenth century, however, Jefferson decided that Americans were unwilling to limit themselves to such traditional ideals. So he gradually accommodated himself to changing realities. As President he helped promote commerce and industry and territorial expansion. Yet he always insisted that such accommodation to new circumstances did not lessen his commitment to republican simplicity as a personal code of conduct. In fact he self-consciously projected a plain republican style in his Presidential role. His letters from the period reflect his concerns and his hopes.

Correspondence

Thomas Jefferson

THOMAS JEFFERSON TO BARON GEISMAR, 6 SEPTEMBER 1785, PARIS

I am now of an age which does not easily accommodate itself to new manners and new modes of living; and I am savage enough to prefer the woods, the wilds, and the independence of Monticello, to all the pleasures of the gay Capital. I shall, therefore, rejoin myself to my native country, with new attachments, and with exaggerated esteem for its advantages; for though there is less wealth there, there is more freedom, more ease, and less misery.

THOMAS JEFFERSON TO DR. JAMES CURRIE, 4 AUGUST 1787, PARIS

I wish the bulk of my extravagant countrymen had as good prospects and resources as you. But with many of them, a feebleness of mind makes them afraid to probe the true state of their affairs, and procrastinate the reformation which alone can save something, to those who may yet be saved. How happy a people were we during the war, from the single circumstance that we could not run in debt! This counteracted all the inconveniences we felt, as the present facility of ruining ourselves overweighs all the blessings of peace. I know no condition happier than that of a Virginia farmer might be, conducting himself as he did during the war. His estate supplies a good table, clothes himself and his family with their ordinary apparel, furnishes a small surplus to buy salt, sugar, coffee, and a little finery for his wife and daughters, enables him to receive and visit friends, and furnishes him pleasing and healthy occupation. To secure all this he needs but one act of self-denial, to put off buying anything till he has the money to pay for it.

THOMAS JEFFERSON TO J. BANNISTER, JR., 15 OCTOBER 1785, PARIS

[The American abroad] acquires a fondness for European luxury and dissipation, and a contempt for the simplicity of his own country; he is fascinated with the privileges of the European aristocrats, and sees, with abhorrence, the lovely equality which the poor enjoy with the rich, in his own country . . . he recollects the voluptuary dress and arts of the European women, and pities

Monticello.

and despises the chaste affections and simplicity of those of his own country ... he returns to his own country a foreigner, unacquainted with the practices of domestic economy, necessary to preserve him from ruin. ...

THOMAS JEFFERSON TO CHARLES WILSON PEALE, 20 AUGUST 1811

I have often thought that if heaven had given me a choice of my position and calling, it should have been on a rich spot of earth, well watered, and near a good market for the productions of the garden. No occupation is so delightful to me as the culture of the earth. ...

Correspondence in Andrew A. Lipscomb, ed., *The Writings of Thomas Jefferson*, 20 vols. (Washington: Jefferson Memorial Association, 1903): 5:128–29, 186–87; 6:229; 13:79.

On the Situation, Feelings, and Pleasures of an American Farmer

J. Hector St. John de Crèvecoeur

Crèvecoeur is most famous not for his account of eighteenth-century Quaker life but for his description of his own

version of republican simplicity on a farm in Revolutionary-
era New York. His lands were overrun by the contending
armies, and he was for a time imprisoned on suspicion of
being an English spy. After his release he went to England
where he published *Letters from an American Farmer*. It
has become justly famous for its idealized portrait of self-
sufficient rural life in young America. Crèvecoeur's description of contented rural simplicity reinforced Jefferson's
vision of the agrarian ideal and helped etch such a mythic
state into the minds of later generations of Americans. As
such it retained its symbolic potency even as it increasingly
lost its basis in social practice.

. . . I owe nothing, but a pepper corn to my country, a small
tribute to my king, with loyalty and due respect; I know no other
landlord than the lord of all land, to whom I owe the most sincere
gratitude. My father left me three hundred and seventy-one acres
of land, forty-seven of which are good timothy meadow, an
excellent orchard, a good house, and a substantial barn. It is my
duty to think how happy I am that he lived to build and to pay for
all these improvements; what are the labours which I have to
undergo, what are my fatigues when compared to his, who had
every thing to do, from the first tree he felled to the finishing of his
house? Every year I kill from 1,500 to 2,000 weight of pork, 1,200
of beef, half a dozen of good wethers in harvest: of fowls my wife
has always a great stock: what can I wish more? My negroes are
tolerably faithful and healthy; by a long series of industry and
honest dealings, my father left behind him the name of a good man;
I have but to tread his paths to be happy and a good man like him.
I know enough of the law to regulate my little concerns with
propriety, nor do I dread its power; these are the grand outlines of
my situation, but as I can feel much more than I am able to
express, I hardly know how to proceed. When my first son was
born, the whole train of my ideas were suddenly altered; never was
there a charm that acted so quickly and powerfully; I ceased to
ramble in imagination through the wide world; my excursions
since have not exceeded the bounds of my farm, and all my
principal pleasures are now centered within its scanty limits: but
at the same time there is not an operation belonging to it in which I
do not find some food for useful reflections. . . . When I con-

template my wife, by my fire-side, while she either spins, knits, darns, or suckles our child, I cannot describe the various emotions of love, of gratitude, of conscious pride which thrill in my heart, and often overflow in involuntary tears. I feel the necessity, the sweet pleasure of acting my part, the part of an husband and father, with an attention and propriety which may entitle me to my good fortune. It is true these pleasing images vanish with the smoke of my pipe, but though they disappear from my mind, the impression they have made on my heart is indelible. When I play with the infant, my warm imagination runs forward, and eagerly anticipates his future temper and constitution. I would willingly open the book of fate, and know in which page his destiny is delineated; alas! where is the father who in those moments of paternal extacy can delineate one half of the thoughts which dilate his heart? I am sure I cannot; then again I fear for the health of those who are become so dear to me, and in their sicknesses I severely pay for the joys I experienced while they were well. Whenever I go abroad it is always involuntary. I never return home without feeling some pleasing emotion, which I often suppress as useless and foolish. The instant I enter on my own land, the bright idea of property, of exclusive right, of independence exalt my mind. Precious soil, I say to myself by what singular custom of law is it that thou wast made to constitute the riches of the free holder? What should we American farmers be without the distinct possession of that soil? It feeds, it clothes us, from it we draw even a great exuberancy, our best meat, our richest drink, the very honey of our bees comes from this privileged spot. No wonder we should thus cherish its possession, no wonder that so many Europeans who have never been able to say that such portion of land was theirs, cross the Atlantic to realize that happiness. . . .

. . . I bless God for all the good he has given me; I envy no man's prosperity, and with no other portion of happiness that I may live to teach the same philosophy to my children; and give each of them a farm, shew them how to cultivate it, and be like their father, good substantial independent American farmers—an appellation which will be the most fortunate one, a man of my class can possess, so long as our civil government continues to shed blessings on our husbandry. Adieu.

J. Hector St. John Crèvecoeur, *Letters from an American Farmer* (1782; New York: Peter Smith, 1968), pp. 29–43.

POOR RICHARD AND
REPUBLICAN SIMPLICITY

Benjamin Franklin

> O happy he! happiest of mortal Men!
> Who far remov'd from Slavery, as from Pride,
> Fears no man's Frown, nor cringing waits to catch
> The gracious Nothing of a great Man's nod;
>
> Tempted nor with the Pride nor Pomp of Power,
> Nor Pageants of Ambition, nor the Mines
> Of grasping Av'rice, nor the poison'd Sweets
> Of pampered Luxury, he plants his Foot
> With Firmness on his old paternal Fields,
> And stands unshaken.

Benjamin Franklin, *Poor Richard Improved... 1755* (Philadelphia, n.d.), pp. 5-9.

Domestic Simplicity

4

Republican simplicity was increasingly in retreat as the nineteenth century progressed. With the demise of the Revolutionary generation of classical republican leaders, simplicity no longer served as the basis for national policy. It remained a frequent subject of social discussion, but it was primarily espoused by religious leaders, moral reformers, and creative writers and artists.

In the Jacksonian era, as the nation continued its pattern of rapid economic and urban expansion, the familiar plea for a revival of traditional simplicity was reassuring to Americans dismayed by the pace and extent of social change. Its virtues were frequently praised in journals, speeches, sermons, poems, paintings, and novels. Lyman Beecher and like-minded evangelical ministers sought to induce pious simplicity through religious revivals. Henry Wadsworth Longfellow, William Cullen Bryant, John Greenleaf Whittier, and other popular poets wrote hearthside verse evoking nostalgia for earlier days when life seemed less urban, hectic, materialistic, and artificial. Likewise, James Fenimore Cooper and Mark Twain developed characters such as Leatherstocking and Huck Finn whose natural simplicity and honesty appealed to readers dismayed by the complexity and artificiality which seemed to permeate nineteenth-century American life. This same idealization of the rustic and the simple was a prevalent theme in the period's art. Landscape painters of the Hudson River School such as Thomas Cole and Asher Durand portrayed pristine wilderness and pastoral scenes that proved soothing to city dwellers yearning for the imagined simplicities of life on the farm or in the woods.

But the most frequent emphasis of those trying to preserve the ideal of republican simplicity in the nineteenth century was on the American middle-class home and family. Beginning in the 1820s and lasting throughout the century, a "cult of domesticity" developed as moral reformers focused on transforming the home into a training ground for enlightened material restraint. The insidious effects of greed and social striving, many reformers concluded, must be addressed during the formative years of childhood. Catharine Sedgwick's best-selling novel *Home* (1835) explicitly stressed this theme, as did the popular song "Home, Sweet Home," written by John Howard Payne in 1823. Likewise, countless child-rearing manuals told pious young mothers that it was their duty to maintain traditional spiritual and moral values in the home while their husbands worked feverishly in the "real" world. Maternal leadership could mold model republican citizens. The family was thus to be the repository of republican virtue, and the mother was to be the curator.

This idyllic, domesticated version of simple living was frequently located in the country, where, as always, it was widely believed that the possibilities for leading the good life were especially enhanced. Cooper was not the only writer who saw in rusticity the key to happiness. Caroline Kirkland, one of the era's most popular writers, wrote a series of novels describing the beneficial effects of pioneer simplicity upon seaboard urbanites who joined the western migration. Yet she realized that most of her countrymen were not interested in experimenting with such a traditional way of life. They preferred to glorify it from afar. So she and other idealists increasingly spent their time and words trying to instill in city mothers an appreciation for republican simplicity. Sarah Josepha Hale, the editor of *Godey's Lady's Book*, explained in her first editorial that her purpose was to "show the various economical and intellectual benefits of a just simplicity." And for some forty years she did just that, stressing to her female readers that they must take the lead in restoring the "plain standards" of the Revolutionary generation.

In part, this emphasis on domestic simplicity reflected the changing nature of the American home during the nineteenth century. As more and more families lived in cities rather than on farms, husbands frequently worked far away from home, ten to twelve hours a day, six days a week. And it was widely assumed that they had little time or energy to devote to moral instruction in the home. At the same time, the rise of American manufacturing began to provide women with inexpensive household goods which they earlier had to produce themselves. The simultaneous increase in female immigrants from Germany and Ireland provided a pool of cheap house servants, thus allowing many middle-class women more free time to devote to the instruction of children.

This cult of domesticity was also enhanced by architects of virtue such as New Yorker Andrew Jackson Downing. He was convinced that a proper physical setting was the first step toward ensuring the survival of republican virtues. Well-designed houses, Downing observed, would provide a visible reminder of the principles of restraint, proportion, simplicity, and utility. His republican residences would be organically related to their physical setting and would disdain all social pretense. Beauty and function, not show, were their guiding purposes. His homes, he maintained, would not be "too large or too luxurious to warp the life or manners of children."

But neither well-designed homes nor the repeated pleas for mothers to teach republican virtues to their children produced the social regeneration envisioned by such idealists. It was too much to expect American homes to become islands of simplicity in the midst of a booming economy and a mad scramble for social status. Even if some homes were transformed into such havens of republican simplicity, they were but temporary sanctuaries. Eventually the children grew up and entered the larger world, and it was naive to think that they all could avoid succumbing to the anxious spirit of gain that dominated the age. In 1857 a foreign traveler observed that the "simplicity, the frugality of the parents, contrasts often disagreeably with the prodigality, the assumption, self-assertion, and conceit of the children." Thus, like the Puritans, Quakers, and classical republicans,

domestic reformers of the nineteenth century found themselves advocating a static set of values in the midst of a
dynamic new culture. Lydia Maria Child, one of the leading
proponents of domestic simplicity, sadly concluded in 1836
that there were only a few Americans, "an honorable few,
who late in life, with Roman severity of resolution, learn the
long-neglected lesson of economy. But how small is the
number, compared with the whole mass of the population!"

The Course of Empire
Thomas Cole

The ideal of classical republican simplicity survived well
into the nineteenth century. One dramatic illustration of its
persistence was "The Course of Empire," a magisterial
series of allegorical paintings produced by Thomas Cole
(1801–48). Cole was the leader of what became known as
the "Hudson River School" of painters during the 1830s
and 1840s. He had arrived in Philadelphia from England
with his family in 1819. They relocated to New York a few
years later. Cole soon began painting scenes of pastoral life
along the Hudson that attracted the attention of prominent
critics and patrons. His early success afforded Cole the
opportunity to study in England, France, and Italy for
several years before returning to the United States in 1832.
Soon thereafter he began work on "The Course of Empire."
In the five paintings he explicitly pondered the problem of
retaining rustic simplicity and republican virtue in an age
of encroaching urbanization and rampant materialism. He
chose the history of Rome's transformation from agrarian
republic to corrupt empire as his subject, and he intended
the paintings to serve as "maledictions on the dollar-
godded utilitarians" he saw dominating contemporary
American life. In the following excerpt from his memor-
andum book, Cole explained the purpose behind "The
Course of Empire."

Thomas Cole, "The Consummation of Empire," *The Course of Empire.*

Thomas Cole, "Destruction," *The Course of Empire.*

The FIRST PICTURE, representing the savage state, must be a view of a wilderness,—the sun rising from the sea, and the clouds of night retiring over the mountains. The figures must be savage, clothed in skins, and occupied in the chase. There must be a flashing chiaroscuro, and the spirit of motion pervading the scene, as though nature were just springing from chaos.

The SECOND PICTURE must be the pastoral state,—the day further advanced—light clouds playing about the mountains—the scene partly cultivated—a rude village near the bay—small vessels in the harbour—groups of peasants either pursuing their labors in the field, watching their flocks, or engaged in some simple amusement. The chiaroscuro must be of a milder character than in the previous scene, but yet have a fresh and breezy effect.

The THIRD must be a noonday,—a great city girding the bay, gorgeous piles of architecture, bridge, aqueducts, temples—the port crowded with vessels—splendid processions, &c.—all that can be combined to show the fulness of prosperity: the chiaroscuro broad.

The FOURTH should be a tempest,—a battle, and the burning of the city—towers falling, arches broken, vessels wrecking in the harbour. In this scene there should be a fierce chiaroscuro, masses and groups swaying about like stormy waves. This is the scene of destruction or vicious state.

The FIFTH must be a sunset,—the mountains riven—the city a desolate ruin—columns standing isolated amid the encroaching waters—ruined temples, broken bridges, fountains, sarcophagi, &c.—no human figure—a solitary bird perhaps: a calm and silent effect. This picture must be as the funeral knell of departing greatness, and may be called the state of desolation.

Richard J. Koke, comp., *American Landscape and Genre Paintings in the New York Historical Society* (Boston: G.K. Hall, 1982), pp. 195-96.

On the Undue and Pernicious Influence of Wealth

The ideal of classical republican simplicity survived in the South as well as the North during the early nineteenth century. This anonymous writer in the region's leading literary journal sought to sustain a Jeffersonian tradition of enlightened restraint and an aristocracy of virtue in the face of a growing worship of wealth and an aristocracy of money. No doubt he was in part referring to a rising planter and commercial elite in the South seemingly preoccupied with pecuniary standards of value.

Every man seems to think he has been placed in this world to promote the selfish views of himself—alone; and not to accomplish but one object—the acquisition of wealth. Wealth! this is the glorious prize for which all are striving. To obtain it, is the first duty of man; to possess it, is happiness. How foolishly do we neglect the certain means of happiness, and engage in the pursuit of a glittering phantom, which either eludes our grasp altogether, or if secured, entails lasting misery upon us.

Cannot experience teach men, that riches do not confer happiness? Will they not be guided by wisdom into the true road to happiness? No—they cannot, will not. They toil for wealth, and yet dissatisfied with what they possess, they still continue to toil on through life, hoarding up immense treasures which they cannot enjoy, and which will, in all probability, prove a curse to their posterity.

Are there not other important, noble and agreeable objects of pursuit? Does the improvement of the mind, and heart, and conduct, afford no pleasures? Do innocence, contentment, evenness of temper, and the domestic and social virtues, possess no charms? Is the practice of virtue, in promoting the welfare of our fellow men, an object unworthy of our attention? These things have little, very little influence upon the mass of mankind. All their motives, feelings, and principles, are subservient to the predominant, unconquerable love of money. All their thoughts and actions converge to one point—money. The universal cry is—money.

It is the duty of every man to provide for himself a competency. It is essential to happiness to be above want. It is a source of pleasure to enjoy "the glorious privilege of being independent." These pre-suppose that a man is in the enjoyment of all the comforts and conveniences of life. If he have them, he is then in the possession of all the real good which money can afford. Wealth may, indeed, furnish luxuries; but they are hurtful. They enervate both mind and body: corrupt the heart and affections, and engender vicious inclinations and indulgences. Luxury is a rich soil, producing an exuberant growth of noxious, poisonous weeds.

Happiness shuns the abode of voluptuous wealth, as well as that of squalid poverty. She dwells, most frequently, with contented competency. Peace, cheerfulness, simplicity, and virtue, are the companions who attend upon her. She delights in serenity and calmness: in the quiet joys of innocence, contentment and benevolence. This is the golden medium of happiness!

Wealth, when honestly acquired and properly used, is not at all objectionable. It indeed may be, but often is not, honestly acquired: and properly to use it, requires a degree of disinterestedness, philosophy, and virtue, which few men possess.

It is insatiate avarice, and the arbitrary, extraordinary estimate placed upon wealth, which are to be deplored as a prolific source of evils.

They cause us to neglect the duties we owe to ourselves, to our families, to the world, and to God. To ourselves—they divert our attention from those things which would secure real happiness. To our families—occupied by the all-absorbing love of money, we neglect their moral, mental, and religious culture and improvement. To the world—the selfishness always attendant upon avarice renders us totally regardless and insensible of the rights, interests, and welfare of our fellow-men. To God—in the ardent pursuit of wealth, we have neither time, opportunity, nor inclination, to perform the sacred duties we owe to Him.

They destroy the peace of individuals and families; are productive of discontent, disquietude, and misery—of injustice, vice, and crime. They mar the pleasures of social intercourse; and above all, produce that state of feeling, that course of conduct, which, when generally prevalent throughout a republic, are dangerous to liberty, and the sure precursors of the downfall of free institutions.

The love of money has been said by foreigners, and not without cause, to be a prominent feature in the character of Americans. We pay to wealth servile homage and adoration. Mammon is the God we worship. It would be well for us if we obeyed the scripture commandment, and worshipped no other Gods but one. But we have a multitude of Gods. We not only worship Mammon, but we worship also the priests of Mammon—those holy personages who enjoy his peculiar favor, and are distinguished by the golden decorations which adorn them. We worship men—we extend our veneration for wealth to the men who possess it. We are gross idolaters, and like the ancient Egyptians, worship calves, and asses, and apes. The natural dignity of man, the noble independence of freemen, are sacrificed upon the polluted altar of idols. . . .

This undue estimate of wealth would not be so injurious to society, if we did not, in overrating it, at the same time undervalue merit. But as our veneration for wealth increases, in the same degree does our regard for intrinsic merit decrease—in the same degree is diminished our respect for those who are so unfortunate as to be poor. . . .

Superciliousness and injury on the part of the rich, create a spirit of resentment on the part of the poor; which combined, tend to mar the pleasures of social intercourse, by preventing an interchange of friendly offices, and by producing personal animosities and family feuds.

On the other hand, the haughty pride and arrogance of the rich are met by many with the most spirited acquiescence, the most tame submission, the most servile sycophancy. The rich man who feeds them, of course thinks, speaks, and acts for them. Such men deserve to wear the yoke of slavery which disgrace them. But God forbid there should be many of this character in our country. They would barter their liberties for a mess of porridge.

"On the Undue and Pernicious Influence of Wealth," *Southern Literary Messenger* 3 (August 1837): 481–82.

THE DARK SIDE OF OUR NATIONAL PROSPERITY
Samuel Osgood

It is certainly the fact, that the dangers which our nation fears, and the trouble it has experienced, have been occasioned in great measure, by our national prosperity. . . . I refer to the corruptions, which increasing wealth is apt to bring in its train—to the foreign luxuries and misnamed refinements, which are fast changing our republican virtue. . . . it is our republican plainness, our stricter morality, our philanthropic and religious institutions that constitute our peculiar strength.

"The Dark Side of Our National Prosperity," *Western Messenger* (1836): 171, 173.

The Architecture of Country Houses
Andrew Jackson Downing

The idealization of art as a means of sustaining republican simplicity in a rapidly changing American society was not limited to painters and writers. Many of the leading domestic architects of the nineteenth century also believed that plain, unassuming, functional homes would help promote the ideal. The most famous of these architects of republican virtues was Andrew Jackson Downing (1815–52). Born in Newburgh, New York, along the Hudson River, Downing inherited a struggling nursery business from his father and soon made it thrive. In the process he emerged as the nation's foremost landscape gardener and domestic architect. Among his clients were many wealthy, cultured landowners of the Hudson valley region who practiced what James Fenimore Cooper called a "refined simplicity." Downing was attracted to their Jeffersonian manner of living, and he was determined to design homes and gardens that would accentuate enlightened republican virtues. When "smiling lawns and tasteful cottages begin to embellish a country," Downing asserted, "we know that order and culture are established." Downing brought an eighteenth-century republican perspective to his drawing table, and he designed three different types of homes—farmhouses, cottages, and villas—for the different social classes he saw represented in America.

In each of the three classes of country houses, there is a predominant character, to which all other expressions, whether of beauty, usefulness, or truth, should be referred. In cottages, this predominant character is *simplicity*. It ought, accordingly, to pervade every portion of cottage architecture. There should be a convenient simplicity of arrangement, to facilitate the simple manner of living; an economical simplicity of construction, to suit the moderate means of the builder or owner; and a tasteful simplicity of decoration, to harmonize with the character of the dwelling and its occupants.

All ornaments which are not simple, and cannot be executed in a substantial and appropriate manner, should be at once rejected; all flimsy and meager decorations which have a pasteboard effect, are as unworthy of, and unbecoming for the house of him who understands the true beauty of a cottage life, as glass breastpins

Downing, *Architecture of Country Houses*

A "Small Bracketed Cottage" designed by Andrew Jackson Downing.

or gilt-pewter spoons would be for his personal ornaments or family service of plate.

As much taste, as much beauty, as can be combined with the comparatively simple habits of cottage life, are truly admirable and delightful in a cottage. But every thing beyond this, every thing only imitated, every thing that is false, forced or foreign to the real feelings or intelligence of the inmates, is not worthy of the least approbation in a cottage. . . .

Now, if we have clearly explained, in a previous part of this work, the great value and importance of truthfulness in domestic architecture, it cannot but be plain to our readers that a farm-house must, first of all, look like a farm-house, or it cannot give us any lasting satisfaction; and that as one of the highest sources of beauty in domestic architecture is derived from its embodying the best traits of character of the man or class of men for whom it is designed, it is equally plain that to raise the farm-house in the scale of truth and beauty, we must make it express that beauty, whatever it may be, which lies in a farmer's life.

How shall we make a farm-house truthful and significant, so that it shall look like a farm-house? Only by studying the characteristics of the farmer's life, and expressing, first of all, in the forms of his dwelling, the peculiar wants and comforts of that life.

Some of these we conceive to be the following: extended space on the ground, to afford room for all the in-door occupation of agricultural life, which will always give the farm-house breadth rather than height; a certain rustic plainness, which denotes a class more occupied with the practical and useful than the elegant arts of life; a substantial and solid construction, which denotes abundance of materials to build with, rather than money to expend in workmanship.

The genuine farmer is peculiarly the man of nature—more sincere, more earnest than men of any other class; because, dealing more with Providence than with men, he is less sophisticated either in manners or heart, and, if less cultivated, is more frank, and gives us more homely truths and less conventional insincerity than dwellers in cities.

The farm-house, to be significant, should therefore show an absence of all pretension. It should not borrow Grecian columns, or Italian balustrades, or Gothic carved work from the villa; or merely pretty ornaments from the cottage ornée. It should rely on its own honest, straightforward simplicity, and should rather aim to be frank, and genuine, and open-hearted, like its owner, than to wear the borrowed ornaments of any class of different habits and tastes. The porch or the veranda of the farm-house should not only be larger, but also simpler, and ruder, and stronger than that of the cottage, because there is more manly strength in the agriculturist's life than in that of any other class; the roof should be higher and more capacious, for it is to overshadow larger families and larger stores of nature's gifts; and, above all, the chimneys should be larger and more generous-looking, to betoken the warm-hearted hospitality of the farmer's home. Their large and simple tops should rather suggest ample hearths and good kitchens than small grates and handsome parlors.

Now, the real elements of beauty in the farm-house must be found in giving expression to the best and most beautiful traits in the farmer's life. And since the farmer's life is neither devoted to the elegant nor the ornamental arts, he should no more be expected to display a variety of architectural ornaments in the construction of his house, than he would be to wear garments made by the most fashionable tailor in Broadway, or to drive to his market town in one of Lawrence and Collis's most modish carriages.

Expecting, as we do, to find every species of domestic architecture typifying the character of the man or class of men inhabiting it, we do not desire any elaborate artistic effect or any thing like carefully studied attempts at architectural style in the farm-house. The farmer's life is not one devoted to aesthetics, and we do not look chiefly for the evidences of carefully elaborated taste and culture in house, as in the dwelling of the scholar and the man of letters.

But we ought to find, in every farm-house, indications of those virtues which adorn the farmer's character, and which, if expressed at all in his dwelling, must give the latter something of the same beauty as the former. His dwelling ought to suggest simplicity, honesty of purpose, frankness, a hearty, genuine spirit of good-will, and a homely and modest, though manly and independent, bearing in his outward deportment. For the true farmer despises affectation; he loves a blunt and honest expression of the truth; and he shows you that he knows the value of a friend, by shaking hands with you, as if his heart acted like a magnetic machine on the chords of his fingers.

It would be false and foolish to embellish highly the dwelling of such a man with the elaborate details of the different schools of architecture. We must leave this more scientific display of art and learning to villas and public edifices, and endeavor to make the farm-house agreeable, chiefly by expressing in its leading forms the strength, simplicity, honesty, frankness, and sterling goodness of the farmer's character. Although we must recognize, first of all, the constant industry which gives so much dignity and independence to his life, in the arrangement of the interior of his house mainly for useful ends, yet we would also introduce every comfort and convenience denoting the intelligence and ease of the successful farmer's life in a country where that life is so truly intelligent and reputable as our own. But in adding the veranda, the bay-window, the other architectural features significant of social cultivation and enjoyment, we should still bear in mind that these features are to be stamped with the strength, simplicity, and downrightness of character which denote that they belong to the dwelling of a man who cannot wear fine ornaments, even upon his house, because they are foreign to his nature—however significant the same ornaments may be of the life of another man or another class of men.

Andrew Jackson Downing, *The Architecture of Country Houses* (New York: Appleton, 1850), pp. 43, 137-40.

A New Home

Caroline Kirkland

Downing's blueprints for tasteful country cottages and villas were widely popular. But the actual formation of republican character required more than good design. Conservators of republican simplicity in the nineteenth century thus placed great emphasis on home and community life, on the role of the family and the environment in shaping American character along traditional lines. And these promoters of uplifting domesticity directed most of their attention to women as the guardians of republican simplicity. Women reformers led this crusade on behalf of domestic idealism, and one of their most persistent voices was Caroline Stansbury Kirkland (1801–64).

The daughter of a New York City bookseller and publisher, Caroline Stansbury married William Kirkland in 1827, and for several years thereafter they operated a seminary, first in Geneva, New York, then in Detroit. In 1837 they relocated to the frontier settlement of Pinckney, sixty miles northwest of Detroit. There Caroline Kirkland began writing a series of thinly disguised autobiographical novels about the trials of an eastern housewife adapting to life in the woods. These books were enormously popular, especially among women readers. Their moral was that Americans needed to quit aping aristocratic European styles of living and embrace an unassuming republicanism. To her, "a dignified simple life" meant "moderation in expense for the express purpose of being liberal where liberality is honorable; plainness of dress resulting at once from good taste and from religious self-denial. . . . plainness of living, lest our splendor should separate us and the good to whom God had not seen fit to give riches."

Kirkland's first novel, *A New Home*, was written under the pseudonym "Mrs. Mary Clavers, an actual settler," and it used her own experiences to tell the story of an eastern woman of refined tastes and sensibilities who reluctantly accompanied her husband to a new pioneer settlement in Michigan "on the outskirts of civilization." The book dealt with issues that millions of Americans faced throughout the nineteenth century as they participated in the westward migration. Initially Mrs. Clavers rebels against the forced simplicities of frontier life, but she gradually finds great merit and joy in such unpretentious living.

One must come quite away from the conveniences and refined indulgences of civilized life to know any thing about them. To be always inundated with comforts, is but too apt to make us proud, selfish, and ungrateful. The mind's health, as well as the body's, is promoted by occasional privation or abstinence. Many a sour-faced grumbler I wot of, would be marvelously transformed by a year's residence in the woods, or even in a Michigan village of as high pretensions as Montacute. I should be disposed to recommend a course of Michigan to the Sybarites, the puny exquisites, the worldworn and sated Epicureans of our cities. If I mistake not, they would make surprising advances in philosophy in the course of a few months' training. I should not be severe either. I should not require them to come in their strictly natural condition as featherless bipeds. I would allow them to bring many a comfort —nay, even some real luxuries; books, for instance, and a reasonable supply of New-York Safety-Fund notes, the most tempting form which "world's gear" can possibly assume for our western, wild-cat wearied eyes. I would grant to each Neophyte a ready-made loggery, a garden fenced with tamarack poles, and every facility and convenience which is now enjoyed by the better class of our settlers, yet I think I might after all hope to send home a reasonable proportion of my subjects completely cured, sane for life.

I have in the course of these detached and desultory chapters, hinted at various deficiencies and peculiarities, which strike, with rather unpleasant force, the new resident in the back-woods; but it would require volumes to enumerate all the cases in which the fastidiousness, the taste, the pride, the self-esteem of the refined child of civilization, must be wounded by a familiar intercourse with the persons among whom he will find himself thrown, in the ordinary course of rural life. He is continually reminded in how great a variety of particulars his necessities, his materials for comfort, and his sources of pain, are precisely those of the humblest of his neighbours. . . .

Interior of an early nineteenth-century home.

This same republican spirit is evinced rather amusingly, in the reluctance to admire, or even to approve, any thing like luxury or convenience which is not in common use among the settlers. Your carpets are spoken of as "one way to hide dirt;" your mahogany tables as, "dreadful plaguy to scour;" your kitchen conveniences, as "lumberin' up the house for nothin';" and so on to the end of the chapter. One lady informed me, that if she had such a pantry full of "dishes," under which general term is included every variety of china, glass and earthenware, she should set up store, and "sell them off pretty quick," for she would not "be plagued with them." Another, giving a slighting glance at a French mirror of rather unusual dimensions, larger by two-thirds, I verily believe, than she had ever seen, remarked, "that would be quite a nice glass, if the frame was done over."

Others take up the matter reprovingly. They "don't think it right to spend money so;" they think too, that "pride never did nobody no good;" and some will go so far as to suggest modes of disposing of your superfluities.

"Any body that's got so many dresses, might afford to give away half of 'em;" or, "I should think you'd got so much land, you might give a poor man a lot, and never miss it." A store of any thing, however simple or necessary, is, as I have elsewhere observed, a subject of reproach, if you decline supplying whomsoever may be deficient.

This simplification of life, this bringing down the transactions of daily intercourse to the original principles of society, is neither very eagerly adopted, nor very keenly relished, by those who have been accustomed to the politer atmospheres. They rebel most determinedly, at first. They perceive that the operation of the golden rule, in circumstances where it is all give on one side, and all take on the other, must necessarily be rather severe; and they declare manfully against all impertinent intrusiveness. But, sooth to say, there are in the country so many ways of being made uncomfortable by one's most insignificant enemy, that it is soon discovered that warfare is even more costly than submission.

But then there are some absolute and evident superfluities, according to the primitive estimate of these regions; in the other, none. The doll of Fortune, who may cast a languid eye on this homely page, from the luxurious depths of a velvetcushioned library-chair, can scarce be expected to conceive how natural it may be, for those who possess nothing beyond the absolute requisites of existence, to look with a certain degree of envy on the extra comforts which seem to cluster round the path of another; and to feel as if a little might well be spared, where so much would still be left. To the tenant of a log-cabin whose family, whatever be its numbers, must burrow in a single room, while a bed or two, a chest, a table, and a wretched handful of cooking utensils, form the chief materials of comfort, an ordinary house, small and plain it may be, yet amply supplied, looks like the very home of luxury. The woman who owns but a suit apiece for herself and her children, considers the possession of an abundant though simple and inexpensive wardrobe, as needless extravagance; and we must scarcely blame her too severely, if she should be disposed to condemn as penurious, any reluctance to supply her pressing need, though she may have no shadow of claim on us beyond that which arises from her being a daughter of Eve. We look at the matter from opposite points of view. Her light shows her very plainly, as she thinks, what is our Christian duty; we must take care that ours does not exhibit too exclusively her envy and her impertinence.

The inequalities in the distribution of the gifts of fortune are not greater in the country than in town, but the contrary; yet circumstances render them more offensive to the less-favoured class. The denizens of the crowded alleys and swarming lofts of our great cities see, it is true, the lofty mansions, the splendid equipages of the wealthy—but they are seldom or never brought into contact or collision with the owners of these glittering advantages. And the extreme width of the great gulf between, is almost a barrier, even to all-reaching envy. But in the ruder stages of society, where no one has yet begun to expend any thing for show, the difference lies chiefly in the ordinary requisites of comfort; and this comes home at once "to men's business and bosoms." The keenness of their appreciation, and the strength of their envy, bear a direct proportion to the real value of the objects of their desire; and when they are in habits of entire equality and daily familiarity with those who own ten or twenty times as much of the material of earthly enjoyment as themselves, it is surely natural, however provoking, that they should not be studious to veil their longings after a share of the good, which has been so bounteously showered upon their neighbours. . . .

. . . I am now a denizen of the wild woods—in my view, "no mean city" to own as one's home; and I feel no ambition to aid in the formation of a Montacute aristocracy, for which an ample field is now open, and all the proper materials are at hand. What lack we! Several of us have as many as three cows; some few, carpets and shanty-kitchens; and one or two, piano-fortes and silver tea-sets. I myself, as dame de la seigneurie, have had secret thoughts of an astral lamp! but even if I should go so far, I am resolved not to be either vain-glorious or over-bearing, although this kind of superiority forms the usual ground for exclusiveness. I shall visit my neighbours just as usual, and take care not to say a single word about dipped candles, if I can possibly help it.

Caroline Kirkland, *A New Home, Who'll Follow? Or, Glimpses of Western Life* (New York: C. S. Francis, 1839), pp. 306–13.

Forest Life

Caroline Kirkland

Like Andrew Jackson Downing, Caroline Kirkland promoted in her writings a version of republican simplicity that stressed self-restraint rather than self-denial. Simplicity in her view did not require poverty, but it did require consciously establishing limits and priorities. In this selection from a later novel, *Forest Life*, she described a model family living in rural republican simplicity.

Our friend Mr. Hay has a noble farm. His cleared and cultivated acres may be counted by hundreds, and his "stock" of all kinds will far outnumber them. A wide tract of forest land hems in his clearing, and this too calls him master. He is wont to boast that he has more land enclosed within a ring-fence than any man in the country, and he boasts still louder that it is all the fruit of his own industry, and loudest of all, that it has never made him proud.

He maintains and insists upon his family's maintaining the simplicity of habits and manners that is usual in the neighborhood, and watches with jealous eye every tendency towards an imitation of those who attempt fashion and style among us. He goes daily into the field with his men, and his wife and daughters spin and wear wool and flax of home production. No imported luxury graces their daily table. Mrs. Hay, to be sure, has her tea, but she has it in the afternoon, before the family supper; and the sugar (for the few who like sweetnin' in their tea) comes from no further off than the farm "sugar-bush." Notwithstanding these strict sumptuary laws however, no family lives in greater comfort and abundance.

Mr. Hay's house is large enough to make a figure any where, though it lacks as yet the beautifying aid of the paint-brush. His barn would make a hotel of tolerable dimensions, and the various outhouses, and sheds, and coops, and pens, that cluster around it, make passing travellers fancy they are coming upon a rising village in the deep woods. A fine young orchard adorns the sloping bank behind the house; whole rows of peach and cherry-trees border the ample door-yard; hedges of currant and gooseberry bushes intersect the garden; thick screens of wild grape and honeysuckle overshadow the porch and drapery the "square-room" windows.

When you enter, you find bare but well-scrubbed floors; the only exception being found in the aforesaid "square room," which is decorated with a home-made carpet of resplendent colors, large enough to reach almost the border of chairs, and shaken every morning on the grass to avoid the ravages of the wasteful broom. A great eight-day clock with a moon on its face is the most conspicuous ornament of the common or "keepin'-room;" but there is, besides this, in a favored corner near the window, a small mirror, round which hang black profiles of all the family, including aunts and uncles; pin-cusions of every size and hue; strings of little birds' eggs; vials of camphor, peppermint and essence of lemon, and perhaps a dozen other small articles much prized by different members of the family; while over the glass wave a few peacocks' feathers, and a whole plume of asparagus.

Pass into the kitchen and you will find Mrs. Hay kneading bread or rolling pie-crust to give her stout handmaid time for some less delicate service; her daughter Marthy-Ann preparing dinner; her daughter Sophia-Jane shelling peas; her daughter Harriet-Lizzy rocking the cradle in which lies yet another daughter, whose name is Apollonia,—not quite Apollyon, but so like it that I almost wonder that people who read John Bunyan should be fond of the appellation. The truth is, we do love high-sounding names, and the more syllables or adjuncts the better.

The kitchen has a great fireplace, with a crane stout enough to swing a five pail kettle of soap, and a great oven too, that will hold at least a dozen country loaves. About the walls are disposed all the conveniences necessary for the full use of fireplace and oven, on the same plenteous scale. A rifle and a shot-gun hang on wooden hooks driven into the rafters overhead; two or three gleaming butcher-knives ornament a leather strap fixed against the chimney. A meal-room near at hand contains several varieties of flour, and a buttery and milk-house supply other rustic dainties in profusion. Is it not to be supposed that Mr. and Mrs. Hay and their five daughters, and their help and their hired men, live well?

Caroline Kirkland, *Forest Life*, 2 vols. (New York: C. S. Francis, 1842), 1:237–40.

SNOW-BOUND

John Greenleaf Whittier

> Our mother, while she turned her wheel
> Or ran the new-knit stocking-heel,
> Told how the Indian hordes came down
> At midnight on Cocheco town,
> And how her own great-uncle bore
> His cruel scalp-mark to fourscore.
> Recalling, in her fitting phrase,
> So rich and picturesque and free,
> (The common unrhymed poetry
> Of simple life and country ways,)
> The story of her early days,—
> She made us welcome to her home;

Old hearths grew wide to give us room;
    We stole with her a frightened look
At the gray-wizard's conjuring-book,
    The fame whereof went far and wide
Through all the simple country side;
    We heard the hawks at twilight play
The boat-horn on Piscataqua,
    The loon's weird laughter far away;
We fished her little trout-brook, knew
    What flowers in wood and meadow grew,
What sunny hillsides autumn-brown
    She climbed to shake the ripe nuts down,
Saw where in sheltered cove and bay
    The ducks' black squadron anchored lay,
And heard the wild geese calling loud
    Beneath the gray November cloud.

The Complete Poetical Works of John Greenleaf Whittier (Boston: Houghton Mifflin, 1848), pp. 401–02.

The Mother's Book

Lydia Maria Child

One of the most effective and consistent promoters of domestic simplicity was Lydia Maria Francis Child (1802–80). Born in Medford, Massachusetts, she began writing sentimental novels in the 1820s. She married David Child, a lawyer, in 1828, and thereafter they were prominent participants in the anti-slavery movement. Lydia Child published numerous tracts against slavery, and along with her husband she edited an abolitionist magazine. But like so many other women activists of the era, she promoted an array of causes ranging from temperance to prison reform to the moral improvement of the home. Her advice books to women went through

numerous editions, and her didactic essays and stories
appeared in every major periodical of the day. Their
persistent theme was that republican simplicity must be
implanted in American youth at an early age.

Human ambition and human policy labor after happiness in
vain; goodness is the only foundation to build upon. The wisdom of
past ages declares this truth, and our own observation confirms it;
all the world acknowledge it; yet how few, how very few, are willing
to act upon it. We say we believe goodness is always happiness, in
every situation of life, and that happiness should be our chief
study; we know that wealth and distinction do not bring
happiness; but we are anxious our children should possess them,
because they appear to confer enjoyment. What a motive for
immortal beings!

If the inordinate love of wealth and parade is not checked
among us, it will be the ruin of our country, as it has been, and will
be, the ruin of thousands of individuals. What restlessness, what
discontent, what bitterness, what knavery and crime, have been
produced by this eager passion for money! Mothers! as you love
your children, and wish for their happiness, be careful how you
cherish this unquiet spirit, by speaking and acting as if you
thought wealth the greatest good. Teach them to consider money
valuable only for its use; and that it confers respectability only
when it is used well. Teach them to regard their childish property
as things held in trust for the benefit and pleasure of their
companions—that the only purpose of having anything to call their
own is that they may use it for the good of others. If this spirit
were more inculcated we should not hear children so often say 'Let
that alone, it is mine, and you sha'n't have it.' Neither should we
see such an unprincipled scrambling for wealth—such willingness
to cast off the nearest and dearest relations in the pursuit of
fashion—such neglect of unfortunate merit—and such servile
adulation to successful villainy. I will not mention religion,—for its
maxims have nothing in common with worldly and selfish
policy,—I will simply ask what republicanism there is in such rules
of conduct?

But there are always two sides to a question. If it is pernicious
to make money and style the standard of respectability, it is
likewise injurious and wrong to foster a prejudice against the
wealthy and fashionable. If we experience the slightest degree of
pleasure in discovering faults or follies in those above us, there
certainly is something wrong in our own hearts. Never say to your

family 'Such a one feels above us'—'Such a one is too proud to come and see us'—&c. In the first place, perhaps it is not true; (for I know by experience that the poor are apt to be unreasonably suspicious of the rich; they begin by being cold and proud to their wealthy acquaintance, for fear the wealthy mean to be cold and proud to them;) and even if it be true, that a rich neighbor is haughty, or even insolent, you should be careful not to indulge bad passions, because he does. Your business is with your own heart—keep that pure—and measure out to the rich man, as well as the poor man, just as much of respect and regard as their characters deserve, and no more.

Do not suffer your mind to brood over the external distinctions of society. Neither seek nor avoid those who are superior in fortune; meet them on the same ground as you do the rest of your fellow-creatures. There is a dignified medium between cringing for notice, and acting like a cat that puts up her back and spits, when no dog is coming.

Perhaps I say more on this subject than is necessary, or useful. I am induced to say it, from having closely observed the effect produced on society by the broad and open field of competition in this country. All blessings are accompanied with disadvantages; and it is the business of the judicious to take the good and leave the evil. In this country every man can make his own station. This is indeed a blessing. But what are some of the attendant dangers? Look at that parent, who is willing to sacrifice her comfort, her principles, nay even her pride, for the sake of pushing her children into a little higher rank of life.

Look at another, too independent for such a course. —Hear how he loves to rail about the aristocracy—how much pleasure he takes in showing contempt of the rich. Is his own heart right? I fear not. I fear that unbending independence, so honorable in itself, is mixed with a baser feeling. The right path is between extremes. I would never creep under a door, neither would I refuse to enter when it was opened wide for my reception.

Poverty and wealth have different temptations; but they are equally strong. The rich are tempted to pride and insolence; the poor to jealousy and envy. The envious and discontented poor invariably become haughty and overbearing when rich; for selfishness is equally at the bottom of these opposite evils. Indeed, it is at the bottom of all manner of evils. . . .

A dress distinguished for simplicity and freshness is abundantly more lady-like than the ill-placed furbelows of fashion. It is very common to see vulgar, empty-minded people perpetually changing their dresses, without ever acquiring the air of a gentlewoman. If there is simplicity in the choice of colors,—if clothes set well, and are properly pinned, tied and arranged,—if they always have a neat, fresh look,—and above all, if the head and the feet are always in order,—nothing more is required for a perfectly lady-like appearance.

Lydia Maria Child, *The Mother's Book* (Boston: Carter and Hendee, 1831), pp. 126–28, 130–31.

DOMESTIC SIMPLICITY
Catherine Beecher

The success of democratic institutions, as is conceded by all, depends upon the intellectual and moral character of the mass of the people. If they are intelligent and virtuous, democracy is a blessing; but if they are ignorant and wicked, it is only a curse. . . . It is equally conceded, that the formation of the moral and intellectual character of the young is committed mainly to the female hand. The mother forms the character of the future man.

Catherine Beecher, *A Treatise on Domestic Economy* (Boston: Marsh and Webb, 1841), p. 13.

The Young Wife
William Alcott

William Andrus Alcott (1798–1859) was one of the most prolific male spokesmen for the cult of domesticity. Born in Connecticut, he began his career as a teacher and later traveled with his more famous cousin, the Transcendentalist reformer Bronson Alcott, giving lectures on education and promoting various pedagogical experiments. He was an earnest reformer, publishing almost fifty books on subjects ranging from education to health reform to domestic improvement. In the following excerpt from *The Young Wife* he stressed that simplicity refers to honesty of expression as well as modes of dress.

When I say that I consider simplicity a virtue in a young wife, I mean not by the term weakness of intellect, or any want of common sagacity. But I mean, rather, great plainness of language, dress and manners—an entire artlessness and freedom from

"The Light of Home," engraving from *Godey's Lady's Book* (July 1860)

everything which savors in the smallest degree of cunning or duplicity.

This simplicity is an ornament of great price in any individual; but it is especially becoming in the young married lady. It is one, moreover, which she should watch over, and be exceedingly studious to preserve.

The necessity of preserving and cultivating simplicity of character, is enhanced by the consideration that, like other gems, it is exceedingly rare among us, and is every day becoming more so. The young wife, whether she comes from the family or the boarding school, is very apt to bring with her almost anything else, rather than this trait; and as she is now to commence an era in her life, it seems highly desirable that she should commence right. Hence it is, that I press upon her attention a due regard to simplicity.

She should study simplicity in dress. But on this point I need not enlarge, as I shall have occasion to recur to it hereafter.

She should study great plainness of speech. She should say just what she thinks. I do not, indeed, undertake to show that she should say *all* she thinks; for that were quite another matter. Only let what is said, be exactly what is thought, and intended and felt.

Nothing can be more foolish, than anything like art or duplicity in the language of a wife to her husband. I know that some husbands like it well enough at first; but it is because they do not discover its tendency. They at length become sick of it themselves; and will, if it be continued, despise her for it.

Let me urge this point the more, from the fact that to be simple requires great self-denial. Everywhere in society this virtue is becoming old-fashioned and vulgar. You will need, therefore, to be armed for battle; otherwise you will surely be swept along in the full tide of a wretched and despicable fashion, till your end is destruction—I mean, morally so. . . .

Cultivate simplicity, in the fear of the Lord, with all the earnestness required by an apostle of old, in his letters to Timothy. In short, if you would go through the world happily, and reach the bar of an approving God, strive with all your power, not only to be what you ought to be, but to be what you seem to be.

William Alcott, *The Young Wife, Or Duties of Women in the Relation of Marriage* (Boston: George Light, 1837), pp. 108–10, 112.

Glances and Glimpses

Harriot Hunt

Even though promoters of domestic simplicity often embellished and idealized their version of the good life, there were many Americans in the nineteenth century who attested to it as an actual way of life. Harriot Hunt (1805–1875) provided one such testimony. She was one of the first female physicians in the country. After working first as a teacher, she opened a medical practice with her sister. Most of their patients were middle-class women suffering from neurasthenia, a debilitating nervousness and anxiety. Hunt later wrote that she was surprised at how many of her patients were improved by "prescriptions for mental states." And her most frequent psychological prescription was a call for simpler living. In her autobiography, *Glances and Glimpses*, she presented a portrait of her own simple home and family life as a child in Boston that embodied the virtues of domestic simplicity. And she used it to point up the contrast with the home environments she observed while ministering to her patients.

It was in that Fleet street home, my sister and myself grew up to youth. As our childish characters developed, and our dispositions unfolded, we were very carefully guarded from temptation. Habits of trust and obedience were thus more easily formed. Our early playmates were chosen with more care—yes, a great deal more care—than is now given to elect a member for Congress. Our hearts were kept enlarged by family needs; and the difference between wants and needs was wisely taught us. We were not suffered to grow up in ignorance of the distinction between the apparent and the real—What Is and What Seems. Our fingers were kept busy out of school and play hours, aiding the shirt-maker—helping her in the fine stitching, ruffled bosoms, and button-holes. In the making of the latter, even now, I am considered an adept. But with all this work, (which would be accounted a terrible hardship in 1855!) there was always blended a merriment and joy, for our mother managed to make us feel that younger eyes were aiding older ones. Children always like to think they can be of service; and love transfigures every task, and makes it pleasure. The books we read were carefully examined, as our eager curiosities seized these intellectual treasures; healthful imagination was encouraged; pains were taken that beautiful pictures of Truth should impress our minds with its power. With scrupulous care, our apparel was ever alike; but with thoughtful wisdom, our individualisms were respected. I was naturally indolent—yes, I may say, lazy; and I well remember the pleasant devices used by my mother to lure me to industry. Loving books, and a sort of dreamy foreshadowing resting on me at a very early period, I was not a useful child in many of those domestic arts which tend to make others happy; but I was not forced from my natural bias to constrained obedience, by rough, rude treatment, but gently led to be of service to others, and, as gently attracted to such service, because it was for others. I am grateful to my mother for this. I think she was wise.

The memory of our early morning walks with our father, our constant attendance at church, our simple and chaste wardrobe, our happy intercourse with our parents, our cheerful, witty, piquant table, shared frequently with many of our kindred, and overrunning with cheerful vivacity, is present with me now. The lonely meal partaken so often since my orphanage, has been endured with life from the past. I call it lonely; it is indeed solitary; but old memories make it festal. . . .

The simplicity of our lives, the nearness of our spirits, and our limitation to home delights, placed us where we were little understood by our neighbors. When we were mere children we read the newspaper to our parents. (How long the President's messages seemed to us then!) While other children were walking out in the evening, we were quietly in bed—too often awake!—and talking over when we should be old enough to be up in the evenings! The early hours we were made to keep, have had a beneficial effect on our whole lives, in the matter of health, and the control of our nervous energies. And thus, too, were formed habits of personal independence. Other children did thus and so:—why we should imitate them was not "in the Dictionary" used at No. 6 Fleet street! I suppose feelings of gratitude that we were individually recognized, tended to quiet our childish natures, when our neighbors' children were living a life so much more congenial, and with more apparent enjoyment. The restrictions put upon us, often caused our dear mother to be termed, prudish. There are persons unalterably true to their Ideal of Duty, they inevitably provoke the fancies and whims of the world about them, and are accused of nearsightedness and want of judgment. But such minds heed little what other people think or say; they do not take the trouble to prove they are right, or prate about the wrong; friends and foes may judge as they please; for within is the fixed light-house, and they keep their course through the shifting currents of opinion, directed by the safe, bright beacon—Conscience.

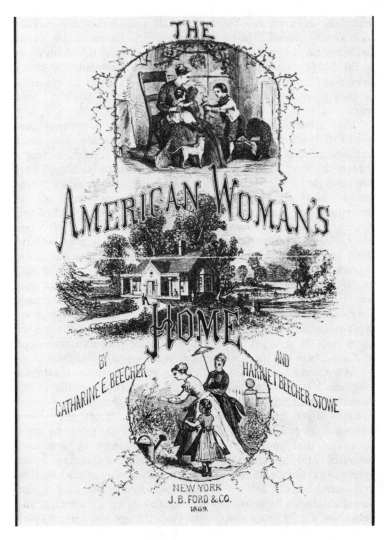

Title page, *The American Woman's Home*, by Catherine Beecher and Harriet Beecher Stowe.

There have been many as choice Homes. There have been many as true Parents. In many a soul their memory shines, like a star, and in many a heart they have lit an undying sunshine of gratitude. My sympathy with such, is electrical. I would take to my bosom every child thus blessed in its opening life; I would gratefully acknowledge the few friends with whom my parents took sweet counsel. But there is a mournful converse. My ear is sick—my heart is pained, with the conditions, and the changes, of social life! My medical profession has opened homes to me; and I have seen them ugly and bare. Sometimes I seem to myself a century plant, comparing the days that are with the days that were.

What are these homes of which I speak? The merest apologies; places for eating, drinking, and sleeping; haunts for ennui, fretfulness, and distrust; habitations where foreign servants control the kitchen and the nursery, while foreign fashions lord it over the parlor and the drawing-room! Elegant localities where vacant folly plays its antics; where hypocrisy lays off its sanctimonious mask, and shows the scowl; where whispering slander poisons the breathing air. Nests for parrots and mocking-birds. Alcoves where pompous pride and fickle vanity perform their private theatricals. Uncultured gardens where indolence, neglect, irritability, and recrimination, gather nettles and nightshade, and heaps of rubbish, choking every vital plant, that would germinate if it could, and make the air as sweet as summer. Dwellings where apathy and indifference are the substitutes for quiet home enjoyments; where fulsome flattery of some one for some end, is planned, and bait and hook prepared for social angling. These are the sad homes of what we call Society!

"A sentence has formed a character, and a character subdued a kingdom." But example is worth all the precept in the world. Parents! your children are worth more to you than the unrealities so many of you follow. See to it, that you not only educate by wise precept that conscience which will be their only guide to noble lives, but that you also educate that conscience by your own example, and by those good and graceful influences whose presence in your dwelling alone can make it worthy of the beautiful and sacred name of Home. Parents, see to it, that you give to your young children a home worthy of the name. Giving them that, you give them all. Failing to give them that, though you bestow every thing else, you give them nothing. Home is the mold of character. If it has cracks and flaws, expect to see the consequences in your children. You may separate precept and example, but, remember! infantile ears are very keen,—childish eyes are very search-ing,—and if your theory and practice are divorced, your young child of seven years knows all about it. Plans are laid to trap trap you by your children when you least suspect it; and you find yourself ashamed of yourself. Before you know it you are weighed in the child's balance—wo to you if you are found wanting! If there is sin and disorder in your life, you will see it all lived over again in your child. That child holds the clue to the intricate labyrinth of deception in itself, built by your ignorance or folly and used against yourself by your neglect or vacillation. My way of life has led me for many years, both as a teacher and a physician, to the observation of houses. The view has been a very sad one. The joy and gratitude I have felt for my own privileges, have been mixed with sorrow for the neglected childhood I have seen around me. I do not care what after delights and alleviations may be in store for the life of a neglected child; there will always be a void—a cheat—a sorrow—a loneliness in its being, which it will feel, though often not understand. Fathers! Mothers! think of this; and while you are striving for houses, lands, wealth, social position, and all those uncertain and perishable accumulations you are wont to gather for your children, give some little time to your own spiritual development,—to that certain and imperishable wealth of parental care which should be bequeathed to them; their use of this treasure will bless your lives and solace your dying hours—it may be, conscious that you have left them the best legacy!

Harriot Hunt, *Glances and Glimpses* (Boston: J. P. Jewett, 1856), pp. 13-21.

Transcendental Simplicity

5

I n the 1830s, at the same time that conservative moralists were promoting domestic simplicity, a group of young poets, preachers, and philosophers centered in Concord, Massachusetts, was developing a quite different version of plain living and high thinking. These Transcendentalists—Ralph Waldo Emerson, Henry David Thoreau, George Ripley, Theodore Parker, Bronson Alcott, Margaret Fuller, Elizabeth Peabody, Ellery Channing, and others—were much more spontaneous and romantic in their quest for the good life. They were skeptical that society at large would ever be converted to such ideal purposes, so they focused their attention on cultivating their own expressions of enlightened simplicity. This resulted in a wide range of practices. As Emerson reported in a letter to the English writer Thomas Carlyle in 1840: "We are all a little wild here with numberless projects of social reform." Indeed, romantic simplicity expressed itself in a variety of colorful forms, and before long the Transcendentalists were labeled eccentric and utopian.

Many of them were. These romantic perfectionists were much more radical and eclectic in their interpretation of simplicity than their Puritan forefathers or the promoters of the cult of domesticity. Some experimented with vegetarianism and sexual abstinence; others emphasized the simplification of clothing, favoring Byron collars, loose, flowing shirts and pants, and gaily colored blouses. A few such as Thoreau and Channing promoted a self-sustaining life in the woods. Emerson, on the other hand, enjoyed the luxury of a legacy from his first wife that enabled him to practice a genteel simplicity.

Whatever its particular form, Transcendental simplicity stressed a life of material and sensual self-control and intellectual and artistic exertion. It drew its inspiration not only from the Greeks and Romans, from Christian teachings, and Oriental religion, but also from the workings of nature. The bountiful wilderness that had proved a boon to economic growth also nurtured the idea that sensitive souls could establish what Emerson called an "original relation with the universe." In the woods the Transcendentalists found a source of aesthetic inspiration, moral goodness, and spiritual reassurance. Nature offered them both a retreat from the growing complexity and artificiality of American life and an opportunity for soul-searching introspection.

Of course this romantic naturalism was not unique to New England. Europeans had been expressing similar themes for years. But what distinguished American Transcendentalists from their Old World counterparts was their explicit debt to their Puritan ancestors. Though most of these intellectual rebels abandoned Calvinist theology, they were inspired by the Puritans' strenuous efforts to control their baser instincts in order to pursue spiritual glory. The Transcendentalists were likewise intent upon developing ways of living that reduced their material and societal needs to a minimum so they could more easily pursue spiritual truths, moral ideals, and aesthetic impulses.

Some of these New England idealists, such as Emerson and Thoreau, preached individual self-reliance; others preferred the communal simplicity offered by the experimental settlements at Brook Farm and Fruitlands. Self-reliant simplicity proved to be more enduring. Transcendentalists and other romantics were much too individualistic by temperament to last long in collective associations. By 1850 the Transcendentalist communities had collapsed.

The varied expressions of Transcendental social philosophy revealed the continuing ambiguity and appeal of the simple life. The ideal of plain living and high thinking encompassed a wide spectrum of practices, and it was only a slight step from enlightened restraint to mere eccentricity. "Everything runs to excess," Emerson concluded. Yet even with its excesses, Transcendental simplicity was a significant expression of American idealism. Its practitioners, however few, unusual, and extreme, revealed once again that simplicity could be much more than a hollow sentiment or a temporary expedient; it could be a living creed. Aspiring, failing, yet persistently striving to elevate their sights above the crassly material, these romantic naturalists displayed an enlivening sense of wonder and an ennobling sense of purpose. Emerson was never more accurate than when he described the Transcendentalists as "collectors of the heavenly spark, with power to convey the electricity to others."

An Emerson Miscellany

Ralph Waldo Emerson (1801–82) was the animating genius behind American Transcendentalism. His ideas were drawn from a variety of sources—Greek and Roman philosophy, German idealism, English romanticism, Oriental mysticism, and New England Puritanism. But he also learned much from his personal experiences. His minister father died in 1811, thus leaving the family destitute and dependent on their own ingenuity and frugality. Emerson later credited the "iron band of poverty, of necessity, of austerity" for steering him away from a life of material indulgence and pointing him toward "the grand, the beautiful, and the good."

Family tradition initially led Emerson into the ministry, but by 1832 he decided that the "cold and cheerless" Unitarian religion was too confining. So he retired from his Boston ministry and, after an excursion to Europe, he settled in Concord with his mother and second wife, Lidian. There he was soon "imparadised." Emerson described his home as "plain, square, and wooden." The house was situated on two acres of land near the Concord River and an inviting countryside, and in the woods and fields he found solace and solitude, inspiration and wonder. But he was no sylvan hermit. In the village of Concord he discovered a sense of republican community and many stimulating friends, especially young Henry Thoreau.

Thanks largely to a legacy from his first wife, who had died tragically in 1831, Emerson developed in Concord the scholarly routine of introspection, writing, community service, lecturing, and occasional preaching for which he quickly became famous. He devoted much of his attention to promoting an Emersonian version of the simple life. "Things are in the saddle and ride mankind," he observed. Americans, he felt, needed to redress the imbalance that had developed between materialism and idealism in their pursuit of the good life. This meant a thoroughgoing reform in perception as well as behavior in order to "correct the whole system of our social living." Like the earlier Puritans, Quakers, and pietistic sects, he thus preached nonconformity to the ways of the world. But Transcendental nonconformity was not tied to a particular theology or a collective social organization. Individuals would have to cultivate their own version of self-reliance, plain living, and high thinking. And in his journal, correspondence, and essays, Emerson wrestled with the implications of such an ethic for his own life and community. "It is hard," he once admitted, "to be simple enough to be good."

"NATURE" (1836)

To go into solitude, a man needs to retire as much from his chamber as from society. I am not solitary whilst I read and write, though nobody is with me. But if a man would be alone, let him look at the stars. The rays that come from those heavenly worlds will separate between him and what he touches. One might think the atmosphere was made transparent with this design, to give man, in the heavenly bodies, the perpetual presence of the sublime. Seen in the streets of cities, how great they are! If the stars should appear one night in a thousand years, how would men believe and adore; and preserve for many generations the remembrance of the city of God which had been shown! But every night come out of these envoys of beauty, and light the universe with their admonishing smile.

The stars awaken a certain reverence, because though always present, they are inaccessible; but all natural objects make a kindred impression, when the mind is open to their influence.

View of Concord, Massachusetts (1836).

Nature never wears a mean appearance. Neither does the wisest man extort her secret, and lose his curiosity by finding out all her perfection. Nature never became a toy to a wise spirit. The flowers, the animals, the mountains, reflected the wisdom of his best hour, as much as they had delighted the simplicity of his childhood.

When we speak of nature in this manner, we have a distinct but most poetical sense in the mind. We mean the integrity of impression made by manifold natural objects. It is this which distinguishes the stick of timber of the wood-cutter from the tree of the poet. The charming landscape which I saw this morning is indubitably made up of some twenty or thirty farms. Miller owns this field, Locke that, and Manning the woodland beyond. But none of them owns the landscape. There is a property in the horizon which no man has but he whose eye can integrate all the parts, that is, the poet. This is the best part of these men's farms, yet to this their warranty-deeds give no title.

To speak truly, few adult persons can see nature. Most persons do not see the sun. At least they have a very superficial seeing. The sun illuminates only the eye of the man, but shines into the eye and the heart of the child. The lover of nature is he whose inward and outward senses are still truly adjusted to each other; who has retained the spirit of infancy even into the era of manhood. His intercourse with heaven and earth becomes part of his daily food.

In the presence of nature a wild delight runs through the man, in spite of real sorrows. Nature says,—he is my creature, and maugre all his impertinent griefs, he shall be glad with me. Not the sun or the summer alone, but every hour and season yields its tribute of delight; for every hour and every change corresponds to and authorizes a different state of the mind, from breathless noon to grimmest midnight. Nature is a setting that fits equally well a comic or mourning piece. In good health, the air is a cordial of incredible virtue. Crossing a bare common, in snow puddles, at twilight, under a clouded sky, without having in my thoughts any occurrence of special good fortune, I have enjoyed a perfect exhilaration. I am glad to the brink of fear. In the woods, too, a man casts off his years, as the snake his slough, and at what period soever of life is always a child. In the woods is perpetual youth. Within these plantations of God, a decorum and sanctity reign, a perennial festival is dressed, and the guest sees not how he should tire of them in a thousand years. In the woods, we return to reason and faith. There I feel that nothing can befall me in life,—no disgrace, no calamity (leaving me my eyes), which nature cannot repair. Standing on the bare ground,—my head bathed by the blithe air and uplifted into infinite space,—all mean egotism vanishes. I become a transparent eyeball; I am nothing; I see all; the currents of the Universal Being circulate through me; I am part or parcel of God. The name of the nearest friend sounds then foreign and accidental: to be brothers, to be acquaintances, master or servant, is then a trifle and a disturbance. I am the lover of uncontained and immortal beauty. In the wilderness, I find something more dear and connate than in streets or villages. In the tranquil landscape, and especially in the distant line of the horizon, man beholds somewhat as beautiful as his own nature.

17 FEBRUARY 1838

My good Henry Thoreau made this else solitary afternoon sunny with his simplicity & clear perception. How comic is simplicity in this doubledealing quacking world. Every thing that boy says makes merry with society though nothing can be graver than his meaning.

26–28 APRIL 1838

Yesterday P.M. I went to the Cliff with Henry Thoreau. Warm, pleasant, misty weather which the great mountain amphitheatre seemed to drink in with gladness. A crow's voice filled all the miles

Asher Durand, *Kindred Spirits.*

of air with sound. A bird's voice, even a piping frog enlivens a solitude & makes world enough for us. At night I went out into the dark & saw a glimmering star & heard a frog & Nature seemed to say, Well do not these suffice? Here is a new scene, a new experience. Ponder it, Emerson, & not like the foolish world hanker after thunders & multitudes & vast landscapes, the sea or Niagara.

TO THOMAS CARLYLE, 10 MAY 1838

In aid of your friendliest purpose [of coming to America], I will set down some of the facts. I occupy, or *improve*, as we Yankees say, two acres only of God's earth; on which is my house, my kitchen-garden, my orchard of thirty young trees, my empty barn. My house is now a very good one for comfort, and abounding in room. Besides my house, I have, I believe, $22,000, whose income in ordinary years is six per cent. I have no other tithe or glebe except the income of my winter lectures, which was last winter $800. Well, with this income, here at home, I am a rich man. I stay at home and go abroad at my own instance. I have food, warmth, leisure, books, friends. Go away from home, I am rich no longer. I never have a dollar to spend on a fancy. As no wise man, I suppose, ever was rich in the sense of *freedom to spend*, because of the inundation of claims, so neither am I, who am not wise. But at home, I am rich,—rich enough for ten brothers. My wife Lidian is an incarnation of Christianity,—I call her Asia,—and keeps my philosophy from Antinomianism; my mother, whitest, mildest, most conservative of ladies, whose only exception to her universal preference for old things is her son; my boy, a piece of love and sunshine, well worth my watching from morning to night;—these, and three domestic women, who cook and sew and run for us, make all my household. Here I sit and read and write, with very little system, and, as far as regards composition, with the most fragmentary result: paragraphs incompressible, each sentence an infinitely repellent particle.

In summer, with the aid of a neighbor, I manage my garden; and a week ago I set out on the west side of my house forty young pine trees to protect me or my son from the wind of January. The ornament of the place is the occasional presence of some ten or twelve persons, good and wise, who visit us in the course of the year. . . .

27 MAY 1839

A great genius must come & preach self reliance. Our people are timid, desponding, recreant whimperers. If they fail in their first enterprises they lose all heart. If the young merchant fails, men say he is RUINED. If the finest genius studies at the Cambridge Divinity College, and is not ordained within a year afterwards in Boston, or New York, it seems to his friend & himself that he is justified in being disheartened & in complaining for the rest of his life.

A sturdy New Hampshire man or Vermonter who in turn tries *all* the professions, who *teams it, farms it, peddles*, keeps a school, preaches, edits a newspaper, goes to Congress, & so forth, in successive years, and always like a cat falls on his feet, is worth a hundred of these Boston dolls. My brave Henry here who is content to live now, & feels no shame in not studying any profession, for he does not postpone his life but lives already—pours contempt on these crybabies of routine & Boston. He has not one chance but a hundred chances. Now let a stern preacher arise who shall reveal the resources of Man, & tell men they are not leaning willows, but can & must detach themselves, that a man, a woman, is a sovereign eternity, born to shed healing to the nations; that he should be ashamed of our compassion; & that the moment he acts from himself, tossing the laws, the books, the idolatries, the customs, out of the window, we pity him, we pity here no more, but thank & revere them; that with the exercise of self trust new powers shall appear.

"SELF-RELIANCE" (1840)

And so the reliance on Property, including the reliance on governments which protect it, is the want of self-reliance. Men have looked away from themselves and at things so long that they have come to esteem the religious, learned and civil institutions as guards of property, and they deprecate assaults on these, because they feel them to be assaults on property. They measure their esteem of each other by what each has, and not by what each is. But a cultivated man becomes ashamed of his property, out of new respect for his nature. Especially he hates what he has if he sees that it is accidental,—came to him by inheritance, or gift, or crime; then he feels that it is not worth having; it does not belong to him, has no root in him and merely lies there because no revolution or robber takes it away. But that which a man is, does always by necessity acquire; and what a man acquires, is living property, which does not wait the beck of rulers, or mobs, or revolutions, or fire, or storm, or bankruptcies, but perpetually renews itself wherever the man breathes. "Thy lot or portion of life," said the Caliph Ali, "is seeking after thee; therefore be at rest from seeking after it." Our dependence on these foreign goods leads us to our slavish respect for numbers. . . .

6 JUNE 1841

I am sometimes discontented with my house because it lies on a dusty road and with its sills & cellar almost in the water of the meadow. But when I creep out of it into the Night or the Morning and see what majestic & what tender beauties daily wrap me in their bosom, how near to me is every transcendant secret of Nature's love & religion, I see how indifferent it is where I eat & sleep. This very street of hucksters & taverns the moon will transform to a Palmyra, for she is the apologist of all apologists & will kiss the elm-trees alone & hides every meanness in a silver edged darkness. Then the good river-god has taken the form of my valiant Henry Thoreau here & introduced me to the riches of his shadowy starlit, moonlit stream, a lovely new world lying as close & yet as unknown to this vulgar trite one of streets & shops as death to life or poetry to prose. . . .

SPRING 1844

Henry [Thoreau] is a good substantial childe, not encumbered with himself. He has no troublesome memory, no wake, but lives extempore, & brings today a new proposition as radical & revolutionary as that of yesterday, but different. The only man of leisure in the town. He is a good Abbot Samson: & carries counsel in his breast. If I cannot show his performance much more manifest than that of the other grand promisers, at least I can see that with his practical faculty, he has declined all the kingdoms of this world. Satan has no bribe for him.

MAY–JUNE 1857

I do not count the hours I spend in the woods, though I forget my affairs there & my books. And, when there, I wander hither & thither; any bird, any plant, any spring, detains me. I do not hurry homewards for I think all affairs may be postponed to this walking. And it is for this idleness that all my businesses exist.

Joel Porte, ed., *Emerson in His Journals* (Cambridge, Mass.: Harvard University Press, 1982), pp. 181, 185, 218–19, 325, 393–94, 476; "Nature," in Stephen E. Whicher, ed., *Selections from Ralph Waldo Emerson* (Boston: Houghton Mifflin, 1960), pp. 23–24; Letter to Carlyle, ibid., p. 124; "Self-Reliance," ibid., p. 167.

MY SYMPHONY

William Henry Channing

To live content with
  small means; to seek
elegance rather than
  luxury, and refinement
rather than fashion;
To be worthy, not respectable,
  and wealthy, not rich;
      to study hard,
      think quietly,
      talk gently,
      act frankly;
to listen to stars and birds,
  to babes and sages with open heart;
    to bear all cheerfully,
      do all bravely, await occasions, never hurry.
      In a word, to let the spiritual, unbidden, and unconscious,
      grow up through the common.
      This is to be my symphony.

William Henry Channing, *My Symphony* (New York: Dodge, n.d.), p. 3.

Brook Farm

Emerson's repeated appeals for contemplative simplicity
were compelling, and his words helped to provoke a wide
array of individual and group efforts to put into practice his
ethic of plain living and high thinking. Brook Farm and
Fruitlands were two colorful attempts to create Transcendental communities. George Ripley, like Emerson a former
Unitarian minister turned Transcendentalist, was the

founder of Brook Farm, located in West Roxbury, about nine miles from Boston. It was a serious attempt to address the relationship between work and culture, an issue that has always been a central concern of those promoting the simple life. Ripley solicited Emerson's participation and financial support, only to discover that the Concord poet and philosopher preferred to travel his own path to goodness. Emerson, for whom at "the name of a society all my repulsions play, all my quills rise and sharpen," offered his moral support to Brook Farm but not his money or participation. Ripley's appeal, as well as the general excitement over ways of simplifying life, inspired Emerson to "accommodate" such virtues in his own household. So he began cultivating a garden, experimenting with a vegetarian diet, and contemplating giving up the use of domestic servants. But neither his temperament nor his constitution was suited to such a new regimen. Son Waldo feared that his clumsy father would hurt himself hoeing in the garden. Indeed, Emerson soon admitted that "God has given me the seeing eye but not the working hand." He also found a meatless diet "too bland" for his taste. And although he declared he could do without household servants, his mother and wife insisted that they could not.

GEORGE RIPLEY TO R. W. EMERSON, 9 NOVEMBER 1840

My Dear Sir,

Our conversation in Concord was of such a general nature, that I do not feel as if you were in complete possession of the idea of the Association which I wish to see established. As we have now a prospect of carrying it into effect, at an early period, I wish to submit the plan more distinctly to your judgment, that you may decide whether it is one that can have the benefit of your aid and cooperation.

Our objects, as you know, are to insure a more natural union between intellectual and manual labor than now exists; to combine the thinker and the worker, as far as possible, in the same individual; to guarantee the highest mental freedom, by providing all with labor, adapted to their tastes and talents, and securing to them the fruits of their industry; to do away with the necessity of menial services, by opening the benefits of education and the profits of labor to all; and thus to prepare a society of liberal, intelligent, and cultivated persons, whose relations with each other would permit a more simple and wholesome life, than can be led amidst the pressure of our competitive institutions.

To accomplish these objects, we propose to take a small tract of land, which, under skillful husbandry, uniting the garden and the farm, will be adequate to the subsistence of the families; and to connect with this a school or college, in which the most complete instruction shall be given, from the first rudiments to the highest culture. Our farm would be a place for improving the race of men that lived on it; thought would preside over the operations of labor, and labor would contribute to the expansion of thought; we should have industry without drudgery, and true equality without its vulgarity. . . .

I can imagine no plan which is suited to carry into effect so many divine ideas as this. If wisely executed, it will be a light over this country and this age. If not the sunrise, it will be a morning star. As a practical man, I see clearly that we must have some such arrangement, or all changes less radical will be nugatory. I believe in the divinity of labor; I wish to "harvest my flesh and blood from the land"; but to do this, I must either be insulated and work to disadvantage, or avail myself of the services of hirelings, who are not of my order, and whom I can scarce make friends; for I must have another to drive the plough, which I hold. I cannot empty a cask of lime upon my grass alone. I wish to see a society of educated friends, working, thinking, and living together, with no strife, except that of each to contribute the most to the benefit of all.

Personally, my tastes and habits would lead me in another direction. I have a passion for being independent of the world, and of every man in it. This I could do easily on the estate which is now offered, and which I could rent at a rate, that with my other resources, would place me in a very agreeable condition, as far as my personal interests were involved. I should have a city of God, on a small scale of my own; and please God, I should hope one day to drive my own cart to market and sell greens. But I feel bound to sacrifice this private feeling, in the hope of a great social good. I shall be anxious to hear from you. Your decision will do much towards settling the question with me, whether the time has come for the fulfillment of a high hope, or whether the work belongs to a future generation. All omens now are favorable; a singular union of diverse talents is ready for the enterprise; everything indicates that we ought to arise and build; and if we let slip this occasion, the unsleeping Nemesis will deprive us of the boon we seek. For myself, I am sure that I can never give so much thought to it again; my mind must act on other objects, and I shall acquiesce in the course of fate, with grief that so fair a light is put out. . . .

Pray write me with as much frankness as I have used towards you, and believe me ever your friend and faithful servant,

George Ripley

R. W. EMERSON TO GEORGE RIPLEY, 15 DECEMBER 1840

My Dear Sir,

It is quite time I made an answer to your proposition that I should join you in your new enterprise. The design appears to me so noble & humane, proceeding, as I plainly see, from a manly & expanding heart & mind that it makes me & all men its friends & debtors. It becomes a matter of conscience to entertain it friendly & to examine what it has for us.

I have decided not to join it & yet very slowly & I may almost say penitentially. I am greatly relieved by learning that your coadjutors are now so many that you will no longer ascribe that importance to the defection of individuals which you hinted in your letter to me . . . might . . . attach to mine.

The ground of my decision is almost purely personal to myself. I have some remains of skepticism in regard to the general practicability of the plan, but these have not much weighed with me. That which determines me is the conviction that the Community is not good for me. Whilst I see it may hold out many inducements for others it has little to offer me which with resolution I cannot procure for myself. It seems to me that it would not be worth my while to make the difficult exchange of my property in Concord for a share in the new Household. I am in many respects suitably placed . . . in an agreeable neighborhood, in a town which I have many reasons to love & which has respected my freedom so far that I may presume it will indulge me farther if I need it. Here I have friends & kindred. Here I have builded & planted: & here I have greater facilities to prosecute such practical enterprizes as I may cherish, than I could probably find by any removal. I cannot accuse my townsmen or my social position of my domestic

From John McAleer, *Ralph Waldo Emerson*

Emerson in 1842.

grievances:—only my own sloth & conformity. It seems to me a circuitous & operose way of relieving myself of some irksome circumstances, to put on your community the task of my emancipation which I ought to take on myself.

The principal particulars in which I wish to mend my domestic life are in acquiring habits of regular manual labor, and in ameliorating or abolishing in my house the condition of hired menial service. I should like to come one step nearer to nature than this usage permits. But surely I need not sell my house & remove my family to Newton in order to make the experiment of labor & self help. I am already in the act of trying some domestic & social experiments which my present position favors. And I think that my present position has even greater advantages than you would offer me for testing my improvements in those small private parties into which men are all set off already throughout the world. . . .

But I own I almost shrink from making any statement of my objections to our ways of living because I see how slowly I shall mend them. My own health & habits & those of my wife & my mother are not of that robustness which should give any pledge of enterprize & ability in reform. And whenever I am engaged in literary composition I find myself not inclined to insist with heat on new methods. Yet I think that all I shall solidly do, I must do alone. I do not think I should gain anything—I who have little skill to converse with people—by a plan of so many parts and which I comprehend so slowly & imperfectly as the proposed Association.

If the community is not good for me neither am I good for it. I do not look on myself as a valuable member to any community which is not either very large or very small & select. I fear that yours would not find me as profitable & pleasant an associate as I should wish to be and as so important a project seems imperatively to require in all its constituents. Moreover I am so ignorant & uncertain in my improvements that I would fain hide my attempts & failures in solitude where they shall perplex none or very few beside myself. The result of our secretest improvements will certainly have as much renown as shall be due to them. . . .

Whilst I refuse to be an active member of your company I must yet declare that of all the . . . philanthropic projects of which I have heard yours is the most pleasing to me and if it is prosecuted in the same spirit in which it is begun, I shall regard it with lively sympathy & with a sort of gratitude.

Yours affectionately,
R W Emerson

O. B. Frothingham, *George Ripley* (Boston: Houghton Mifflin, 1882), pp. 307–12; *The Letters of Ralph Waldo Emerson*, ed. Ralph L. Rusk (New York: Columbia University Press, 1939), 2:368–71.

Brook Farm—Another View

Nathaniel Hawthorne

Though Emerson declined to participate in Brook Farm, George Ripley went ahead with his plans. The community was an engaging expression of the recurring ideal of communal simplicity, and many of its residents found considerable fulfillment and enlightenment before a fire and mounting debts brought the community's demise in the late 1840s. During the first few years Brook Farm included about 150 adults and children. Philosophers, poets, clergymen, reformers, artists, and writers worked together milking cows, pitching manure, cleaning stables, cooking, and washing. Wages were equalized and leisure time was devoted to contemplation and artistic creation. One Brook Farmer later recalled that most of the residents "were happy, contented, well-off and carefree; doing a great work in the world, enthusiastic and faithful, we enjoyed every moment of every day."

But a few participants were not so enthusiastic. Nathaniel Hawthorne joined the community hoping to find more free time to write than his job at the Boston Customs House allowed. He also wanted to save some money in order to marry Sophia Peabody. Yet his experience at Brook Farm proved disillusioning in both respects. It was, as he later said, "the most romantic episode of my own life," and his witty and wry descriptions of the episode in his journal reveal that naivete often accompanies romanticism. Rural simplicity may offer elevating surroundings, but it also entails hard and frequently wearisome work.

Brook Farm, Oak Hill, *April 13th, 1841.*—... I have not yet taken my first lesson in agriculture, except that I went to see our cows foddered, yesterday afternoon. We have eight of our own; and the number is now increased by a transcendental heifer belonging to Miss Margaret Fuller. She is very fractious, I believe, and apt to kick over the milk-pail. ... I intend to convert myself into a milkmaid this evening, but I pray Heaven that Mr. Ripley may be moved to assign me the kindliest cow in the herd, otherwise I shall perform my duty with fear and trembling.

I like my brethren in affliction very well; and, could you see us sitting around our table at meal-times, before the great kitchen fire, you would call it a cheerful sight. Mrs. B— is a most comfortable woman to behold. She looks as if her ample person were stuffed full of tenderness,—indeed, as if she were all one great, kind heart.

April 14th, 10 A.M.—... I did not milk the cows last night, because Mr. Ripley was afraid to trust them to my hands, or me to their horns, I know not which. But this morning I have done wonders. Before breakfast, I went out to the barn and began to chop hay for the cattle, and with such "righteous vehemence," as Mr. Ripley says, did I labor, that in the space of ten minutes I broke the machine. Then I brought wood and replenished the fires; and finally went down to breakfast, and ate up a huge mound of buckwheat cakes. After breakfast, Mr. Ripley put a four-pronged instrument into my hands, which he gave me to understand was called a pitchfork; and he and Mr. Farley being armed with similar weapons, we all three commenced a gallant attack upon a heap of manure. This office being concluded, and I having purified myself, I sit down to finish this letter. . . .

Miss Fuller's cow hooks the other cows, and has made herself ruler of the herd, and behaves in a very tyrannical manner. . . . I shall make an excellent husbandman,—I feel the original Adam reviving within me.

April 16th.—. . . I have milked a cow!!! . . . The herd has rebelled against the usurpation of Miss Fuller's heifer; and, whenever they are turned out of the barn, she is compelled to take refuge under our protection. So much did she impede my labors by keeping close to me, that I found it necessary to give her two or three gentle pats with a shovel; but still she preferred to trust herself to my tender mercies, rather than venture among the horns of the herd. She is not an amiable cow; but she has a very intelligent face, and seems to be of a reflective cast of character. I doubt not that she will soon perceive the expediency of being on good terms with the rest of the sisterhood.

I have not yet been twenty yards from our house and barn; but I begin to perceive this is a beautiful place. The scenery is of a mild and placid character, with nothing bold in its aspect; but I think its beauties will grow upon us, and make us love it the more, the longer we live here. There is a brook, so near the house that we

Josiah Walcott, *Brook Farm* (1844).

shall be able to hear its ripple in the summer evenings, . . . but, for agricultural purposes, it has been made to flow in a straight and rectangular fashion, which does it infinite damage as a picturesque object. . . .

April 22nd—. . . What an abominable hand do I scribble! but I have been chopping wood, and turning a grindstone all the forenoon; and such occupations are likely to disturb the equilibrium of the muscles and sinews. It is an endless surprise to me how much work there is to be done in the world; but, thank God, I am able to do my share of it,—and my ability increases daily. What a great, broad-shouldered, elephantine personage I shall become by and by!

May 4th.—. . . My cold no longer troubles me, and all the morning I have been at work under the clear, blue sky, on a hill-side. Sometimes it almost seemed as if I were at work in the sky itself, though the material in which I wrought was the ore from our gold-mine. Nevertheless, there is nothing so unseemly and disagreeable in this sort of toil as you could think. It defiles the hands, indeed, but not the soul. This gold ore is a pure and wholesome substance, else our mother Nature would not devour it so readily, and derive so much nourishment from it, and return such a rich abundance of good grain and roots in requital of it. . . .

The farm is growing very beautiful now,—not that we yet see anything of the peas and potatoes which we have planted; but the grass blushes green on the slopes and hollows. I wrote that word "blush" almost unconsciously; so we will let it go as an inspired utterance. . . .

June 1st.—. . . I have been too busy to write a long letter by this opportunity, for I think this present life of mine gives me an antipathy to pen and ink, even more than my Custom House experience did. . . . In the midst of toil, or after a hard day's work in the gold-mine, my soul obstinately refuses to be poured out on paper. That abominable gold mine! Thank God, we anticipate getting rid of its treasures in the course of two or three days! Of all hateful places that is the worst, and I shall never comfort myself for having spent so many days of blessed sunshine there. It is my opinion that a man's soul may be buried and perish under a dung-heap, or in a furrow of the field, just as well as under a pile of money.

August 12th.—. . . I am very well, and not at all weary, for yesterday's rain gave us a holiday; and, moreover, the labors of the farm are not so pressing as they have been. And, joyful thought! in a little more than a fortnight I shall be free from my bondage,—. . . free to enjoy Nature,—free to think and feel! . . . Even my Custom House experience was not such a thraldom and weariness; my mind and heart were free. Oh, labor is the curse of the world, and nobody can meddle with it without becoming proportionately brutified! Is it a prayer-worthy matter that I have spent five golden months in providing food for cocks and horses? It is not so. . . .

Salem, September 3d.—. . . But really I should judge it to be twenty years since I left Brook Farm; and I take this to be one proof that my life there was an un-natural and unsuitable, and therefore an unreal, one. It already looks like a dread behind me. The real Me was never an associate of the community; there had been a spectral Appearance there, sounding the horn at daybreak, and milking the cows, and hoeing potatoes, and raking hay, toiling in the sun, and doing me the honor to assume my name. But the spectre was not myself. Nevertheless, it is somewhat remarkable that my hands have, during the past summer, grown very brown and rough, insomuch that many people persist in believing that I, after all, was the aforesaid spectral horn-sounder, cow-milker, potato-hoer, and hay-raker. But such people do not know a reality from a shadow.

Nathaniel Hawthorne, *The American Notebooks* (Cambridge, Mass.: Houghton Mifflin, 1896), pp. 227–38.

Fruitlands

Brook Farm was one of several efforts to create simple-living communities during the 1840s. Fruitlands was a much more spartan attempt to combine collective plain living with high thinking. Its organizers were the tirelessly quixotic Transcendental reformer Bronson Alcott and Charles Lane, an English journalist, reformer, and educator. Alcott was determined to form a communal brotherhood that would cultivate a divine economy. Lane agreed to help finance the venture, and in the summer of 1843 they founded Fruitlands on ninety acres outside the village of Harvard, Massachusetts. Unlike Brook Farm, however, its regimen verged on the ascetic. Alcott declared that Brook Farm was not "sufficiently ideal."

So Bronson Alcott, his wife Abigail, their four daughters, Anna, Elizabeth, Louisa May, and Abby May, joined Charles Lane, his son, and a motley assortment of a half dozen or so other courageous, well-intentioned, but rather bizarre idealists, in an attempt to lead a truly simple life. They refused to wear clothes made of cotton or wool because the former was the product of slave labor and the latter was forcibly taken from sheep. Hence they wore linen. They also adopted a strict vegetarian diet.

The daily routine at Fruitlands was rigidly struc-tured—at least in theory. Each day was to begin at dawn with a plunge into the cold pond, followed by a music lesson and a breakfast of nuts and grains. The residents would then work until noon, eat lunch, and then engage in some "interesting and deep-searching conversation." Late afternoon would bring more outside work, and the day was to end with supper and more discussion. It was an idyllic plan, and when Emerson visited the community a few weeks after its creation, he wrote in his journal: "Young men and young women, should visit them and be inspired. I think there is as much merit in beautiful manners as in hard work. I will not prejudge them successful. They look well in July; we will see them in September." It was a prophetic statement.

CHARLES LANE TO HENRY D. THOREAU, JUNE 7, 1843

It [Fruitlands] is very remotely placed, without a road, surrounded by a beautiful green landscape of fields and woods, with the distance filled up with some of the loftiest mountains in the State. At present there is much hard manual labor, so much so that, as you see, my usual handwriting is very greatly suspended. Our house accommodations are poor and scanty; but the greatest want is good female society. Far too much labor devolves on Mrs. Alcott. Besides the occupations of each succeeding day, we form in this ample theatre of hope, many forthcoming scenes. The nearer little copse is designed as the site of the cottages. Fountains can be made to descend from their granite sources on the hill-slope to every apartment if desired. Gardens are to displace the warm grazing glades on the South, and numerous human beings instead of cattle, shall here enjoy existence. . . .

On the estate are about 14 acres of wood,—a very sylvan realization, which only wants a Thoreau's mind to elevate it to classic beauty. The farther wood offers to the naturalist and the poet an exhaustless hunt; and a short cleaning of the brook would connect our boat with the Nashua. Such are the designs which Mr. Alcott and I have just sketched, as resting from planting we walked around this reserve. . . .

Though to me our mode of life is luxurious in the highest degree, yet generally it seems to be thought that the setting aside of all impure diet, dirty habits, idle thoughts, and selfish feelings is a source of self-denial scarcely to be encountered, or even thought of, in such an alluring world as this. . . .

Alcott's and Lane's vision of an ideal transcendental community was flawed from the start. The two philosophers were so rigid in their expectations and so ethereal in outlook that they vastly underestimated the problems facing such an undertaking. Alcott, Lane, and most of the other male Fruitlanders spent more time cultivating their conversations than their crops. They also were away from the settlement for extended periods, trying, unsuccessfully, to recruit new residents. Consequently, the burden of sustaining the community fell on the shoulders of Abigail Alcott and her young girls. By the early winter the food supply had run out. As the north winds began to sweep across Fruitlands, the residents found themselves ill-prepared for a prolonged winter siege. Lane thereupon sought shelter in a nearby Shaker settlement. Alcott was so depressed by the disintegration of his communal dream that he fasted for three days. Then, as if having received a vision, he led his family back to Concord.

Louisa May Alcott later wrote "Transcendental Wild Oats," the most comprehensive and satirical description of the Fruitlands episode. Part of it is excerpted below.

Any housewife can imagine the emotions of Sister Hope [Mrs. Alcott], when she took possession of a large, dilapidated kitchen, containing an old stove and the peculiar stores out of which food was to be evolved for her little family of eleven. Cakes of maple sugar, dried peas and beans, barley and hominy, meal of all sorts, potatoes, and dried fruit. No milk, butter, cheese, tea, or meat appeared. Even salt was considered a useless luxury and spice entirely forbidden by lovers of Spartan simplicity. A ten years' experience of vegetarian vagaries had been good training for this new freak, and her sense of the ludicrous supported her through many trying scenes.

Unleavened bread, porridge, and water for breakfast; bread, vegetables, and water for dinner; bread, fruit, and water for supper was the bill of fare ordained by the elders. No teapot profaned that sacred stove, no gory steak cried aloud for vengeance from her chaste gridiron; and only a brave woman's taste, time, and temper were sacrificed on that domestic altar.

The vexed question of light was settled by buying a quantity of bayberry wax for candles; and, on discovering that no one knew how to make them, pine knots were introduced, to be used when absolutely necessary. Being summer, the evenings were not long, and the weary fraternity found it no great hardship to retire with the birds. The inner light was sufficient for most of them. But Mrs. Lamb [Mrs. Alcott] rebelled. Evening was the only time she had to herself, and when the tired feet rested the skillful hands, mended torn frocks and little stockings, or anxious heart forgot its burden in a book.

So "mother's lamp" burned steadily, while the philosophers built a new heaven and earth by moonlight; and through all the metaphysical mists and philanthropic pyrotechnics of that period Sister Hope played her own little game of "throwing light," and none but the moths were the worse for it.

Such farming probably was never seen before since Adam delved. The band of brothers began by spading garden and field; but a few days of it lessened their ardor amazingly. Blistered hands and aching backs suggested the expediency of permitting the use of cattle 'til the workers were better fitted for noble toil by a summer of the new life.

Brother Moses [Joseph Palmer] brought a yoke of oxen from his farm,—at least, the philosophers thought so till it was discovered that one of the animals was a cow; and Moses confessed that he "must be let down easy, for he couldn't live on garden sarse entirely."

Great was Dictator Lion's [Charles Lane] indignation at this lapse from virtue. But time pressed, the work must be done; so the meek cow was permitted to wear the yoke and the recreant brother continued to enjoy forbidden draughts in the barn, which dark proceeding caused the children to regard him as one set apart for destruction.

The sowing was equally peculiar, for, owing to some mistake, the three brethren, who devoted themselves to this graceful task, found when about half through the job that each had been sowing a different sort of grain in the same field; a mistake which caused much perplexity, as it could not be remedied; but, after a long consultation and a good deal of laughter, it was decided to say nothing and see what would come of it.

The garden was planted with a generous supply of useful roots and herbs; but, as manure was not allowed to profane the virgin soil, few of these vegetable treasures ever came up. Purslane reigned supreme, and the disappointed planters ate it philosophically, deciding that Nature knew what was best for them, and would generously supply their needs, if they could only learn to digest her "sallets" and wild roots.

The orchard was laid out, a little grafting done, new trees and vines set, regardless of the unfit season and entire ignorance of the husbandmen, who honestly believed that in the autumn they would reap a bounteous harvest.

Slowly things got into order, and rapidly rumors of the new experiment went abroad, causing many strange spirits to flock thither, for in those days communities were the fashion and transcendentalism raged wildly. Some came to look on and laugh, some to be supported in poetic idleness, a few to believe sincerely and work heartily. Each member was allowed to mount his favorite hobby and ride it to his heart's content. Very queer were some of the riders, and very rampant some of the hobbies.

One youth, believing that language was of little consequence if the spirit was only right, startled new-comers by blandly greeting them with "Good-morning, damn you," and other remarks of an equally mixed order. A second irrepressible being held that all the emotions of the soul should be freely expressed, and illustrated his theory by antics that would have sent him to a lunatic asylum, if, as an unregenerate wag said, he had not already been in one. When his spirit soared, he climbed trees and shouted; when doubt assailed him, he lay upon the floor and groaned lamentably. At joyful periods, he raced, leaped, and sang; when sad, he wept aloud; and when a great thought burst upon him in the watches of the night, he crowed like a jocund cockerel, to the great delight of the children and the great annoyance of the elders. One musical brother fiddled whenever so moved, sang sentimentally to the four little girls, and put a music-box on the wall when he hoed corn.

Brother Pease [Samuel Bower] ground away at his uncooked food, or browsed over the farm on sorrel, mint, green fruit, and new vegetables. Occasionally he took his walks abroad, airily attired in an unbleached cotton *poncho*, which was the nearest approach to the primeval costume he was allowed to indulge in. At midsummer he retired to the wilderness, to try his plan where the woodchucks were without prejudices and huckleberry-bushes were hospitably full. A sunstroke unfortunately spoilt his plan, and he returned to semi-civilization a sadder and wiser man.

Forest Absalom [Abram Everett] preserved his Pythagorean silence, cultivated his fine dark locks, and worked like a beaver, setting an excellent example of brotherly love, justice, and fidelity by his upright life. He it was who helped Sister Hope with her heavy washes, kneaded the endless succession of batches of bread, watched over the children, and did the many tasks left undone by the brethren, who were so busy discussing and defining great duties that they forgot to perform the small ones.

Moses White [Joseph Palmer] placidly plodded about, "chorin' around," as he called it, looking like an old-time patriarch, with his silver hair and flowing beard, and saving the community from many a mishap by his thrift and Yankee shrewdness.

Brother Lion [Charles Lane] domineered over the whole concern; for, having put the most money into the speculation, he was resolved to make it pay,—as if anything founded on an ideal basis could be expected to do so by any but enthusiasts.

Abel Lamb [Bronson Alcott] simply revelled in the Newness, firmly believing that his dream was to be beautifully realized and in time not only little Fruitlands, but the whole happy earth, be turned into a Happy Valley. He worked with every muscle of his body, for *he* was in deadly earnest. He taught with his whole head and heart; planned and sacrificed, preached and prophesied, with a soul full of the purest aspirations, most unselfish purposes, and desired for a life devoted to God and man, too high and tender to bear the rough usage of this world.

It was a little remarkable that only one woman ever joined this community. Mrs. Lamb merely followed wheresoever her husband led,—"as ballast for his balloon," as she said, in her bright way. . . .

About the time the grain was ready to house, some call of the Oversoul wafted all the men away. An easterly storm was coming up and the yellow stacks were sure to be ruined. Then Sister Hope gathered her forces. Three little girls, one boy (Timon's son) and herself, harnessed to clothes-baskets and Russia-linen sheets, were the only teams she could command; but with these poor appliances the indomitable women got in the grain and saved food for her young, with the instinct and energy of a mother-bird with a brood of hungry nestlings to feed.

This attempt at regeneration had its tragic as well as comic side, though the world only saw the former.

With the first frosts, the butterflies, who had sunned themselves in the new light through the summer, took flight, leaving the few bees to see what honey they had stored for winter use. Precious little appeared beyond the satisfaction of a few months of holy living.

At first it seemed as if a chance to try holy dying also was to be offered them. Timon, much disgusted with the failure of the scheme, decided to retire to the Shakers, who seemed to be the only successful community going. . . .

Then the tragedy began for the forsaken little family. Desolation and despair fell upon Abel. As his wife said, his new beliefs had alienated many friends. Some thought him mad, some unprincipled. Even the most kindly thought him a visionary, whom it was useless to help till he took more practical views of life. All stood aloof, saying: "let him work out his own ideas, and see what they are worth."

He had tried, but it was a failure. The world was not ready for Utopia yet, and those who attempted to found it only got laughed at for their pains. In other days, men could sell all and give to the poor, lead lives devoted to holiness and high thought, and, after the persecution was over, find themselves honored as saints or martyrs. But in modern times these things are out of fashion. To live for one's principles, at all costs, is a dangerous speculation; and the failure of an ideal, no matter how humane and noble, is harder for the world to forgive and forget than bank robbery or the grand swindles of corrupt politicians. . . .

Clara Sears, comp., *Bronson Alcott's Fruitlands* (Boston: Houghton Mifflin, 1915), pp. 22-23, 156-62, 166-69.

Walden

Henry David Thoreau

The most famous version of Transcendental simplicity, of course, was that practiced by Henry David Thoreau. He remains the most conspicuous and persuasive exponent of simple living in the American experience. Where Emerson spoke of self-reliance while subsisting on a legacy, and the Brook Farmers and Fruitlanders practiced communal simplicity for a few years, Thoreau earned his way his whole life by using his practical skills and by limiting his desires. Like Emerson, Thoreau was deeply influenced by the Puritan conscience. He, too, believed that body and soul were in a perpetual struggle for man's heart. True virtue resided with those who successfully resisted needless material and sensual temptations in order to concentrate on spiritual or inward development. It was this Puritan strain

of moral toughness leading to self-control that differen-
tiated Thoreau from most European romantics as well as
the later American "hippies" who so revered his wilderness
adventure.

After graduating from Harvard in 1837, Thoreau taught
in a small private academy with his brother for several
years until the latter's failing health forced the closing of
the school. In 1841 he moved in with the Emersons in
exchange for serving as their handyman and gardener. But
he was not comfortable there in the midst of "a very
dangerous prosperity." Nor was he interested in joining
Brook Farm or Fruitlands. Such corporate, regimented life
repelled him. He was eager to discover a self-sustaining, yet
liberating mode of life, and he began to consider a life of
simple sufficiency in the woods as a temporary option. In
October, 1844, when Emerson bought some land along
Walden Pond, Thoreau saw his chance. Emerson allowed
him to "squat" on the property in exchange for clearing
part of it. In the summer of 1845 Thoreau moved into his
cabin. Nature would now provide his path to an ideal world
and an inner discovery.

Those who know *Walden* only by reputation too often
assume that Thoreau lived at Walden Pond the life of a
hermit bent on leading a primal existence. Yet it is
important to remember that his cabin was only a mile or so
from town. He returned often to visit family and friends,
and they also were guests in his cabin. His primary purpose
was not "to live cheaply nor to live dearly there, but to
transact some private business with the fewest obstacles."
The "private business" was the writing of his first book, *A
Week on the Concord and Merrimack Rivers*. His broader
purpose was to discover how many of the so-called necessities of life he could forego in order to experience the
wonders of nature and the joys of self-culture.

Most of the luxuries, and many of the so called comforts of life,
are not only not indispensable, but positive hindrances to the

elevation of mankind. With respect to luxuries and comforts, the wisest have ever lived a more simple and meagre life than the poor. The ancient philosophers, Chinese, Hindoo, Persian, and Greek, were a class than which none has been poorer in outward riches, none so rich in inward. We know not much about them. It is remarkable that *we* know so much of them as we do. The same is true of the more modern reformers and benefactors of their race. None can be an impartial or wise observer of human life but from the vantage ground of what *we* should call voluntary poverty. Of a life of luxury the fruit is luxury, whether in agriculture, or commerce, or literature, or art. There are nowadays professors of philosophy, but not philosophers. Yet it is admirable to profess because it was once admirable to live. To be a philosopher is not merely to have subtle thoughts, nor even to found a school, but so to love wisdom as to live according to its dictates, a life of simplicity, independence, magnanimity, and trust. It is to solve some of the problems of life, not only theoretically, but practically. The success of great scholars and thinkers is commonly a courtier like success, not kingly, not manly. They make shift to live merely by conformity, practically as their fathers did, and are in no sense the progenitors of a nobler race of men. But why do men degenerate ever? What makes families run out? What is the nature of the luxury which enervates and destroys nations? Are we sure that there is none of it in our own lives? The philosopher is in advance of his age even in the outward form of his life. He is not fed, sheltered, clothed, warmed, like his contemporaries. How can a man be a philosopher and not maintain his vital heat by better methods than other men? . . .

. . . My purpose in going to Walden Pond was not to live cheaply nor to live dearly there, but to transact some private business with the fewest obstacles; to be hindered from accomplishing which for want of a little common sense, a little enterprise and business talent, appeared not so sad as foolish. . . .

Though we are not so degenerate but that we might possibly live in a cave or a wigwam or wear skins to-day, it certainly is better to accept the advantages, though so dearly bought, which the invention and industry of mankind offer. In such a neighborhood as this, boards and shingles, lime and bricks are cheaper and more easily obtained than suitable caves, or whole logs, or bark in sufficient quantities, or even well-tempered clay or flat stones. I speak understandingly on this subject, for I have made myself acquainted with it both theoretically and practically. With a little more wit we might use these materials so as to become richer than the richest are now, and make our civilization a blessing. The civilized man is a more experienced and wiser savage. But to make haste to my own experiment.

Near the end of March, 1845, I borrowed an axe and went down to the woods by Walden Pond, nearest to where I intended to build my house, and began to cut down some tall, arrowy, white pines, still in their youth, for timber. It is difficult to begin without borrowing, but perhaps it is the most generous course thus to permit your fellow-men to have an interest in your enterprise. The owner of the axe [Bronson Alcott], as he released his hold on it, said that it was the apple of his eye; but I returned it sharper than I received it. It was a pleasant hillside where I worked, covered with pine woods, through which I looked out on the pond, and a small open field in the woods where pines and hickories were springing up. The ice in the pond was not yet dissolved, though there were some open spaces, and it was all dark-colored and saturated with water. There were some slight flurries of snow during the days that I worked there; but for the most part when I came out to the railroad, on my way home, its yellow sand-heap stretched away gleaming in the hazy atmosphere, and the rails shone in the spring sun, and I heard the lark and peewee and other birds already come to commence another year with us. They were pleasant spring days, in which the winter of man's discontent was thawing as well as the earth, and the life that had lain torpid began to stretch itself. One day, when my axe had come off and I had cut a green hickory for a wedge, driving it with a stone, and had placed the whole to soak in a pond-hole in order to swell the wood, I saw a striped snake run into the water, and he lay on the bottom, apparently without inconvenience, as long as I stayed there, or more than a quarter of an hour; perhaps because he had not yet fairly come out of the torpid state. It appeared to me that for a like reason men remain in their present low and primitive condition; but if they should feel the influence of the spring of springs arousing them, they would of necessity rise to a higher and more ethereal life. . . .

I went to the woods because I wished to live deliberately, to front only the essential facts of life, and see if I could not learn what it had to teach, and not, when I came to die, discover that I had not lived. I did not wish to live what was not life, living is so dear; nor did I wish to practise resignation, unless it was quite necessary. I wanted to live deep and suck out all the marrow of life, to live so sturdily and Spartan-like as to put to rout all that was not life, to cut a broad swath and shave close, to drive life into a corner, and reduce it to its lowest terms, and, if it proved to be mean, why then to get the whole and genuine meanness of it, and

WALDEN;

OR,

LIFE IN THE WOODS.

By HENRY D. THOREAU,

AUTHOR OF "A WEEK ON THE CONCORD AND MERRIMACK RIVERS."

I do not propose to write an ode to dejection, but to brag as lustily as chanticleer in the morning, standing on his roost, if only to wake my neighbors up. — Page 92.

BOSTON:

TICKNOR AND FIELDS.

M DCCC LIV.

Title page from first edition of *Walden* (1854), with drawing of Thoreau's cabin by his sister, Sophia.

publish its meanness to the world; or if it were sublime, to know it by experience, and be able to give a true account of it in my next excursion. For most men, it appears to me, are in a strange uncertainty about it, whether it is of the devil or of God, and have *somewhat hastily* concluded that it is the chief end of man here to "glorify God and enjoy him forever."

Still we live meanly, like ants; though the fable tells us that we were long ago changed into men; like pygmies we fight with cranes; it is error upon error, and clout upon clout, and our best virtue has for its occasion a superfluous and evitable wretchedness. Our life is frittered away by detail. An honest man has hardly need to count more than his ten fingers, or in extreme cases he may add his ten toes, and lump the rest. Simplicity, simplicity, simplicity! I say, let your affairs be as two or three, and not a hundred or a thousand; instead of a million count half a dozen, and keep your accounts on your thumb-nail. In the midst of this chopping sea of civilized life, such are the clouds and storms and quicksands and thousand-and-one items to be allowed for, that a man has to live, if he would not flounder and go to the bottom and not make his port at all, by dead reckoning, and he must be a great calculator indeed who succeeds. Simplify, simplify. Instead of three meals a day, if it be necessary eat but one; instead of a hundred dishes, five; and reduce other things in proportion. Our life is like a German Confederacy, made up of petty states, with its boundary forever fluctuating, so that even a German cannot tell you how it is bounded at any moment. The nation itself, with all its so-called internal improvements, which, by the way, are all external and superficial, is just such an unwieldy and overgrown establishment, cluttered with furniture and tripped up by its own traps, ruined by luxury and heedless expense, by want of calculation and a worthy aim, as the million households in the land; and the only cure for it, as for them, is in a rigid economy, a stern and more Spartan simplicity of life and elevation of purpose. It lives too fast. Men think that it is essential that the *Nation* have commerce, and export ice, and talk through a telegraph, and ride thirty miles an hour, without a doubt, whether *they* do or not; but whether we should live like baboons or like men, is a little uncertain. . . .

Our village life would stagnate if it were not for the unexplored forests and meadows which surround it. We need the tonic of wildness,—to wade sometimes in marshes where the bittern and the meadow-hen lurk, and hear the booming of the snipe; to smell the whispering sedge where only some wilder and more solitary fowl builds her nest, and the mink crawls with its belly close to the ground. At the same time that we are earnest to explore and learn all things, we require that all things be mysterious and unexplorable, that land and sea be infinitely wild, unsurveyed and unfathomed by us because unfathomable. We can never have enough of Nature. We must be refreshed by the sight of inexhaustible vigor, vast and Titanic features, the sea-coast with its wrecks, the wilderness with its living and its decaying trees, the thundercloud, and the rain which lasts three weeks and produces freshets. We need to witness our own limits transgressed, and some life pasturing freely where we never wander. . . .

I left the woods for as good a reason as I went there. Perhaps it seemed to me that I had several more lives to live, and could not spare any more time for that one. It is remarkable how easily and insensibly we fall into a particular route, and make a beaten track for ourselves. I had not lived there a week before my feet wore a path from my door to the pond-side; and though it is five or six years since I trod it, it is still quite distinct. It is true, I fear, that others may have fallen into it, and so helped keep it open. The surface of the earth is soft and impressible by the feet of men; and so with the paths which the mind travels. How worn and dusty, then, must be the highways of the world, how deep the ruts of tradition and conformity! I did not wish to take a cabin passage, but rather to go before the mast and on the deck of the world, for there I could best see the moonlight amid the mountains. I do not wish to go below now.

I learned this, at least, by my experiment: that if one advances confidently in the direction of his dreams, and endeavors to live the life which he has imagined, he will meet with a success unexpected in common hours. He will put some things behind, will pass an invisible boundary; new, universal, and more liberal laws will begin to establish themselves around and within him; or the old laws be expanded, and interpreted in his favor in a more liberal sense, and he will live with the license of a higher order of beings. In proportion as he simplifies his life, the laws of the universe will appear less complex, and solitude will not be solitude, nor poverty poverty, nor weakness weakness. If you have built castles in the air, your work need not be lost; that is where they should be. Now put the foundations under them.

Henry David Thoreau, "Walden," in *The Writings of Henry David Thoreau* (Boston: Houghton Mifflin, 1906), 2:44–46, 100–102, 355–56.

Thoreau's Journal

Before moving to Walden Pond, Thoreau, like so many of the Transcendentalists, had often praised the simple life close to nature without specifying its practical meaning or

The shore at Walden Pond.

appreciating its practical difficulties. During his two-year
stay and after, however, he learned that many of his pre-
conceptions were misconceptions. For instance, he initially

thought that the Indian led the perfect existence, in harmony with nature and the spirits. But many of the Indians he came across during his excursions were not so noble. Nor were many of the white countryfolk as inspiring as he had thought. He rarely encountered any rustics whose vision was elevated beyond mere survival. Plain living did not necessarily lead to high thinking. This was a frustrating realization. Yet it helped him begin to see the complexity of simple living. It entailed far more than living in the woods. Ideally, the simple life could be lived best not in the wilds or in the city, but in "partially cultivated country" like Concord. His farmer neighbor George Minott seemed to personify his maturing vision of what simplicity ideally represented. And by 1853 Thoreau had come to recognize that simplicity is first a quality of the mind and only secondarily a manifestation of one's standard of living.

Journal, 4 October 1851—Minott is, perhaps, the most poetical farmer—who most realizes to me the poetry of the farmer's life—that I know. He does nothing with haste and drudgery, but as if he loved it. He makes the most of his labor, and takes infinite satisfaction in every part of it. He is not looking forward to the sale of his crops or any pecuniary profit, but he is paid by the constant satisfaction which his labor yields him. He has not too much land to trouble him,—too much work to do,—no hired man nor boy,—but simply to amuse himself and live. He cares not so much to raise a large crop as to do his work well. He knows every pin and nail in his barn. If another linter is to be floored, he lets no hired man rob him of that amusement, but he goes slowly to the woods and at his leisure, selects a pitch pine tree, cuts it, and hauls it or gets it hauled to the mill; and so he knows the history of his barn floor.

Farming is an amusement which has lasted him longer than gunning or fishing. He is never in a hurry to get his garden planted and yet [it] is always planted soon enough, and none in the town is kept so beautifully clean.

He always prophesies a failure of the crops, and yet is satisfied with what he gets. His barn floor is fastened down with oak pins, and he prefers them to iron spikes, which he says will rust and give way. He handles and amuses himself with every ear of his corn

Crayon portrait of Thoreau (1854), by Samuel Rowse.

crop as much as a child with his playthings, and so his small crop goes a great way. He might well cry if it were carried to market. The seed of weeds is no longer in his soil.

He loves to walk in a swamp in windy weather and hear the wind groan through the pines. He keeps a cat in his barn to catch the mice. He indulges in no luxury of food or dress or furniture, yet he is not penurious but merely simple. If his sister dies before him, he may have to go to the almshouse in his old age; yet he is not poor, for he does not want riches. He gets out of each manipulation in the farmers' operations a fund of entertainment which the speculating drudge hardly knows. With never-failing rheumatism and trembling hands, he seems yet to enjoy perennial health.

Journal, 1 September 1853—There are two kinds of simplicity,—one that is akin to foolishness, the other to wisdom. The philosopher's style of living is only outwardly simple, but inwardly complex. The savage's style is both outwardly and inwardly simple. A simpleton can perform many mechanical labors, but is not capable of profound thought. It was their limited view, not in respect to *style*, but to the *object* of living. A man who has equally limited views with respect to the end of living will not be helped by the most complex and refined style of living. It is not the tub that makes Diogenes, the Jove-born, but Diogenes the tub.

The Journal of Henry David Thoreau, eds. Bradford Torrey and Francis H. Allen, 15 vols. (1906; Salt Lake City: Peregrine Smith, 1984), 3:41–42; 5:410–11.

Progressive Simplicity

6

Many Northerners, including most of the Transcendentalists, greeted the outbreak of the Civil War with tempered optimism. Like the earlier Revolutionary patriots, they saw in martial conflict the possibility of societal regeneration. The evil of slavery would finally be confronted, and in the process Americans would also come to reassess their spiritual and material priorities. But as the Revolution had shown, wars maim ideals as well as people. The Civil War proved disappointing to those who initially saw it as a catalyst for sustained moral revival. The struggle to save the Union and free the slaves helped spawn a new era of urban and industrial development as well as westward expansion. Entrepreneurial opportunities were seemingly endless, and Americans rushed to take advantage of them. Appomattox was thus followed not by a golden age of material restraint and moral intensity but rather by a gilded age of political corruption and private greed. By 1871 Mark Twain could announce: "What is the chief end of man?—to get rich. In what way? dishonestly if he can; honestly if he must. Who is God, the one and only true? Money is God."

Yet proponents of simple living and traditional folkways remained persistent during the post-Civil War era. By the end of the nineteenth century, in fact, a remarkable resurgence in the appeal of simple living developed among the growing middle class. This revival coincided with the political and social reform movement known as Progressivism that swept across the country between 1890 and 1920. At the same time that activists were purging governments of entrenched corruption, regulating corporations in the public interest, protecting workers and consumers, and conserving natural resources, many were also promoting simpler living as an appropriate personal ethic for good republican citizens. This Progressive Era revival of simplicity included a cluster of practices and values that have remained associated with the concept: conscientious consumption, uncluttered domestic life, material contentment, an aesthetic appreciation for the plain and functional and a preference for handicraft rather than mass production, social service and philanthropy, and invigorating contact with nature.

In large measure this renewed middle-class interest in simplicity was generated by the increasing tensions of modern metropolitan life. The city offered many economic, educational, and cultural advantages, but it also tended to be crowded, filthy, hectic, and enervating. Harried middle-class urban dwellers, especially those of comfortable but modest means—doctors, lawyers, professors, teachers, social workers, bureaucrats, journalists, small business-men—pursued simplicity primarily for its therapeutic effects. Few believed it would ever attract the majority of the citizenry. But it could be of great value to those eager for a way out of the suffocating materialism and harassing complexities of metropolitan life. This middle-class sim-plicity did not require living in a hut like Thoreau or enduring the austerities of a John Woolman. By spending time and money wisely, middle-class Americans could learn to live simply but comfortably in modern America. This meant developing a taste for the essential, the beautiful, and the good as well as pursuing vital forms of public service and personal recreation.

Among the most popular forms of such recreation was "getting back to nature." In 1893 the historian Frederick Jackson Turner had declared that the frontier had been the most positive force in the shaping of American character. But now the frontier era was over. The continent had been settled and civilized, and Turner wondered if American ideals and institutions could be sustained in a dramatically different urban environment. Many other Americans came to share Turner's anxieties about the impact of moderni-zation upon American values.

Theodore Roosevelt, for example, was convinced that there was a crisis of virility at the turn of the century. The metropolitan American was fast becoming an "overcivilized man, who had lost the great, fighting, masterful virtues," and he called for a revival of the "strenuous life" as an antidote to the "mere money-getting American." He and others sharply criticized the growing feminization of American culture. The cult of domesticity had gone too far. Overprotective mothers and female schoolteachers now dominated the formative years of childhood and threatened to produce a generation of passive and dependent men. Roosevelt was especially upset with the new breed of educational experts who advocated letting children develop in their own way and at their own pace. Newly affluent parents were giving their children too much license and too many material expressions of affection. Such permissive attitudes in the homes and schools only encouraged the development of self-indulgent and timid Americans. So Roosevelt enthusiastically supported the rise of college athletics, the back-to-nature movement, and new organizations such as the Boy Scouts intended to inject pioneer hardihood and simplicity into coddled urbanites. He also glorified the uplifting effects of warfare upon American character.

Yet there were other spokesmen for renewed simplicity whose proposals were less agitated and militant. Impassioned naturalists and exemplars of plain living such as John Burroughs, John Muir, and "David Grayson," the pseudonym of the novelist and Progressive journalist Ray Stannard Baker, helped revitalize a transcendental reverence for enriching and ennobling contact with the outdoors. God and goodness, they and others claimed, were more accessible in the woods. And the countryside also offered fresh air, relaxation, reflection, and a stimulus to exhilarating physical activity for nervous urbanites. Strenuous exertion was deemed vital both to moral fiber and mental alertness.

Such a craving for real and immediate experience led thousands of urbanites into the country during the Progressive Era—camping, hiking, hunting, fishing, relaxing. It also led many of them to the workbench. The Arts and Crafts Movement began in England as a crusade on behalf of good taste against the ugliness and artificiality of modern metropolitan life. It was led by the art critic and historian John Ruskin and his disciple William Morris, both of whom sought to revive the medieval handicraft tradition as an alternative to the dehumanizing factory system and the shoddiness of its mass-produced products. They and others also decried the conspicuous consumption practiced by affluent Victorians. Morris instead promoted an aesthetic based on use and beauty rather than gaudiness.

By the turn of the century, American reformers were becoming avid supporters of the Arts and Crafts perspective. Gustav Stickley, a stonemason turned woodworker, took the lead in promoting the ideas of Ruskin and Morris in the United States. To do so he began making sturdy, rustic "Craftsman" furniture at his shop in upstate New York, and he began publishing a journal entitled *The Craftsman: An Illustrated Monthly Magazine for the Simplification of Life.* Stickley, Joseph Worcester, Charles Keeler, and other American craft reformers saw in aesthetic improvement and simpler living the means for the urban middle classes to turn away from the shams and decadence of modern civilization.

The Arts and Crafts Movement was only one example of many efforts to promote middle-class simplicity among urban and suburban dwellers. A number of prominent Progressive reformers, including Florence Kelley, Julia Lathrop, Louis Brandeis, and John R. Commons helped form the National Consumers League. Though its main objective was to exert consumer pressure on management in order to improve the quality of their products and the treatment of their workers, the Consumers League also encouraged affluent Americans to be more conscientious about their spending, to avoid costly display and overindulgence, and to stress quality and utility rather than quantity and gaudiness in their purchases.

Another influential voice for such Progressive simplicity was Edward Bok, the intense editor of the *Ladies' Home Journal.* Between 1889 and 1919 Bok used his editorial prerogative to launch a crusade on behalf of middle-class simplicity. Like the earlier advocates of domestic simplicity, he preached to his female readers the virtues of a simplified home and personal life. For a generation they listened. His message was direct and consistent: the simple life was joyous and good, and too many Americans, seduced by the clutter and false values of Victorian materialism, had drifted away from it.

Bok's appeal for renewed simplicity and self-reliance was given a needed boost by the onset of World War I. Wars bring out the best and worst in people. World War I was no exception to this truism. As had happened in the past, many idealists hoped that the conflict would promote a revival of republican simplicity and self-sacrifice. Shortly after Congress declared war on Germany in 1917, President Woodrow Wilson challenged the nation to revive old virtues: "This is the time for America to correct her unpardonable fault of wastefulness and extravagance. Let every man and every woman assume the duty of careful, provident use and expenditure as a public duty." Edith Bolling Wilson, the President's second wife, persuaded the cabinet members' wives to pledge with her to "reduce living to its simplest form and to deny ourselves luxuries in order to free those who produce them for the cultivation of necessities." Edward Bok urged his readers to follow the Wilsons' example. He called on them to organize Red Cross auxiliaries, engage in food and fuel conservation, buy Liberty Bonds, and participate in the Victory Garden program. To advise readers about the opportunities for patriotic simplicity, Bok created a regular column in the *Journal* entitled "The Woman and the War."

But Bok's efforts on behalf of simple living, like those of other idealistic Progressives, ultimately fell short of their goals. The accumulated momentum of modern urban and industrial life was difficult to restrain. Though there was indeed considerable evidence of patriotic simplicity, it quickly ended with the close of the war. During 1919 America went on an unprecedented buying spree. And in the process, Bok's plea for middle-class simplicity was brusquely ignored by the larger society. Still, if middle-class simplicity did not provoke a dramatic shift from the status quo of cosmopolitan life, it was a significant departure for many and a profound transformation for a few. Even in its most superficial forms, Progressive simplicity did reflect a yearning for more lasting values and enriching experiences than orthodox corporate and community life had to offer. If Burroughs, Stickley, Bok and other propagandists succeeded in luring a few indulgent urbanites out of their cluttered houses and "nervous" frame of mind and into the countryside and a more enlightened approach to getting and spending, they considered it an important first step in restoring balance and sanity to the American dream. "We can never make life simple," Bok confessed, "but we can make it simpler than we do."

Strenuous Simplicity

William James

The Harvard philosopher William James (1842–1910) lived through the vulgar excesses of the Gilded Age and the social and economic upheavals of the 1890s, and by the first years of the twentieth century, he was convinced that affluent, sedentary, urban Americans needed to reform their private lives by reviving a strenuous version of simple living. Like Theodore Roosevelt, his former student, he castigated the overly indulgent approach to child-rearing that had developed among the financially successful. His study of the past convinced James that the people deserving of admiration and emulation were those who "courted the arduous," who suffered hardships willingly, who refused the easy way, who resisted fatalism and conquered great physical and psychological obstacles. But unlike Roosevelt and other militarists, James did not sanction warfare as a revitalizing activity. Instead he promoted what he called a "moral equivalent of war," organizing civic armies of young Americans who would perform hard and invigorating work in nature for public benefit. Through such a program, he suggested, "hardihood and discipline would be wrought into the growing fibre of the people; no one would remain blind as the luxurious classes are now blind." Though it was never adopted during his own lifetime, James's "moral equivalent of war" concept was later used by Franklin Roosevelt in creating the Civilian Conservation Corps and by Jimmy Carter in publicizing his energy program. In the following excerpt from his influential study, *The Varieties of Religious Experience* (1902), James made an eloquent plea for a modern version of pious simplicity.

The immediate aim of the soldier's life is, as Moltke said, destruction, and nothing but destruction; and whatever constructions wars result in are remote and non-military. Consequently the soldier cannot train himself to be too feelingless to all those usual sympathies and respects, whether for persons or for things, that make for conservation. Yet the fact remains that war is a school of strenuous life and heroism; and, being in the line of aboriginal instinct, is the only school that as yet is universally available. But when we gravely ask ourselves whether this wholesale organization of irrationality and crime be our only bulwark against effeminacy, we stand aghast at the thought, and think more kindly of ascetic religion. One hears of the mechanical equivalent of heat. What we now need to discover in the social realm is the moral equivalent of war: something heroic that will speak to men as universally as war does, and yet will be as compatible with their spiritual selves as war has proved itself to be incompatible. I have often thought that in the old monkish poverty-worship, in spite of the pedantry which infested it, there might be something like that moral equivalent of war which we are seeking. May not voluntarily accepted poverty be "the strenuous life," without the need of crushing weaker peoples?

Poverty indeed *is* the strenuous life—without brass bands or uniforms or hysteric popular applause or lies or circumlocutions; and when one sees the way in which wealth-getting enters as an ideal into the very bone and marrow of our generation, one wonders whether a revival of the belief that poverty is a worthy religious vocation may not be "the transformation of military courage," and the spiritual reform which our time stands most in need of.

Among us English-speaking peoples especially do the praises of poverty need once more to be boldly sung. We have grown literally afraid to be poor. We despise any one who elects to be poor in order to simplify and save his inner life. If he does not join the general scramble and pant with the money-making street, we deem him spiritless and lacking in ambition. We have lost the power even of imagining what the ancient idealization of poverty could have meant: the liberation from material attachments, the unbribed soul, the manlier indifference, the paying our way by what we are or do and not by what we have, the right to fling away our life at any moment irresponsibly—the more athletic trim, in short, the moral fighting shape. When we of the so-called better classes are scared as men were never scared in history at material ugliness and hardship; when we put off marriage until our house can be artistic, and quake at the thought of having a child without a bank-account and doomed to manual labor, it is time for thinking men to protest against so unmanly and irreligious a state of opinion.

It is true so far as wealth gives time for ideal ends and exercise to ideal energies, wealth is better than poverty and ought to be chosen. But wealth does this in only a portion of the actual cases. Elsewhere the desire to gain wealth and the fear to lose it are our chief breeders of cowardice and propagators of corruption. There are thousands of conjunctures in which a wealth-bound man must be a slave, whilst a man for whom poverty has no terrors becomes a free man. Think of the strength which personal indifference to poverty would give us if we were devoted to unpopular causes. We need no longer hold our tongues or fear to vote the revolutionary or reformatory ticket. Our stocks might fall, our hopes of promotion vanish, our salaries stop, our club doors close in our faces; yet, while we lived, we would imperturbably bear witness to the spirit, and our example would help to set free our generation. The cause would need its funds, but we its servants would be potent in proportion as we personally were contented with our poverty.

I recommend this matter to your serious pondering, for it is certain that the prevalent fear of poverty among the educated classes is the worst moral disease from which our civilization suffers.

William James, *The Varieties of Religious Experience* (1902; New York: Random House, 1932), pp. 356-61.

THEODORE ROOSEVELT ON SIMPLICITY

McCLURE'S (1898)

There is not in the world a more ignoble character than the mere money-getting American, insensible to every duty, regardless of every principle, bent only on amassing a fortune, and putting his fortune only to the basest uses. . . . Such a man is only the more dangerous if he occasionally does some deed like founding a college or endowing a church, which makes those good people who are also foolish forget this iniquity.

THEODORE ROOSEVELT TO WILLIAM HOWARD TAFT, 9 JUNE 1903

Mrs. Roosevelt and I are now going back to Oyster Bay. We do not take the White House servants with us. We have two maids and live as any gentlefolk of small means should live. When I leave the Presidency I shall not mind in the least going back to the utmost simplicity of life, and I wish to live simply as President; and I feel that you can render a real service by living, as you will, in a manner which is in the real sense of the word democratic inasmuch as it is dignified because of its very simplicity.

THEODORE ROOSEVELT TO CECIL ARTHUR SPRING RICE, 11 APRIL 1908

I am simply unable to understand the value placed by so many people upon great wealth. I very thoroly[sic] understand the need of sufficient means to enable the man or woman to be comfortable; I also entirely understand the pleasure of having enough more than this so as to add certain luxuries, and above all, that greatest of all luxuries, the escape from the need of considering at every turn whether it is possible to spend a dollar or two extra; but when the last limit has been reached, then increase in wealth means but little, certainly as compared with all kinds of other things.

Ray Stannard Baker, "Theodore Roosevelt," *McClure's* 12 (November 1898):32; Elting Morison, ed., *The Letters of Theodore Roosevelt,* 8 vols. (Cambridge, Mass.: Harvard University Press, 1951-54), 3:486; 6:1002.

What Life Means to Me

John Burroughs

The dramatic surge of interest in nature study and outdoor recreation at the turn of the century was inspired in large measure by the charismatic poet, essayist, and naturalist John Burroughs (1837–1921). This hardy grey-bearded poet of the countryside was universally revered among the middle-class reading public as an exemplar of plain living, keen insight, and pristine integrity. As a writer in the *Outlook* stressed: "The simplicity of Mr. Burroughs's nature and the simplicity of his spirit, as well as his innate kindliness, have made him the companion and neighbor of the whole country."

Many found in Burroughs's nature writings qualities lacking in Thoreau's—a congenial normality, a ripe and comfortable domesticity, a spontaneous warmth for other human beings. Readers also appreciated the fact that Burroughs was a true man of the soil. On his farm at "Riverby," about eighty miles up the Hudson from Manhattan, he tended a vineyard and harvested berries. At the same time he consciously followed Thoreau's advice and limited his material desires in order to have greater control over his own time. And like Thoreau, Emerson, and the other earlier romantics, Burroughs found in nature the inspiration and guide for his own ethic of simple living.

Burroughs's most complete statement about his own preference for a nature-inspired simple life was published in *Cosmopolitan* in 1906, some fifteen years before his death. The essay, reprinted below, received more reader response than any he ever wrote. It teaches patience and acceptance, contentment, the joy to be found in simple pleasures and everyday occurrences. It also presents an eloquent critique of the dominant trends of the time, especially the mad scramble for money, the mania of corporate growth, and the sharpening class divisions of modern urban-industrial America.

I have had a happy life, and there is not much of it I would change if I could live it over again. I think I was born under happy stars, with a keen sense of wonder, which has never left me, and which only become jaded a little now and then, and with no exaggerated notion of my own deserts. I have shared the common lot and have found it good enough for me. Unlucky is the man who is born with great expectations and who finds nothing in life quite up to their mark.

One of the best things a man can bring into the world with him is natural humility of spirit. About the next best thing he can bring, and they usually go together, is an appreciative spirit—a loving and susceptible heart. If he is going to be a reformer and stir up things, and slay the dragons, he needs other qualities more. But if he is going to get the most out of life in a worthy way, if he is going to enjoy the grand spectacle of the world from first to last, then he needs his life pitched in a low key and well attuned to common universal things. The strained, the loud, the farfetched, the extravagant, the frenzied—how lucky we are to escape them, and to be born with dispositions that cause us to flee from them!

I would gladly chant a paean for the world as I find it. What a mighty, interesting place to live in! If I had my life to live over again, and had my choice of celestial abodes, I am sure I should take this planet and I should choose these men and women for my friends and companions. This great rolling sphere with its sky, its stars, its sunrises and sunsets, and with its outlook into infinity—what could be more desirable? What more satisfying? Garlanded by the seasons, embosomed in sidereal influences, thrilling with life, with a heart of fire and a garment of azure seas, and fruitful continents—one might ransack the heavens in vain for a better or a more picturesque abode. As Emerson says, it is "well worth the heart and pith of great men to subdue and enjoy it."

Oh, to share the great, sunny, joyous life of the earth! to be as happy as the birds are! as contented as the cattle on the hills! as the leaves of the trees that dance and rustle in the wind! as the waters that murmur and sparkle to the sea! To be able to see that the sin and sorrow and suffering of the world are a necessary part of the natural course of things, a phase of the law of growth and development that runs through the universe, bitter in its personal application, but illuminating when we look upon life as a whole! Without death and decay how could life go on? Without what we call sin (which is another name for imperfection) and the struggle consequent upon it, how could our development proceed? I know the waste, the delay, the suffering in the history of the race are appalling, but they only repeat the waste, the delay, the conflict through which the earth itself has gone and is still going and which finally issues in peace and tranquility. Look at the grass, the flowers, the sweet serenity and repose of the fields—at what a price it has all been bought, of what a warring of the elements, of what overturnings, and pulverizings and shiftings of land and sea, and slow grindings of the mills of the gods of the foreworld it is all the outcome!

I have had, I say, a happy life. When I was a young man (twenty-five), I wrote a little poem called "Waiting," which has had quite a history, and the burden of which is, "my own shall come to me." What my constitution demands, the friends, the helps, the fulfillments, the opportunities, I shall find somewhere, sometime. It was a statement of the old doctrine of the elective affinities. Those who are born to strife and contention find strife and contention ready at their hand; those who are born for gentleness and love find gentleness and love drawn to them. The naturally suspicious and distrustful find the world in conspiracy against them; the unkind, the hard-hearted see themselves in their fellows about them. The tone in which we speak to the world the world speaks to us. Give your best and you will get the best in return. Give in heaping measure and in heaping measure it shall be returned. We all get our due sooner or later, in one form or another. "Be not weary in well doing;" the reward will surely come, if not in worldly goods, then in inward satisfaction, grace of spirit, peace of mind.

All the best things of my life have come to me unsought, but I hope not unearned. That would contradict the principle of equity I have been illustrating. A man does not, in the long run, get wages he has not earned. What I mean is that most of the good things of my life—friends, travel, opportunity—have been unexpected. I do not feel that fortune has driven sharp bargains with me. I am not a disappointed man. Blessed is he who expects little, but works as if he expected much. Sufficient unto the day is the *good* thereof. I have invested myself in the present moment, in the things near at hand, in the things that all may have on equal terms. If one sets one's heart on the exceptional, the far-off—on riches, on fame, on power—the chances are he will be disappointed; he will waste his time seeking a short cut to these things. There is no short cut. For anything worth having one must pay the price, and the price is always work, patience, love, self-sacrifice—no paper currency, no promises to pay, but the gold of real service.

I am not decrying ambition, the aiming high, only there is no use aiming unless you are loaded, and it is the loading, and the kind of material to be used, that one is first to be solicitous about.

"Serene I fold my hands and wait;" but if I have waited one day, I have hustled the next. If I have had faith that my own would come to me, I have tried to make sure that it was my own, and not that of another. Waiting with me has been mainly a cheerful acquiescence in the order of the universe as I found it—a faith in the essential veracity of things. I have waited for the sun to rise and for the seasons to come; I have waited for a chance to put in my oar. Which way do the currents of my being set? What do I love that is worthy and of good report? I will extend myself in this direction; I will annex this territory. I will not wait to see if this or that pays, if this or that notion draws the multitude. I will wait only till I can see my way clearly. In the meantime I will be clearing my eyes and training them to know the real values of life when they see them.

Waiting for some one else to do your work, for what you have not earned to come to you, is to murder time. Waiting for something to turn up is equally poor policy, unless you have already set the currents going that will cause a particular something to turn up. The farmer waits for his harvest after he has sown it. The sailor waits for a breeze after he has spread his sail. Much of life is taken up in waiting—fruitful waiting.

I have never sought wealth, I have been too much absorbed in enjoying the world about me. I had no talent for business anyhow—for the cutthroat competition that modern business for the most part is—and probably could not have attained wealth had I desired it. I dare not aver that I had really rather be cheated than to cheat, but I am quite sure I could never knowingly overreach a man, and what chance of success could such a tenderfoot have in the conscienceless struggle for money that goes on in the business world? I am a fairly successful farmer and fruit grower. I love the soil, I love to see the crops grow and mature, but the marketing of them, the turning of them into money, grinds my soul because of the sense of strife and competition that pervades the air of the market place. If one could afford to give one's fruit away, after he had grown it to perfection, to people who would be sure to appreciate it, that would be worth while and would leave no wounds. But that is what I have in a sense done with my intellectual products. I have not written one book for money (yes, one, and that was a failure); I have written them for love, and the modest sum they have brought me has left no sting.

I look upon this craze for wealth that possesses nearly all classes in our time as one of the most lamentable spectacles the world has ever seen. The old prayer, "Give me neither poverty nor riches," is the only sane one. The grand mistake we make is in supposing that because a little money is a good thing, unlimited means is the sum of all good, or that our happiness will keep pace with the increase of our possessions. But such is not the case, because the number of things we can really make our own is limited. We cannot drink the ocean be we ever so thirsty. A cup of water from the spring is all we need. A friend of mine once said that if he outlived his wife he should put upon her tombstone, "Died of Things"—killed by the multitude of her possessions. The number of people who are thus killed is no doubt very great. When Thoreau found that the specimens and curiosities that had accumulated upon his mantlepiece needed dusting, he pitched them out of the window.

The massing of a great fortune is a perilous enterprise. The giving away of a great fortune is equally a perilous enterprise, not to the man who gives it—it ought to be salutary to him—but to his beneficiaries.

Very many of the great fortunes of our time have been accumulated by a process like that of turning all the streams into your private reservoir; they have caused a great many people somewhere to be short of water and have taken away the power of many busy, peaceful wheels. The ideal condition is an even distribution of wealth. When you try to give away your monstrous fortune, to open your dam, then danger begins, because you cannot return the waters to their natural channels. You must make new channels and you may do more harm than good. It never can go now where it would have gone. The wealth is in a measure redistributed, without enriching those from whom it originally came.

Beyond the point of a moderate competency, wealth is a burden. A man may possess a competency; great wealth possesses him. He is the victim. It fills him with unrest; it destroys or perverts his natural relations to his fellows; it corrupts his simplicity, it thrusts the false values of life before him; it gives him power which it is dangerous to exercise; it leads to self-indulgence; it hardens the heart; it fosters a false pride; to give it away is perilous; to keep it is to invite care and vexation of spirit. For a rich man to lead the simple life is about as hard as for a camel to go through the needle's eye. How many things stand between him and the simple open air of our common humanity! Marcus Aurelius thought a man might be happy even in a palace; but it takes a Marcus Aurelius—a man whose simplicity of character is incorruptible—to be so. Yet I have no disposition to rail at wealth as such, though the penalties and dangers that attend it are very obvious. I never expect to see it go out of fashion. Its unequal distribution in all times, no doubt, results from natural causes. . . .

I am bound to praise the simple life, because I have lived it and found it good. When I depart from it evil results follow. I love a small house, plain clothes, simple living. Many persons know the

Barrus, *Our Friend John Burroughs*

John Burroughs and John Muir in the Yosemite.

luxury of a skin bath—a plunge in the pool or the wave un-hampered by clothing. That is the simple life—direct and immediate contact with things, life with the false wrappings torn away—the fine house, the fine equipage, the expensive habits, all cut off. How free one feels, how good the elements taste, how close one gets to them, how they fit one's body and one's soul! To see the fire that warms you, or better yet, to cut the wood that feeds the fire that warms you; to see the spring where the water bubbles up that slakes your thirst, and to dip your pail into it; to see the beams that are the stay of your four walls, and the timbers that uphold the roof that shelters you; to be in direct and personal contact with the sources of your material life; to want no extras, no shields; to find the universal elements enough; to find the air and the water exhilarating; to be refreshed by a morning walk, or an evening saunter; to find a quest of wild berries more satisfying than a gift of tropic fruit; to be thrilled by the stars at night; to be elated over a bird's nest, or over a wild flower in spring—these are some of the rewards of the simple life.

John Burroughs, "What Life Means to Me," *Cosmopolitan* 40 (1905–06):654–58.

THE GOSPEL OF NATURE
John Burroughs

There can be little doubt, I think, but that intercourse with nature and a knowledge of her ways tends to simplicity of life. We come more and more to see through the follies and vanities of the world and to appreciate the real values. We load ourselves up with so many false burdens, our complex civilization breeds in us so many false or artificial wants, that we become separated from the real sources of our strength and health as by a gulf.

For my part, as I grow older I am more and more inclined to reduce my baggage, to lop off superfluities. I become more and more in love with simple things and simple folk—a small house, a hut in the woods, a tent on the shore. The show and splendor of great houses, elaborate furnishings, stately halls, oppress me, impose upon me. They fix the attention upon false values, they set up a false standard of beauty; they stand between me and the real feeders of character and thought. A man needs a good roof over his head winter and summer, and a good chimney and a big woodpile in winter. The more open his four walls are, the more fresh air he will get, and the longer he will live.

How the contemplation of nature as a whole does take the conceit out of us! How we dwindle to mere specks and our little lives to the span of a moment in the presence of the cosmic bodies and the interstellar spaces! How we hurry! How we husband our time. A year, a month, a day, an hour may mean so much to us. Behold the infinite leisure of nature.

John Burroughs, "The Gospel of Nature," *Century* 84 (1912):195–204.

Adventures in Contentment
David Grayson

Nature writing was extremely popular at the turn of the century, not only in the form of reflective essays but also in hearthside novels set in the countryside. One of the most popular of the novelists of the soil was Ray Stannard Baker (1870–1946). He began his career as a muckraking journalist for *McClure's*, advocating government regulation of corporations and promoting labor unions. At the same time he was engaged in such investigative reporting, Baker was writing short stories and novels under the pseudonym "David Grayson." Grayson, an obviously literate gentleman farmer, who reads Marcus Aurelius, William Penn, Jefferson, Emerson, and Thoreau, spread the gospel of rustic simplicity. And he attracted many converts. One reader reported that he and his wife had become "David Graysonized." They lived simply, but were happy with their "moderate income and enjoyed life to the full." In the following excerpt from *Adventures in Contentment* (1906), Grayson describes his philosophy of rustic, yet progressive, simple living.

The great point of advantage in the life of the country is that if a man is in reality simple, if he love true contentment, it is the place of all places where he can live his life most freely and fully, where he can *grow*. The city affords no such opportunity; indeed, it often destroys, by the seductiveness with which it flaunts its carnal graces, the desire for the higher life which animates every good man.

While on the subject of simplicity it may be well to observe that simplicity does not necessarily, as some of those who escape from the city seem to think, consist in doing without things, but rather in the proper use of things. One cannot return, unless with affectation, to the crudities of a former existence. We do not believe in Diogenes and his tub. Do you not think the good Lord has given us the telephone (that we may better reach that elbow-rub of brotherhood which is the highest of human ideals) and the railroad (that we may widen our human knowledge and sympathy)—and even the motor-car? (though, indeed, I have sometimes imagined that the motor-cars passing this way had a different origin!). He may have given these things to us too fast, faster than we can bear; but is that any reason why we should denounce them all and return to the old, crude, time-consuming ways of our ancestors? I am no reactionary. I do not go back. I neglect no tool of progress. I am too eager to know every wonder in this universe. The motorcar, if I had one, could not carry me fast enough! I must yet fly!

After my experience in the country, if I were to be cross-examined as to the requisites of a farm, I should say that the chief thing to be desired in any sort of agriculture, is good health in the farmer. What, after all, can touch that! How many of our joys that we think intellectual are purely physical! This joy o' the morning that the poet carols about so cheerfully, is often nothing more than the exuberance produced by a good hot breakfast. Going out of my kitchen door some mornings and standing for a moment, while I survey the green and spreading fields of my farm, it seems to me truly as if all nature were making a bow to me. It seems to me that there never was a better cow than mine, never a more really perfect horse, and as for pigs, could any in this world herald my approach with more cheerful gruntings and squealings!

But there are other requisites for a farm. It must not be too large, else it will keep you away from your friends. Provide a town not too far off (and yet not too near) where you can buy your flour and sell your grain. If there is a railroad convenient (though not so near that the whistling of the engines reaches you), that is an added advantage. Demand a few good old oak trees, or walnuts, or even elms will do. No well-regulated farm should be without trees; and having secured the oaks—buy your fuel of your neighbors. Thus you will be blessed with beauty both summer and winter.

As for neighbors, accept those nearest at hand; you will find them surprisingly human, like yourself. If you like them you will be surprised to find how much they all like you (and will upon occasion lend you a spring-tooth harrow or a butter tub, or help you with your plowing); but if you hate them they will return your hatred with interest. I have discovered that those who travel in pursuit of better neighbours never find them.

Somewhere on every farm, along with the other implements, there should be a row of good books, which should not be allowed to rust with disuse: a book, like a hoe, grows brighter with employment. And no farm, even in this country where we enjoy the even balance of the seasons, rain and shine, shine and rain, should be devoid of that irrigation from the currents of the world's thought which is so essential to the complete life. From the papers which the postman puts in the box flow the true waters of civilisation. You will find within their columns how to be good or how to make pies: you will get out of them what you look for! And finally, down the road from your farm, so that you can hear the bell on Sunday mornings, there should be a little church. It will do you good even though, like me, you do not often attend. It's a sort of Ark of the Covenant; and when you get to it, you will find therein the True Spirit—if you take it with you when you leave home. Of course you will look for good land and comfortable buildings when you buy your farm: they are, indeed, prime requisites. I have put them last for the reason that they are so often first. I have observed, however, that the joy of the farmer is by no means in proportion to the area of his arable land. It is often a nice matter to decide between acres and contentment: men perish from too much as well as from too little. And if it be possible there should be a long table in the dining-room and little chairs around it, and small

Howard Heath, *A Place in the Country.*

beds upstairs, and young voices calling at their play in the fields—if it be possible.

"David Grayson" (Ray S. Baker), *Adventures in Contentment* (New York: Doubleday, Page, 1906), pp. 245–46.

The Craftsman Idea

Gustav Stickley

Gustav Stickley (1858–1942) shared Burroughs's and Grayson's philosophy of living. And Burroughs admired Stickley's program of aesthetic simplicity. His "Riverby" home was graced with a "Craftsman" rocker. Stickley believed that Progressive simplicity entailed elevating the taste of the bourgeoisie. They needed to realize that the superfluous ornamentation and clutter prevailing in

American furnishings and homes were contributing to the
enervating psychological state that sent so many to
doctors and counselors. He and the others associated with
The Craftsman idea, as they called it, stressed honesty of
construction, beauty of finish, and straightforward simplicity. In each issue of *The Craftsman* Stickley presented
plans for houses "which will simplify the work of home life
and add to it its wholesome joy and comfort." Soon
thousands of "Craftsman" homes were built across the
country. Stickley published a collection of these plans in
1910. In an essay in that volume, reprinted below, he
provided a comprehensive explanation of the Progressive
simplicity promoted by the Arts and Crafts movement.

There is no question now as to the reality of the world-wide
movement in the direction of better things. We see everywhere
efforts to reform social, political and industrial conditions; the
desire to bring about better opportunities for all and to find some
way of adjusting economic conditions so that the heart-breaking
inequalities of our modern civilized life shall in some measure be
done away with. But while we take the greatest interest in all
efforts toward reform in any direction, we remain firm in the
conviction that the root of all reform lies in the individual and that
the life of the individual is shaped mainly by home surroundings
and influences and by the kind of education that goes to make real
men and women instead of grist for the commercial mill.

That the influence of the home is of the first importance in the
shaping of character is a fact too well understood and too generally
admitted to be offered here as a new idea. One need only turn to the
pages of history to find abundant proof of the unerring action of
Nature's law, for without exception the people whose lives are
lived simply and wholesomely, in the open, and who have in a high
degree the sense of the sacredness of the home, are the people who
have made the greatest strides in the development of the race.
When luxury enters in and a thousand artificial requirements come
to be regarded as real needs, the nation is on the brink of
degeneration. . . . In our own country, to which has fallen the
heritage of all the older civilizations, the course has been swift, for
we are yet close to the memory of the primitive pioneer days when
the nation was building, and we have still the crudity as well as the
vigor of youth. But so rapid and easy has been our development

and so great our prosperity that even now we are in some respects very nearly in the same state as the older peoples who have passed the zenith of their power and are beginning to decline. In our own case, however, the saving grace lies in the fact that our taste for luxury and artificiality is not as yet deeply ingrained. We are intensely commercial, fond of all the good things of life, proud of our ability to "get there," and we yield the palm to none in the matter of owning anything that money can buy. But, fortunately, our pioneer days are not ended even now and we still have a goodly number of men and women who are helping to develop the country and make history merely by living simple natural lives close to the soil and full of the interest and pleasure which come from kinship with Nature and the kind of work that calls forth all their resources in the way of self-reliance and the power of initiative. Even in the rush and hurry of life in our busy cities we remember well the quality given to the growing nation by such men and women a generation or two ago and, in spite of the chaotic conditions brought about by our passion for money-getting, extravagance and show, we have still reason to believe that the dominant characteristics of the pioneer yet shape what are the salient qualities in American life.

To preserve these characteristics and to bring back to individual life and work the vigorous constructive spirit which during the last half-century has spent its activities in commercial and industrial expansion, is, in a nut-shell, the Craftsman idea. We need to straighten out our standards and to get rid of a lot of rubbish that we have accumulated along with our wealth and commercial supremacy. It is not that we are too energetic, but that in many ways we have wasted and misused our energy precisely as we have wasted and misused so many of our wonderful natural resources. All we really need is a change in our point of view toward life and a keener perception regarding the things that count and the things which merely burden us. This being the case, it would seem obvious that the place to begin a readjustment is in the home, for it is only natural that the relief from friction which would follow the ordering of our lives along more simple and reasonable lines would not only assure greater comfort, and therefore greater efficiency, to the workers of the nation, but would give the children a chance to grow up under conditions which would be conducive to a higher degree of mental, moral and physical efficiency.

Therefore we regard it as at least a step in the direction of bringing about better conditions when we try to plan and build houses which will simplify the work of home life and add to its wholesome joy and comfort. We have already made it plain to our readers that we do not believe in large houses with many rooms elaborately decorated and furnished, for the reason that these seem so essentially an outcome of the artificial conditions that lay such harassing burdens upon modern life and form such a serious menace to our ethical standards. Breeding as it does the spirit of extravagance and of discontent which in the end destroys all the sweetness of home life, the desire for luxury and show not only burdens beyond his strength the man who is ambitious to provide for his wife and children surroundings which are as good as the best, but taxes to the utmost the woman who is trying to keep up the appearances which she believes should belong to her station in life. Worst of all, it starts the children with standards which, in nine cases out of ten, utterly preclude the possibility of their beginning life on their own account in a simple and sensible way. Boys who are brought up in such homes are taught, by the silent influence of their early surroundings, to take it for granted that they must not marry until they are able to keep up an establishment of equal pretensions, and girls also take it as a matter of course that marriage must mean something quite as luxurious as the home of their childhood or it is not a paying investment for their youth and beauty. Everyone who thinks at all deplores the kind of life that marks a man's face with the haggard lines of anxiety and makes him sharp and often unscrupulous in business, with no ambition beyond large profits and a rapid rise in the business world. Also we all realize regretfully the extravagance and uselessness of many of our women and admit that one of the gravest evils of our times is the light touch-and-go attitude toward marriage, which breaks up so many homes and makes the divorce courts in America a by-word to the world. But when we think into it a little more deeply, we have to acknowledge that such conditions are the logical outcome of our standards of living and that these standards are always shaped in the home.

That is why we have from the first planned houses that are based on the big fundamental principles of honesty, simplicity and usefulness,—the kind of houses that children will rejoice all their lives to remember as "home," and that give a sense of peace and comfort to the tired men who go back to them when the day's work is done. Because we believe that the healthiest and happiest life is that which maintains the closest relationship with out-of-doors, we have planned our houses with outdoor living rooms, dining rooms and sleeping rooms, and many windows to let in plenty of air and sunlight. . . .

Craftsman home design, February 1905.

We have set forth the principles that rule the planning of the Craftsman house and have hinted at the kind of life that would naturally result from such an environment. But now comes one of the most important elements of the whole question,—the surroundings of the home. We need hardly say that a house of the kind we have described belongs either in the open country or in a small village or town, where the dwellings do not elbow or crowd one another any more than the people do. We have planned houses for country living because we firmly believe that the country is the only place to live in. The city is all very well for business, for amusement and some formal entertainment,—in fact for anything and everything that, by its nature, must be carried on outside of the home. But the home itself should be in some place where there is peace and quiet, plenty of room and the chance to establish a sense of intimate relationship with the hills and valleys, trees and brooks and all the things which tend to lessen the strain and worry of modern life by reminding us that after all we are one with Nature.

Also it is a fact that the type of mind which appreciates the value of having the right kind of a home, and recognizes the right of growing children to the most natural and wholesome surroundings, is almost sure to feel the need of life in the open, where all the conditions of daily life may so easily be made sane and constructive instead of artificial and disintegrating. People who think enough about the influence of environment to put interest and care into the planning of a dwelling which shall express all that the word "home" means to them, are usually the people who like to have a personal acquaintance with every animal, tree and flower on the place. They appreciate the interest of planting things and seeing them grow, and enjoy to the fullest the exhilarating anxiety about crops that comes only to the man who planted them and means to use them to the best advantage. Then again, such people feel that half the zest of life would be gone if they were to miss the fulness of joy that each returning spring brings to those who watch eagerly for the new green of the grass and the blossoming of the trees. They feel that no summer resort can offer pleasures equal to that which they find in watching the full flowering of the year; in seeing how their own agricultural experiments turn out, and in triumphing over each success and each addition to the beauty of the place that is their own. Few of these people, too, would care to miss the sense of peace and fulfilment in autumn days, when the waning beauty of the year comes into such close kinship with the mellow ripeness of a well-spent life that has borne full fruit. And what child is there in the world who would spend the winter in the city when there are ice-covered brooks to skate on, the comfort of jolly evenings by the fire and the never-ending wonder of the snow? And all the year round there are the dumb creatures for whom we have no room or time in the city,—the younger brothers of humanity who submit so humbly to man's dominion and look so placidly to him for protection and sustenance.

Thank heaven, though, we are not so far away from our natural environment that it needs much to take us back to it. We have many evidences of the turning of the tide of home life from the city toward the country. Even workers in the city are coming more and more to realize that it is quite possible to maintain their place in the business world and yet give their children a chance to grow up in the country. Also the economic advantage of building a permanent home instead of paying rent year after year is gaining an ever-increasing recognition, so that in a few years the American people may cease to deserve the reproach of being a nation of flat-dwellers and sojourners in family hotels. The instinct for home and for some tie that connects us with the land is stronger than any passing fashion, and although we have in our national life phases of artificiality that are demoralizing they affect only a small

An object lesson in domestic simplicity from Stickley in *The Craftsman* (1907). "Complexity, confusion, and chaos" opposed to "cohesion and harmony."

percentage of the whole people, and when their day is over they will be forgotten as completely as if they had never existed. Psychologists talk learnedly of "Americanitis" as being almost a national malady, so widespread is our restlessness and feverish activity; but it is safe to predict that, with the growing taste for wholesome country life, it will not be more than a generation or two before our far-famed nervous tension is referred to with wonder as an evidence of past ignorance concerning the most important things of life.

And when we have turned once more to natural living instead of setting up our puny affairs and feverish ambitions to oppose the quiet, irresistible course of Nature's law, we will not need to turn hungrily to books for stories of a bygone Golden Age, nor will we need to deplore the vanishing of art and beauty from our lives, for when the day comes that we have sufficient courage and perception to throw aside the innumerable petty superfluities that hamper us now at every turn and the honesty to realize what Nature holds for all who turn to her with a reverent spirit and an open mind, we will find that art is once more a part of our daily life and that the impulse to do beautiful and vital creative work is as natural as the impulse to breathe.

Therefore it is not idle theorizing to prophesy that, when healthful and natural conditions are restored to our lives, handicrafts will once more become a part of them, because two powerful influences will be working in this direction as they have worked ever since the earliest dawn of civilization. One is the imperative need for self-expression in some form of creative work that always comes when the conditions of life are such as to allow full development and joyous vigor of body and mind. The other is that which closer relationship with Nature seems to bring; a craving for greater intimacy with the things we own and use. Machine-made standards fall away of themselves as we get away from artificial conditions. It is as if wholesome living brought with it not only quickened perceptions but also a sense of personal affection for all the familiar surroundings of our daily life. It is from such feeling that we get the treasured heirlooms which are handed down from generation to generation because of their associations and what they represent.

Naturally the primitive conditions of pioneer life in any nation include handicrafts as a matter of course, from the simple fact that people had to make for themselves what they needed or go without. We realize that in this age of invention and of labor-saving machinery it is neither possible nor desirable to such conditions, but we believe that it is quite possible for a higher form of handicrafts to exist under the most advanced modern conditions and that achievements as great as those of the old craftsmen who made famous the Mediaeval guilds are by no means out of the reach of modern workers when they once realize the possibilities that lie in this direction. Our theory is that modern improvements and conveniences afford a most welcome and necessary relief from the routine drudgery of household and farm work by disposing quickly and easily of what might much better be done by machinery than by hand, and that therefore there should be sufficient leisure left for the enjoyment of life and for the doing of work that is really worth while, which are among the things most essential to all-round mental and moral development. Almost the greatest drawback to farm life as it is today is the lack of interest and of mental alertness. Especially is this the case during the winter months, when work on the farm is slack and much time is left to be spent in idleness or in some trifling occupation. Consider what the effect would be if it were made possible at such times to take up some form of creative work that would not only bring into play every atom of interest and ability, but would also serve a practical purpose by adding considerably to the family income!

This, in brief, is the whole idea of the Craftsman home,—a pleasant comfortable dwelling situated on a piece of ground large enough to yield, under proper cultivation, a great part of the food supply for the family. Such a home, by its very nature, would be permanent and, with the right kind of education and healthful occupation for the children, would do much to stop the flow of population into the great commercial centers and insure a more even division of prosperity throughout the land. . . .

Gustav Stickley, *Craftsman Homes* (New York: Craftsman Publishing Company, 1909), pp. 194–205.

THE SANE LIFE
Marguerite Bigelow

That life is sane which is thrifty, provident, practical, as well as simple, generous and idealistic:

Which asks no advice and makes no apologies, follows no stale conventional standard, but, standing firmly, challenges the best in other lives and appropriates the best for its own.

That life is sane which has in it enough fresh air to breathe freely, enough sunshine to kill disease, enough rain to make it fruitful, enough wind to arouse the spirit:

Which seeks sound labor for every day, and wholesome play for every holiday, realizing that both work and play in their just ratio are essential, and that both may be beautiful.

That life is sane which claims for its own a few good books, pictures or statues, or the right to enjoy them,—a little good music, and, above all, good friends:

Which recognizes its end in service and its fulfillment in love.

> That life is sane which meets the natural course of events naturally, glorifying, as it passes, birth, growth, maturity, parenthood, death, step by step, with perfect ultimate faith.
> And this sane life may be lived even now.
> Marguerite Ogden Bigelow, "The Sane Life," *Craftsman* 17 (1910):646.

The Simple Home

Charles Keeler

Interest in the *Craftsman* idea was not limited to the Northeast; it was a national phenomenon at the turn of the century, and one of the earliest and most dynamic centers of the Arts and Crafts movement in the United States was in San Francisco. There, a like-minded group of architects, craftsmen, designers, and artists was determined to provide a plain and functional alternative to the excesses of the "General Grant Gothic" that had governed American domestic architecture and furnishings since the Civil War. Charles Keeler (1871–1937), a Berkeley poet, naturalist, and self-appointed crusader for artistic simplicity, was particularly impressed with these local craftsmen and architects promoting what became known as the San Francisco Bay Region style. Like Andrew Jackson Downing before them—and Gustav Stickley, their counterpart in New York—California designers such as Joseph Worcester, Bernard Maybeck, Ernest Coxhead, Willis Polk, and Julia Morgan were determined to develop structures and interiors that blended in with their native environment. Keeler's house in Berkeley was designed by Maybeck, and his experience living in such a "simple" home led him to write a book about the virtues of plain living and design.

A movement toward a simpler, a truer, a more vital art expression, is now taking place in California. It is a movement which involves painters and poets, composers and sculptors, and only lacks co-ordination to give it a significant influence upon modern life. One of the first steps in this movement, it seems to me, should be to introduce more widely the thought of the simple home—to emphasize the gospel of the simple life, to scatter broadcast the faith in simple beauty, to make prevalent the conviction that we must live art before we can create it. . . .

The ideal home is one in which the family may be most completely sheltered to develop in love, graciousness and individuality, and which is at the same time most accessible to friends, toward whom hospitality is as unconscious and spontaneous as it is abundant. Emerson says that the ornament of a house is the friends who frequent it.

In the conventional home, both the richness of family intercourse and the freedom of hospitality is restrained. A life hedged in with formality is like a plant stifled by surrounding weeds. Many people mistake formality for politeness, or even for good morals. There is a vast difference between good etiquette and right conduct. How depressing it is to go into a home where every act is punctuated with the formalism of polite society!

The home must suggest the life it is to encompass. The mere architecture and furnishings of the house do not make the man any more than do his clothes, but they certainly have an effect in modifying him. A large nature may rise above his environment and live in a dream world of his own fashioning, but most of us are mullusks after all, and are shaped and sized by the walls which we build about us. When we enter a room and see tawdry furniture, sham ornaments and vulgar daubs of pictures displayed, do we not feel convinced that the occupants of the home have a tawdry and vulgar streak in their natures? Or if all is cold and formal in architecture and furnishings, do we not instinctively nerve ourselves to meet the shock of a politely proper reception?

The average modern American home is a reflex in miniature of the life of the people. It is quickly made and lightly abandoned. If it were constructed like the Japanese house of bamboo and paper, or like a native hut of thatch, it might charm from its simplicity and lack of ostentation; or if, like the homes of our ancestors, it were made of mortised logs chinked with mud, it would have a rude dignity and inevitableness which would put it in harmony with the surrounding nature. But these things no longer satisfy. We must all have palaces to house us—petty makeshifts, to be sure, with imitation turrets, spires, porticos, corbels and elaborate bracket-work excrescences—palaces of crumbling plaster, with walls papered in gaudy patterns and carpets of insolent device—palaces furnished in cracking veneer, with marble mantels and elaborate chandeliers. It is a shoddy home, the makeshift of a shoddy age. It is the natural outgrowth of our prosperous democracy. Machinery has enabled us to manifold shams to a degree heretofore undreamed. We ornament our persons with imitation pearls and diamonds; we dress in felt wadding that, for a week or two, looks like wool; we wear silk that tears at a touch, and our homes are likewise adorned with imitations and baubles. We botch our carpentering and trust to putty, paint and paper to cover up the defects. On Sundays we preach about the goodly apple rotten at the heart, and all the week we make houses of veneer and stucco. Our defense is that we do not expect to tarry long where we are encamped, so why build for the grandchildren of the stranger?

Happily, a change is coming into our lives. Nowhere in the country is it more marked than in California. From small beginnings it has spread slowly at first, but soon with added momentum. The thought of the simple life is being worked out in the home. In the simple home all is quiet in effect, restrained in tone, yet natural and joyous in its frank use of unadorned material. Harmony of line and balance of proportion is not obscured by meaningless ornamentation; harmony of color is not marred by violent contrasts. Much of the construction shows, and therefore good workmanship is required and the craft of the carpenter is restored to its old-time dignity.

Blessed is he who lives in such a home and who makes life conform to his surroundings,—who is hospitable not only to friends, but to the sweet ministration of the elements, who holds abundant intercourse with sun and air, with bird voices sounding from the shrubbery without and human voices within singing their answer! In such a home, inspiring in its touch with art and books, glorified by mother love and child sunshine, may the human spirit grow in strength and grace to the fullness of years. . . .

Let the work be simple and genuine, with due regard to right proportion and harmony of color; let it be an individual expression of the life which it is to environ, conceived with loving care for the uses of the family. Eliminate in so far as possible all factory-made accessories in order that your dwelling may not be typical of American commercial supremacy, but rather of your own fondness for things that have been created as a response to your love of that which is good and simple and fit for daily companionship. Far better that our surroundings be rough and crude in detail, provided that they are a vital expression conceived as part of an harmonious scheme, than that they be finished with mechanical precision and lacking in genuine character. Beware the gloss that covers over a sham! . . .

Of all reforms needed in the life of the home, that of the relation of the man to his family is most pressing. Modern materialism demands of far too many men an unworthy sacrifice. That the wife and children may live in ostentation the man must be a slave to business, rushing and jostling with the crowd in the scramble for wealth. A simpler standard of living will give him more time for art and culture, more time for his family, more time to live.

The day is ripe for the general adoption of this idea of the simple home. People are growing weary of shams and are longing for reality. They will never get it till they learn that the ideal is the real, that beauty is truth, and that love is the inspiration for beauty. Let those who would see a higher culture in California, a deeper life, a nobler humanity, work for the adoption of the simple home among all classes of people, trusting that the inspiration of its mute walls will be a ceaseless challenge to all who dwell within their shadow, for beauty and character.

Charles Keeler, *The Simple Home* (1904; Salt Lake City: Gibbs M. Smith, Inc., 1979), pp. xiv, 3,6.

A CONSUMER'S SYMPHONY

To govern selection by excellence rather than expense; to prefer simplicity; to make use serve beauty, and beauty usefulness; to believe in goodness, abhor sham, make surroundings contribute to life; in short to conserve, even in the midst of commercial stress and strife, those eternal verities which make for advanced living.

Rho Fisk Zueblin, "Duties of the Consumer," *The Craftsman* 7 (1904):91.

Is It Worth While?

Edward Bok

There were many spokesmen for Progressive simplicity at the turn of the century, but none was more persistent or enthusastic than Edward Bok (1863–1930), the editor of *The Ladies' Home Journal.* Bok promoted a variety of progressive reform causes, but like Stickley, Keeler, and others, he was especially concerned that middle-class Americans were smothering themselves in superfluous possessions and activities. He, too, was influenced by the ideas of William Morris and the Arts and Crafts movement, and he repeatedly urged his women readers to strip their homes and lives of such clutter and reassess their priorities. He reassured them that he was not countenancing a fruit-and-nuts primitivism. No, he recognized the need for "a healthful diet, simple, serviceable clothing, a clean, healthy dwelling place, open-air exercise and good reading." But in most cases, he insisted, Americans added far too much to these essentials. And in doing so they introduced needless complications and anxieties. As possessions increase, Bok maintained, so do desires and cares, and a person must therefore work harder, worry more, and communicate less with family and friends. The following editorial represents a typical appeal for his version of middle-class simplicity.

There are no people on the face of the earth who litter up the rooms of their homes with so much useless, and consequently bad, furnishing as do the Americans. The curse of the American home to-day is useless bric-a-brac. A room in which we feel that we can freely breathe is so rare that we are instinctively surprised when we see one. It is the exception, rather than the rule, that we find a restful room.

As a matter of fact, to this common error of overfurnishing so many of our homes are directly due many of the nervous breakdowns of our women. The average American woman is a perfect slave to the useless rubbish which she has in her rooms. This rubbish, of a costly nature where plenty exists, and of a cheap and tawdry character in homes of moderate incomes, is making housekeeping a nerve-racking burden. A goodly number of these women are conscious of their mistakes. Others, if not absolutely conscious, feel that something is wrong in their homes, yet they know not exactly what it is. But all are loath, yes, I may say afraid, to simplify things. They fear the criticism of the outside world that their homes are sparsely furnished; they dread the possibility that their rooms may be called "bare." They fear to give way to common-sense. It is positively rare, but tremendously exhilarating, to find a woman, as one does now and then, who is courageous enough to furnish her home with an eye single to comfort and practical utility, and who refuses to have her home lowered to a plane of mediocrity by filling it with useless bric-a-brac and jimcracks, the only mission of which seems to be to offend the eye and accumulate dust.

Ladies' Home Journal

DO's & DON'Ts

The twelve-year-old at left in this lesson in taste from a 1907 Ladies' Home Journal is wearing "appropriate and inconspicuous" clothes, in which she is able to "do things," while the unfortunate child at right is wearing "too dreadfully much of everything."

A simple couch is contrasted with one that "affronts the eye."

A "strong and honest" sideboard versus an "unfortunate affair."

Edward Bok's version of domestic simplicity.

A serious phase of this furnishing is that hundreds of women believe these jimcracks ornament their rooms. They refuse to believe that useless ornamentation always disfigures and never ornaments. Simplicity is the only thing that ornaments. It does more: it dignifies. The most artistic rooms are made not by what is in them, but by what has been left out of them. One can never quarrel with simplicity. A tasteful effect is generally reached by what has been left undone. And that is the lesson most needed in America to-day: not what we can put into a room, but what we can leave out of it. . .

Now to suggest a departure from these atrocities is to suggest to many something so radical that they are absolutely afraid. Yet we must reach a more intelligent height with regard to furnishing our homes. True, it would mean a general clearing-out in many of our rooms. But that would be a blessing. We must get to that point where we will allow nothing in our homes except those things for which we have an actual use. This does not mean that our homes would be "too plain," as many will object. Simplicity is not plainness: it is, I repeat, the highest form of good art and good taste. Nothing can improve the beauty of a simple line. No one can quarrel with it. It is beyond criticism. This is easy to believe and see if we will only allow ourselves to get away from the present notion that the ornate is the ornamental. We must believe that what is ornate is never ornamental, and never in good taste. Ornateness is simply artificiality, and nothing artificial can be ornamental. Therefore, if we buy for actual use, for utility, we reach the highest point attainable in good art and taste.

This is the lesson we must learn, and then we will the more easily understand what William Morris meant when he said that we must have fewer things in our homes, but have them better. If we buy for utility we reach the first essential of fewer things. And if we buy fewer things we can naturally afford to buy better things. It is infinitely better and cheaper to have one good, well-made chair than a dozen glued-together affairs. The money paid for a really good piece of furniture is never wasted. It is one of the best investments a man or woman can make, for with simplicity comes good taste, and nothing goes to make for perfect good taste so surely as a simple effect. What we need is restraint. It is a great pity that the ideas and work of William Morris in the way of house-furnishing are not more familiar to our people. Recently "a William Morris wave," or "craze," has been developing, and it is a fad that we cannot push with too much vigor. Morris's ideas about what should go into a room and a house were about as sane as those of any man of the past decade. He insisted that we should have fewer things and have them better. His motto was "not how cheap, but how good." He was an ardent believer in simplicity, and thereby became one of the leading modern apostles of good taste. . . .

More simplicity in our homes would make our lives simpler. Many women would live fuller lives because they would have more time. As it is, hundreds of women of all positions in life are to-day the slaves of their homes and what they have crowded into them. Instead of being above inanimate objects of wood and clothes and silks, their lives are dominated by them. They are the slaves of their furniture and useless bric-a-brac. One hears men constantly complain of this. The condition is not a safe one for wives. No woman can afford to allow a lot of unnecessary furnishings to rule her life. She should be their master. Comfort is essential to our happiness. But with comfort we should stop. Then we are on the safe side. But we get on and over the danger line when we go beyond. Not one-tenth of the things that we think are essential to our happiest living are really so. In fact, we should be an infinitely happier and healthier people if the nine-tenths were taken out of our lives. It is astonishing how much we can do without, and be a thousand times the better for it. And it doesn't require much to test this gospel of wisdom. We need only to be natural: to get back to our real, inner selves. Then we are simple. It is only because we have got away from the simple and the natural that so many of our homes are cluttered up as they are, and our lives full of things that are not worth the while. We have bent the knee to show, to display, and we have lowered ourselves in doing it: surrounded ourselves with the trivial and the useless: and filling our lives with the poison of artificiality and the unnatural, we have pushed the Real: the Natural: the Simple: the Beautiful—the best and most lasting things—out of our lives. Now, I ask, in all fairness: Is it worth while?

Edward Bok, "Is It Worth While?" *The Ladies' Home Journal* 17 (November 1900):18.

A Woman's Questions

Edward Bok

Bok's challenge to his women readers to simplify their lives provoked dozens of letters to the editor. Many of them identified with his portrait of the harried middle-class household and yearned for the simplicities he described, but they remained doubtful about the practicality of such a reform program. In an attempt to assuage their concerns and bolster their courage, he selected one such letter to share with his readers.

One woman has written a letter, which is a very fair sample of several score which have come to this office during the past few months. They have all been about the editorial "Is it Worth While?" which was printed on this page last November asking that women should readjust their homes and lives on simpler lines. In every letter the desire for a simpler life is clearly manifest. But in each there is a note of hesitancy. This feeling is very well expressed in the extracts which I shall quote from the letter of this particular correspondent.

She begins by saying:

"We women want simpler lives. There's no doubt of that. But we are dismayed by the difficulties confronting the woman who essays to 'come out and be separate.' "

Just here is struck the first false note. To be simpler in our lives is not a call to "come out and be separate." It is a call to come out and be true—to be ourselves. It is this false notion of being separate, of being apart, of being unlike the rest of the world, that is keeping thousands of women in an unnatural and injurious bondage. The woman who, feeling that her life is complicated with unprofitable things, will simplify that life, will find the moment she steps out of her bondage that she is not alone. Far from it indeed. She will find herself of a sisterhood that numbers more votaries than she has ever dreamed of: a sisterhood that she will know not of until she has become part of it.

Like attracts like in this world. If we live false lives we attract those who live similar lives. If our lives ring true the chords we strike attract those who also live on equal heights. The true lesson for us to learn is to live for the things we believe: not for what may be thought of those things by others. That is where our chief trouble lies: we are too much concerned by what the world may think of us. We are fearful lest some action of ours may be misunderstood. We are unwilling to stand by our convictions. We forget the thing itself. We forget that we are what we are by the things we do. It matters exceedingly little what the world thinks of us. But it does matter, and it matters much, to ourselves whether the lives we lead are true or false. An action born of a false motive never has the slightest influence. It dies at its birth. The men and women who, by their lives, have influenced the world have been those who have lived earnest and honest lives, and who never for one moment allowed to come into their thoughts the notion of whether the world would approve or disapprove. No life truly lived is lived apart and alone. It has the companionship of the best. . . .

The writer of this letter continues:

"You may tell us that some of the most distinguished and worthy among us adorn their homes only with the fruits of simple taste. They can well afford to do so. Why need they care? They will not be dropped from visiting lists."

No, they will "not be dropped from visiting lists" because, thank God, the women of such homes never have "visiting lists," and, therefore, cannot be dropped from them. They value spontaneity of friendship and natural social intercourse as something above the cold conventionality and formality of "visiting lists." They value their friends as something more than a lot of miscellaneous folks in a book. Such folks pay their friends the compliment of remembering them in their hearts: it isn't necessary to put their names in a book. Their "visiting list" consists of friends who are friends: friends that remain friends in need: friends that become friends not because of social grade nor fancied station, but because they have something within them that goes out and meets the same something in some one else. We call it finding "kindred spirits." They "visit" where the heart prompts: not where conventionality dictates. And they are "distinguished" among us only by reason of the fact that they distinguish the true from the false, and the gold from the tinsel. They value "visits" when "visits" mean that people come to their houses because they want to come, not because custom dictates that they should come.

It is a pathetic conclusion which my correspondent gives to her letter:

"Thousands of women see clearly the force of the needs which you point out, and see them with an intensity born of defeated hopes and thwarted lives. But they find themselves helpless against the ever-increasing tide of complex and artificial standards of living. Woman knows and feels it is a difficult task to hold her way in the swift currents of prevailing customs. But they are forced upon her."

No, they are not, if my correspondent will pardon the bluntness of my comment. Nothing in the world can be forced upon us if we will not have it so. I repeat: our lives are what we make of them ourselves. If we are weak and accept the artificial our lives will be so. And just in proportion as we make our lives artificial we make them profitless and unhappy. A happy life cannot be lived in an atmosphere surcharged with artificiality. That is impossible. No hope is defeated unless we thwart its highest fulfillment and development by our own actions. It is with us, and with us only, whether we allow the "swift currents of prevailing customs" to make our lives complex. They do, unquestionably, and they are dwarfing the inner lives of thousands of women, and killing thousands of others. But it is cowardly and unjust to lay the blame and the responsibility upon those "customs." It is optional with us to accept or reject them. There are certain social laws which seem to make these "customs" right, but every phase of a higher law, the Divine law, proves them wrong. There must be certain laws and customs for the protection of the social body. These are likewise for our own individual protection and are right, and ordinary commonsense teaches us what these are.

It is begging the question to say, as my correspondent says, that:

"Unity of aim and effort against the encroachments of artificial and trivial standards can, I fancy, alone stem the tide that threatens to engulf us."

It is peculiarly characteristic of too many of us that where an evil is seen we always want to conquer it in twos and threes—ever in company, never alone. "Unity of aim and effort," yes, but of the individual. To wait for numbers is to wait forever. What is food for one is poison for another. There are folks whose very natures rebel at the simple. They want the ornate: the gaudy: the complex. There will always be such. Their natures are so attuned to everything that is superficial and flashy that they would positively be unhappy in an atmosphere where everything is true, and pure, and sweet, and simple, and healthy. There is plenty of room in the world for such. There is always companionship to be found for the man or woman whose highest purposes cannot rise above his or her material possessions. The loud clapping of cymbals attracts more folks than the soft note of the lute. But the lute gives the purest note. It depends upon the note we want to strike in our lives—the note that gives forth blatant noise, or the note that gives forth purest melody. But it rests with us: with no one else. There is the life of pretense with its coterie of deformed spirits, where one is measured by artificial standards, with each standard farther away from the Divine than the preceding one. And there is the life of honest endeavor: of men and women: where, as they say in the Far West, "every man that isn't a man is a woman." In other words, a world of real people, where each man and woman is measured by his or her own true worth, where friendships are honest and where laughs are hearty and tears are real: where lives are happiest because they are lived simplest: where the air is clear, and where people look you in the eye, and where the clothes you wear do not signify.

After all one can say, we must come back to the old truism: that men and women are like water: they always find their true level.

And where you live happiest, that is your level. There's polluted water, and there's clear water. But one law is inexorable: the closer you get to Nature, the truest and simplest thing there is because it is closest to God, the clearer always you will find the water.

Edward Bok, "A Woman's Questions," *Ladies' Home Journal* 18 (April 1901):18.

PATRIOTIC SIMPLICITY DURING WORLD WAR I
Edward Bok

Our dolls and playthings must be put aside. We have had our time for the dance and the dinner and the pretty frock. But that time is over. It is the hour for serious thought: for well-doing: for thoughts of others: for service.

The time for wasteful housekeeping is over. . . . With less we can easily do. And how simply and better we can do without is a lesson that will be new to some and good for all. We have had a succession of softening years of prosperity. It will do us all good to have a period of the hardening process that comes with sacrifice. . . . [It] is regrettable that it takes a war to induce simple living.

We are getting into our minds at last that ideals are more important than we thought: that Life is more than meat and that body is more than raiment.

Aside from the patriotic duty involved—a chance to help save our country in time of stress—we have a marvelous opportunity to serve the health of ourselves and families.

Edward Bok, *Ladies' Home Journal* 34 (June 1917):7, 26; 34 (November 1917):7; 35 (May 1918):24.

Simplicity Between the Wars

7

Patriotic simplicity was typically short-lived. No sooner was the Great War over than the aura of self-sacrifice and civic duty quickly dissipated. The mood of the nation during the 1920s was not at all sympathetic to the ideal of simple living. Enforced frugality and rationing during the war generated a pent-up demand for goods and services that resulted in what one observer called "an orgy of extravagant spending" after 1919. The Republican administrations under Harding, Coolidge, and Hoover shaped federal policies so as to promote a resurgence of corporate capitalism and the burgeoning consumer culture, and by 1923 the nation was catapulted into an era of unprecedented prosperity and high living. Coolidge baldly stated his public philosophy when he said that wealth "is the chief end of man." Such a brazen materialism was heard often during the 1920s. A new consumption ethic was rapidly displacing the production ethic of the nineteenth century. The dramatic expansion of production afforded by new technologies and theories of industrial management flooded the country with a welter of commodities which threatened to cause economic havoc unless the public accelerated its spending habits. As a newspaper editorial asserted: "Consumption is a new necessity."

The indulgent requirements of this consumer culture philosophy made appeals for simple living appear almost traitorous. Still, the middle-class versions of simplicity promoted during the Progressive era retained much of their attraction. Millions of Americans continued to enjoy the invigorating effects of periodic contact with nature in the form of camping, hiking, and summer outings. But those advocating simple living as an alternative to modern urban industrial life rather than merely a recreational activity were rapidly dwindling.

Yet there were a few hardy idealists who persevered in their insistence that the good life was not just the pursuit of more and more goods and larger and larger business enterprises. An articulate group of southern intellectuals clustered at Vanderbilt University, known as the Nashville Agrarians, grew increasingly disgusted with modern American society as the 1920s progressed. They especially resented the intrusion of northern urban-industrial culture into their native region. To Allen Tate, John Crowe Ransom, Donald Davidson, Frank Owsley, Robert Penn Warren, Andrew Lytle, and others among the Vanderbilt group of poets, historians, economists, and critics, it was imperative for the South to retain its tradition of dignified plain living and high thinking rather than succumb to the encroaching northern culture of indiscriminate production and consumption. This was the compelling theme of their famous manifesto, *I'll Take My Stand*, published in 1930.

Although reviewers and critics derisively dismissed the Nashville Agrarians as sentimental and naive reactionaries, there were others who shared their critique of contemporary American society. Ralph Borsodi, a New York social theorist, emerged in the 1920s as an outspoken critic of urban-industrial life, and, unlike many of the Vanderbilt academics, he put his own agrarian alternative into practice. In 1920 he and his wife left Manhattan and moved with their two sons to the countryside near Suffern, New York. There they developed a self-sustaining homestead. In the process, Borsodi claimed, they discovered true simplicity and independence. And his own successful experience led him to encourage others to try his version of homesteading simplicity.

But few heeded his call until the onset of the Great Depression. That economic and social disaster served to revitalize the almost dormant ethic of simple living. The devastating effects of the Depression challenged the whole ethos of the consumer and corporate culture. Desperate conditions called for desperate solutions, and there was no lack of proposals and panaceas.

Among the many varied responses to the Depression was a concerted attempt by government officials and private citizens to restore Jeffersonian simplicity as a goal of national social policy. Franklin Roosevelt and many of his advisers saw in the economic crisis a means of promoting a return to the land and to greater self-reliance. Early in 1933 the New Deal "brain trust" began putting forth new programs designed to revivify simple living in the country. These ranged from the Civilian Conservation Corps to the Tennessee Valley Authority to the Subsistence Homesteads Division to the Resettlement Administration. Far more than mere efforts to attack unemployment, these New Deal programs were intended in large measure to promote a dramatic reform in the nature of American social life. They would transplant people from the cities back to the land, provide them with fulfilling work, restore their self-esteem, and instill a renewed sense of civic virtue and community cohesion.

Many Americans applauded such efforts. During the early 1930s a loose coalition of groups promoting a restoration of Jeffersonian decentralist values emerged. They included the Nashville Agrarians, the Catholic Rural Life movement, homesteading advocates such as Borsodi, and promoters of the growing cooperative movement. These traditionalists initially supported Roosevelt's efforts to revitalize country life and the farm economy. And they saw in his homesteading programs and the Civilian Conservation Corps encouraging attempts to halt the spread of unfettered urban industrial materialism and restore balance and sanity to the American way of life.

But as the New Deal developed in all its conflicting facets, these decentralists grew more and more disenchanted with the contradictions and compromises they discovered in Roosevelt's programs. As journalist Dorothy Thompson recognized, "Two souls dwell in the bosom of this Administration, as indeed they do in the bosom of the American people. The one loves the Abundant Life, as expressed in the cheap and plentiful products of large-scale mass production and distribution. . . . The other soul yearns for former simplicities, for decentralization, for the interests of the 'little man,' revolts against high-pressure sales-manship, denounces 'monopoly' and 'economic empires' and seeks the means of breaking them up."

Gradually, these two strands making up the New Deal began to splay, much to the chagrin of the neo-Jeffersonians. The Agrarians, Borsodi, and others broke with the New Deal by the late 1930s and began promoting private initiatives designed to encourage greater self-reliance and simplicity. And most of the New Deal's efforts to do the same were either discarded or had their appropriations sharply reduced as the nation girded itself for a possible war in Europe.

The efforts of these self-styled "decentralists" and New Dealers to resettle Americans in the countryside joined one of the nation's oldest dreams—country simplicity—to the traditional Jeffersonian assumption that a virtuous republican society requires that a majority of the people be economically independent and therefore politically free. Almost a half century before E. F. Schumacher's humanist economics captured the imagination of thousands of American readers, these idealists in the 1930s were insisting that small was indeed beautiful—and American. Despite sharp differences over the role of government in facilitating such objectives, the neo-Jeffersonians helped sustain the myth of republican simplicity as a national program. And in many cases they themselves translated that myth into living reality.

That most of their countrymen were unwilling to share their dream and join in their social experiments, even during the Depression, reveals how far the myth of collective simplicity had diverged from actuality by the 1930s. Whatever can be said about the merits of their proposals, however, those promoting a decentralist agrarian philosophy were making a strong protest on behalf of traditional American values, particularly the assumption that men and women should have greater control over their lives and livelihoods. That control involves the problems of food, clothing and shelter. How one spends one's time is a fundamental moral decision. Insofar as this decentralist version of simplicity sought to give some people, perhaps unusual individuals, more control over their own lives, it will continue to serve as an enticing option or ideal.

Introduction to *I'll Take My Stand*
Twelve Southerners

The Nashville Agrarians, as they came to be called, were led by John Crowe Ransom, Allen Tate, Robert Penn Warren, and Donald Davidson, four poets who during the early 1920s had joined together to publish a little magazine known as *The Fugitive*. At that time they were more interested in literary experimentalism than their regional identity. But during the late 1920s they grew more sensitive to their southern heritage and to the larger forces shaping modern American society. Technology was the new God. Materialism seemed rampant; it was infecting not only the public mood but also the arts. Culture was being ignored in the evanescent quest for quick profits. And the South, their homeland, which had for over a century remained remarkably insulated from the degenerating effects of urban-industrial change and its attendant secular materialism, was rapidly being invaded by the new order. Perhaps most disturbing to the Agrarians was that many prominent southerners eagerly welcomed and encouraged the invasion. Thus they decided to "take their stand" against the encroachments of urban-industrial life. The Fugitives became Agrarians and had no trouble enlisting other sons of the South to their cause—poet and cultural critic John Gould Fletcher, government administrator Henry Blue Kline, psychologist Lyle Lanier, writer and professor Andrew Lytle, historian and political scientist Herman Nixon, historian Frank Owsley, biographer John Wade, and playwright and critic Stark Young.

In defending their traditional vision of the good life, the Twelve Southerners portrayed the old South in idyllic terms. To them it was a regional society based on subsistence agriculture, the fellowship of family, a sense of belonging to a historical tradition, and a deeply felt belief in a stern God—all bound together in an organic vision of community. Their dreamy South, of course, was too good to be true; it had no seamy or scheming characters such as Flem Snopes, Jeeter Lester, or Thomas Sutpen. It had no pellagra, hookworm, or illiteracy. It had no slave rebellions or tyrannical overseers. And such a sentimental portrait understandably provoked scorn and laughter from reviewers.

Yet beneath the veil of nostalgia in *I'll Take My Stand* was a penetrating critique of the values of the emerging twentieth-century consumer culture. And in rebuking the excesses of that powerful social force, they spoke eloquently to the spiritual crisis of the twentieth century. As latter-day Jeffersonians, the Nashville Agrarians helped to sustain a vision of a decentralized, simple American society that transcended the merely material and remained tied to the land and devoted to God.

Nobody now proposes for the South, or for any other community in this country, an independent political destiny. That idea is thought to have been finished in 1865. But how far shall the South surrender its moral, social, and economic autonomy to the victorious principle of Union? That question remains open. The South is a minority section that has hitherto been jealous of its minority right to live its own kind of life. The South scarcely hopes to determine the other sections, but it does propose to determine itself, within the utmost limits of legal action. Of late, however, there is the melancholy fact that the South itself has wavered a little and shown signs of wanting to join up behind the common or American industrial ideal. It is against that tendency that this book is written. The younger Southerners, who are being converted frequently to the industrial gospel, must come back to the support of the Southern tradition. They must be persuaded to look very critically at the advantages of becoming a "new South" which will be only an undistinguished replica of the usual industrial community.

But there are many other minority communities opposed to industrialism, and wanting a much simpler economy to live by. The communities and private persons sharing the agrarian tastes are to be found widely within the Union. Proper living is a matter of the intelligence and the will, does not depend on the local climate or geography, and is capable of a definition which is general and not Southern at all. Southerners have a filial duty to discharge to their own section. But their cause is precarious and they must seek alliances with sympathetic communities everywhere. The members of the present group would be happy to be counted as members of a national agrarian movement. . . .

Even the apologists of industrialism have been obliged to admit that some economic evils follow in the wake of the machines. These are such as overproduction, unemployment, and a growing inequality in the distribution of wealth. But the remedies proposed by the apologists are always homeopathic. They expect the evils to disappear when we have bigger and better machines, and more of them. Their remedial programs, therefore, look forward to more industrialism. . . .

Turning to consumption, as the grand end which justifies the evil of modern labor, we find that we have been deceived. We have more time in which to consume, and many more products to be consumed. But the tempo of our labors communicates itself to our satisfactions, and these also become brutal and hurried. The constitution of the natural man probably does not permit him to shorten his labor-time and enlarge his consuming-time indefinitely. He has to pay the penalty in satiety and aimlessness. The modern man has lost his sense of vocation.

Religion can hardly expect to flourish in an industrial society. Religion is our submission to the general intention of a nature that is fairly inscrutable; it is the sense of our role as creatures within it. But nature industrialized, transformed into cities and artificial habitations, manufactured into commodities, is no longer nature but a highly simplified picture of nature. We receive the illusion of having power over nature, and lose the sense of nature as something mysterious and contingent. The God of nature under these conditions is merely an amiable expression, a superfluity, and the philosophical understanding ordinarily carried in the religious experience is not there for us to have.

Nor do the arts have a proper life under industrialism, with the general decay of sensibility which attends it. Art depends, in general, like religion, on a right attitude to nature; and in particular on a free and disinterested observation of nature that occurs only in leisure. Neither the creation nor the understanding of works of art is possible in an industrial age except by some local and unlikely suspension of the industrial drive.

The amenities of life also suffer under the curse of a strictly-business or industrial civilization. They consist in such practices as manners, conversation, hospitality, sympathy, family life, romantic love—in the social exchanges which reveal and develop sensibility in human affairs. If religion and the arts are founded on right relations of man-to-nature, these are founded on right relations of man-to-man.

Apologists of industrialism are even inclined to admit that its actual processes may have upon its victims the spiritual effects just described. But they think that all can be made right by extraordinary educational efforts, by all sorts of cultural institutions and endowments. They would cure the poverty of the contemporary spirit by hiring experts to instruct it in spite of itself in the historic culture. But salvation is hardly to be encountered on that road. The trouble with the life-pattern is to be located at its economic base, and we cannot rebuild it by pouring in soft materials from the top. The young men and women in colleges, for example, if they are already placed in a false way of life, cannot make more than an inconsequential acquaintance with the arts and humanities transmitted to them. Or else the understanding of these arts and humanities will but make them the more wretched in their own destitution. . . .

The tempo of the industrial life is fast, but that is not the worst of it; it is accelerating. The ideal is not merely some set form of industrialism, with so many stable industries, but industrial progress, or an incessant extension of industrialization. It never proposes a specific goal; it initiates the infinite series. We have not merely capitalized certain industries; we have capitalized the laboratories and inventors, and undertaken to employ all the labor-saving devices that come out of them. But a fresh labor-saving device introduced into an industry does not emancipate the laborers in that industry so much as it evicts them. Applied at the expense of agriculture, for example, the new processes have reduced the part of the population supporting itself upon the soil to a smaller and smaller fraction. Of course no single labor-saving process is fatal; it brings on a period of unemployed labor and unemployed capital, but soon a new industry is devised which will put them both to work again, and a new commodity is thrown upon the market. The laborers were sufficiently embarrassed in the meantime, but, according to the theory, they will eventually be taken care of. It is now the public which is embarrassed; it feels obligated to purchase a commodity for which it had expressed no desire, but it is invited to make its budget equal to the strain. All might yet be well, and stability and comfort might again obtain, but for this: partly because of industrial ambitions and partly because the repressed creative impulse must break out somewhere, there will be a stream of further labor-saving devices in all industries, and the cycle will have to be repeated over and over. The result is an increasing disadjustment and instability....

Opposed to the industrial society is the agrarian, which does not stand in particular need of definition. An agrarian society is hardly one that has no use at all for industries, for professional vocations, for scholars and artists, and for the life of cities. Technically, perhaps, an agrarian society is one in which agriculture is the leading vocation, whether for wealth, for pleasure, or for prestige—a form of labor that is pursued with intelligence and leisure, and that becomes the model to which the other forms approach as well as they may. But an agrarian regime will be secured readily enough where the superfluous industries are not allowed to rise against it. The theory of agrarianism is that the culture of the soil is the best and most sensitive of vocations, and that therefore it should have the economic preference and enlist the maximum number of workers....

For, in conclusion, this much is clear: If a community, or a section, or a race, or an age, is groaning under industrialism, and well aware that it is an evil dispensation, it must find the way to throw it off. To think that this cannot be done is pusillanimous. And if the whole community, section, race, or age thinks it cannot be done, then it has simply lost its political genius and doomed itself to impotence.

Twelve Southerners, *I'll Take My Stand: The South and the Agrarian Tradition* (New York: Harper, 1930), pp. x-xx.

THE SIMPLE LIFE—AND HOW!

Charles Stokes

We will start, in order to save time and nebulous argument, by admitting that we are all sick and tired of this present complicated life, and yearn for a simpler one. The next point that arises is: How can we get it?

How to get there never seems to have worried the social philosophers who have tried to imagine an ideal state. They could tell you what was wrong, and what was ideal; but how you got from one to the other, using means that were already at hand and methods adapted to current conditions, was apparently too prosaic for them to bother with. The Simple Life, to be sure, is not a new idea; but how far have we got towards it?

To arise and preach it now, when every day in every way life is getting speedier, jazzier, and more and more delighted with its own cleverness, seems to be harder than ever. Who wants to go back to the Simple Life when the Dizzy Life is so much more fascinating? The answer is: we must make the Simple Life attractive! If you are one of the Utopians, you will probably answer: "We have done that already. Read our books! We have made the Simple Life so attractive that logically no one could resist it. Yet no one seems to want it." I merely ask: "Did you ever advertise it?"

Advertising! There's the solution. Surely you know that advertising will sell anything? It has launched most of the world's major problems, from poorer teeth—breakfast-food advertising—to traffic congestion-automobile advertising. Why not harness its enormous force to sell Simplicity? It would do it. And you and I could enjoy a traitor's revenge, in using advertising to bring back what it has been most instrumental in destroying—the Simple Life.

Charles Stokes, "The Simple Life—And How!" *New Republic*, 10 July 1929, pp. 203–05.

Flight from the City

Ralph Borsodi

Ralph Borsodi (1888–1977) was the son of Hungarian immigrant parents who had arrived in New York City in the 1870s. Largely self-educated, he early on developed an adoration for Jefferson and his decentralist agrarian philosophy. In 1911, while working as a marketing consultant at Macy's Department store, Borsodi married a western farm girl. Myrtle Mae Borsodi would thereafter become the heroine of the kitchen, loom, and sewing room in her husband's writings and a publishing home economist in her own right.

In 1920 the Borsodis decided to flee the inflated prices and filth of Manhattan and move to the countryside near Suffern. There they sought economic security and independence, family unity, healthful and varied work and recreation, and the aesthetic and spiritual satisfactions of rural life. They succeeded. The Borsodis, through their own ingenuity and grit, established a nearly self-sufficient homestead. In 1933, as millions of Americans struggled to survive in the midst of the Great Depression, Ralph Borsodi published *Flight from the City*, a practical manual on homesteading as well as a philosophical statement of the relationships between self-sufficiency and self-worth.

In many respects the Borsodis represented the persistence of the Thoreauvian ideal. They, too, revered life in the woods and abhorred the factory system. Yet they differed from most of the earlier romantics in their approach to technology. Borsodi wanted to "domesticate" the machine, to use motors and appliances to enhance his family's economic independence, ease their physical burdens, and create more time for productive leisure. The Borsodis' purpose was to synthesize the best of country and city life. And they believed that, if more people followed their example, the runaway urban-industrial system would be reined in and perhaps would come to promote quality rather than quantity.

In 1920 the Borsodi family—my wife, my two small sons, and myself—lived in a rented home. We bought our food and clothing and furnishings from retail stores. We were dependent entirely upon my income from a none too certain white-collar job.

We lived in New York City—the metropolis of the country. We had the opportunity to enjoy the incredible variety of foodstuffs which pour into that great city from every corner of the continent; to live in the most luxurious apartments built to house men and women in this country; to use the speedy subways, the smart restaurants, the great office buildings, the libraries, theaters, public schools—all the thousand and one conveniences which make New York one of the most fantastic creations in the history of man. Yet in the truest sense, we could not enjoy any of them.

How could we enjoy them when we might be without a job; when we lacked the zest of living which comes from real health and suffered all the minor and sometimes major ailments which come from too much excitement, too much artificial food, too much sedentary work, and too much of the smoke and noise and dust of the city; when we had to work just as hard to get to the places in which we tried to entertain ourselves as we had to get to the places in which we worked; when our lives were barren of real beauty—the beauty which comes only from contact with nature and from the growth of the soil, from flowers and fruits, from gardens and trees, from birds and animals?

We couldn't. Even though we were able for years and years, like so many others, to forget the fact—to ignore it amid the host of distractions which make up city life.

And then in 1920, the year of the great housing shortage, the house in which we were living was sold over our heads. New York in 1920 was no place for a houseless family. Rents, owing to the shortage of building which dated back to the World War, were outrageously high. Evictions were epidemic—to enable rapacious landlords to secure higher rents from new tenants—and most of the renters in the city seemed to be in the courts trying to secure the protection of the Emergency Rent Laws. We had the choice of looking for an equally endurable home in the city, of reading endless numbers of classified advertisements, of visiting countless real estate agents, of walking weary miles and climbing endless flights of steps, in an effort to rent another home, or of flight from the city. And while we were trying to prepare ourselves for the struggle with this typical city problem, we were overcome with longing for the country—for the security, the health, the leisure, the beauty we felt it must be possible to achieve there. Thus we came to make the experiment in living which we had often discussed but which we had postponed time and again because it involved so radical a change in our manner of life.

Instead, therefore, of starting the irritating task of house and apartment hunting, we wrote to real estate dealers within commuting distance of the city. We asked them for a house which could be readily remodeled; a location near the railroad station because we had no automobile; five to ten acres of land with fruit trees, garden space, pasturage, a woodlot, and if possible a brook; a location where electricity was available, and last but not least, a low purchase price. Even if the place we could afford only barely complied with these specifications, we felt confident that we could achieve economic freedom on it and a degree of comfort we never enjoyed in the city. All the other essentials of the good life, not even excepting schooling for our two sons, we decided we could produce for ourselves if we were unable to buy in a neighborhood which already possessed them.

We finally bought a place located about an hour and three-quarters from the city. It included a small frame house, one and a half stories high, containing not a single modern improvement—there was no plumbing, no running water, no gas, no electricity, no steam heat. There were an old barn, and a chicken-house which was on the verge of collapse, and a little over seven acres of land. There was a little fruit in the orchard—some apples, cherries, and plums, but of the apples at least there were plenty. . . . Yet "Sevenacres," as we called the place, was large enough for our initial experiment. Four years later we were able to select a more suitable site and begin the building of the sort of home we really wanted.

We began the experiment with three principal assets, courage—foolhardiness, our city friends called it; a vision of what modern methods and modern domestic machinery might be made to do in the way of eliminating drudgery, and the fact that my wife had been born and had lived up to her twelfth year on a ranch in the West. She at least had had childhood experience of life in the country.

But we had plenty of liabilities. We had little capital and only a modest salary. We knew nothing about raising vegetables, fruit, and poultry. All these things we had to learn. While I was a handy man, I had hardly ever had occasion to use a hammer and saw (a man working in an office rarely does), and yet if our experiment was to succeed it required that I should make myself a master of all trades. We cut ourselves off from the city comforts to which we had become so accustomed, without the countryman's material and spiritual compensations for them.

We went to the country with nothing but our city furniture. We began by adding to this wholly unsuitable equipment for pioneering, an electric range. This was the first purchase in the long list of domestic machines with which we proposed to test our theory that it was possible to be more comfortable in the country than in the city, with security, independence, and freedom to do the work to which we aspired thrown in for good measure.

Discomforts were plentiful in the beginning. The hardships of those early years are now fading into a romantic haze, but they were real enough at the time. A family starting with our handicaps had to expect them. But almost from the beginning there were compensations for the discomforts.

Before the end of the first year, the year of the depression of 1921 when millions were tramping the streets of our cities looking for work, we began to enjoy the feeling of plenty which the city-dweller never experiences. We cut our hay; gathered our fruit; made gallons and gallons of cider. We had a cow, and produced our own milk and butter, but finally gave her up. By furnishing us twenty quarts of milk a day she threatened to put us in the dairy business. So we changed to a pair of blooded Swiss goats. We equipped a poultry-yard, and had eggs, chickens, and fat roast capons. We ended the year with plenty not only for our own needs but for a generous hospitality to our friends—some of whom were out of work—a hospitality which, unlike city hospitality, did not involve purchasing everything we served our guests.

To these things which we produced in our first year, we have since added ducks, guineas, and turkeys; bees for honey; pigeons for appearance; and dogs for company. We have in the past twelve years built three houses and a barn from stones picked up on our place; we weave suitings, blankets, carpets, and draperies; we make some of our own clothing; we do all of our own laundry work; we grind flour, corn meal, and breakfast cereals; we have our own workshops, including a printing plant; and we have a swimming-pool, tennis-court, and even a billiard-room.

In certain important respects our experiment was very different from the ordinary back-to-the-land adventure. We quickly abandoned all efforts to raise anything to sell. After the first year, during which we raised some poultry for the market, this became an inviolable principle. We produced only for our own consumption. If we found it difficult to consume or give away any surplus, we cut down our production of that particular thing and devoted the time to producing something else which we were then buying. We used machinery wherever we could, and tried to apply the most approved scientific methods to small-scale production. We acted on the theory that there was always some way of doing what we wanted to do, if we only sought long enough for the necessary information, and that efficient machinery would pay for itself in the home precisely as it pays for itself in the factory.

The part which domestic machinery has played in making our adventure in homesteading a success cannot be too strongly emphasized. Machinery enabled us to eliminate drudgery; it furnished us skills which we did not possess, and it reduced the costs of production both in terms of money and in terms of labor. Not only do we use machines to pump our water, to do our laundry, to run our refrigerator—we use them to produce food, to produce clothing, to produce shelter.

Some of the machines we have purchased have proved unsatisfactory—something which is to be expected since so little

Ralph Borsodi weaving at his own hand loom. He made the suit he is wearing.

real thought has been devoted by our factory-dominated inventors and engineers to the development of household equipment and domestic machinery. But taking the machines and appliances which we have used as a whole, it is no exaggeration to say that we started our quest of comfort with all the discomforts possible in the country, and, because of the machines, we have now achieved more comforts than the average prosperous city man enjoys.

What we have managed to accomplish is the outcome of nothing but a conscious determination to use machinery for the purpose of eliminating drudgery from the home and to produce for ourselves enough of the essentials of living to free us from the thralldom of our factory-dominated civilization.

What are the social, economic, political, and philosophical implications of such a type of living? What would be the consequence of a widespread transference of production from factories to the home?

If enough families were to make their homes economically productive, cash-crop farmers specializing in one crop would have to abandon farming as a business and go back to it as a way of life. The packing-houses, mills, and canneries, not to mention the railroads, wholesalers, and retailers, which now distribute agricultural products would find their business confined to the production and distribution of exotic foodstuffs. Food is our most important industry. A war of attrition, such as we have been carrying on all alone, if extended on a large enough scale, would put the food industry out of its misery, for miserable it certainly is, all the way from the farmers who produce the raw materials to the men, women, and children who toil in the canneries, mills, and packing-towns, and in addition reduce proportionately the congestion, adulteration, unemployment, and unpleasant odors to all of which the food industry contributes liberally.

If enough families were to make their homes economically productive, the textile and clothing industries, with their low wages, seasonal unemployment, cheap and shoddy products, would shrink to the production of those fabrics and those garments which it is impractical for the average family to produce for itself.

If enough families were to make their homes economically productive, undesirable and non-essential factories of all sorts would disappear and only those which would be desirable and essential because they would be making tools and machines, electric light bulbs, iron and copper pipe, wire of all kinds, and the myriad of things which can best be made in factories, would remain to furnish employment to those benighted human beings who prefer to work in factories.

Domestic production, if enough people turned to it, would not only annihilate the undesirable and non-essential factory by depriving it of a market for its products. It would do more. It would release men and women from their present thralldom to the factory and make them masters of machines instead of servants to them; it would end the power of exploiting them which ruthless, acquisitive, and predatory men now possess; it would free them for the conquest of comfort, beauty and understanding.

Ralph Borsodi, *Flight from the City: An Experiment in Creative Living on the Land* (1933; New York: Harper and Row, 1972), pp. 1–9.

BACK TO THE LAND
Franklin D. Roosevelt

And so we plan for the future of agriculture—security for those who have spent their lives on farming; opportunity for real careers for young men and women on the farms; a share for farmers in the good things of life abundant enough to justify and preserve our instinctive faith in the land.

In all our plans we are guided, and will continue to be guided, by the fundamental belief that the American farmer, living on his own land, remains our ideal of self-reliance and of spiritual balance—the source from which the reservoirs of the Nation's strength are constantly renewed. It is from the men and women of our farms, living close to the soil that this Nation, like the Greek giant Antaeus, touches Mother Earth and rises with strength renewed a hundredfold.

We want to perpetuate that ideal, we want to perpetuate it under modern conditions, so that man may be strong in the ancient virtues and yet lay hold of the advantages which science and new knowledge offer a well-rounded life.

Samuel I. Rosenman, ed., *The Public Papers and Addresses of Franklin Delano Roosevelt*, 13 vols. (New York: Random House, 1938–50), 5:438–39.

New Deal Homesteads

M. L. Wilson

As Ralph Borsodi indicated, the Roosevelt Administration during the early 1930s was attempting to promote a return to the land as one means of easing the plight of the urban unemployed and the homeless. In pursuit of this goal the Department of Interior established a Division of Subsistence Homesteads to help settle penurious urban and rural families in planned homestead communities subsidized by the federal government. Unemployed workers would thereby be transformed into virtuous Jeffersonian yeomen. They would build their own homes, raise vegetable gardens, revive domestic handicrafts, and recreate the ideal organic community life envisioned by the Nashville Agrarians, Borsodi, and other neo-Jeffersonians.

Milburn L. Wilson, an agricultural economist who during the 1920s had organized a privately financed homesteading settlement in Montana, was appointed

director of the program. He hoped to use his agency to
create a new community life that would replace the
competitive materialism of modern industrial society with
a more simple and civic-minded village economy. Mutualism would supplant individualism.

It was an ambitious goal, perhaps the most ambitious of
the New Deal. And a few of the government-sponsored
homestead communities lived up to Wilson's ideal vision.
But most did not. Trying to create Jeffersonian agrarian
communities in the 1930s generated a host of unexpected
problems—bureaucratic red-tape, disputatious residents,
cost overruns. About a hundred such communities were
eventually established, but most of them were short-lived.
Many residents could not shed their engrained individualism and refused to participate in community social or
political affairs. Others found homesteading too demanding
or boring and returned to the cities.

The proponents of the subsistence homesteads movement are
quite generally agreed that there are some psychological and philosophical values which attach to the soil; that one of the most
nearly normal manners in which human beings express themselves
is by carrying though the cycle of the seasons the production of a
garden; that there are fundamental values which attach to a family
exhibiting the skill, the initiative and the discipline necessary to
the timely operations of garden production and to the consumption
by the family of something which is actually produced by the
family. Aside from the economic and social arguments pro and con
with reference to decentralization of industry, it is contended that
there is an important place in our national economy for this new
frontier which is just as definitely a frontier as was the country
west of the Alleghenies after the American Revolution. This
frontier contemplates a new type of life which has not been widely
recognized in America, a type of life which is somewhat similar to
European village life.

If we are to move in this direction, we have a wide frontier
ahead of us because the automobile, cheap electricity, rapid
communication of various types, now make possible a new type of
community in which the industries can be in the center, and the
families, instead of living on town lots, can live on plots of land in

subsistence homesteads for ten or fifteen miles in every direction.

This new pattern of life, therefore, is a sort of village life, but more than this it may develop the handicrafts and skills of which we have but little in this country. I am convinced that there are opportunities for hand-weaving, for wood-working, and much handicraft production in the United States provided it can be organized in some guild-like manner. This is the kind of production in which the worker can express his individuality. There is no doubt a market for the handicraft goods alongside the same kind of goods made by the most efficient machine scale organization. Subsistence homestead communities can be a sort of new synthesis of present day ideals and aspirations for community life. A survey of the magazines and periodicals of fifty years ago indicates a yearning for horseless carriages and rapid means of communication and for many things now common-place in national life.

The yearning now among wide classes of people is for security, for wholesome recreation, for constructive use of leisure time, and for things which seem to be best typified by what might be called the community idea. This represents a revolt against the crass materialism and the shallowness of the Jazz Age. It really amounts to a new community synthesis of employment of work, of education, of recreation and other factors which go into the better living to which we all aspire, in keeping with generally accepted ideas, many of which are very difficult to develop in our present industrial or agricultural organization.

This new pattern of life, of course, would not increase agricultural production. I doubt if it would have scarcely any effect on the staples which are the result of commercial agriculture. It might somewhat reduce the consumption power of commercially produced vegetables, poultry, etc., but it is doubtful if any movement of this kind would grow faster than the natural adjustment of producers in the fields which would be effected.

Whether or not we are getting ready to embark upon a national enterprise of building subsistence homestead communities is yet to be determined. Present legislation provides only a fund sufficient for test, experiment and demonstration. There is much evidence of a deep-seated national demand for suburban types of houses and for the subsistence homestead communities. If we are to move in this direction, it will require a coordinated and cooperative type of leadership and service which can be given by the colleges of agriculture, the specialists in the various fields of education, recreation, housing sanitation, community planning, etc. . . .

Farm Security Administration, courtesy of the Library of Congress

Ida Valley Farms, Shenandoah Homesteads, 1941, Luray, Virginia.

What is the place of this new pattern of life in our future national economy? This question is more in the field of speculation rather than exposition and description. Such national drifts largely fall in the category of "philosophies of civilization." The contrast between the opposing philosophies of pessimism and conditioned optimism was never greater than at present. The pessimists look upon subsistence homesteads as a retreat from the age of machinery and science and as the type of adjustment which will give security but not neccessarily raise the standard of living. On the other hand, the group, which I choose to call the conditioned optimists, looks upon subsistence homesteads as a part of a new and higher standard of living, as an adjustment to the age of science and the machine which does not in the least detract from all of the efficiencies of technology and its flow of goods, and by which we can restore security, opportunity for constructive use of leisure time opportunities of a social value to be developed in education, in art, in recreation and kindred fields. The conditioned optimists, therefore, regard it as a natural, sensible adjustment which restores to the machine age many of the values which were lost in the Jazz Age. From the economic standpoint, if we are to be gripped in economic nationalism, then our unemployment will probably be of long standing and some such type of social adjustment must take place.

Friends of the subsistence homestead idea are very skeptical if this new pattern of life can develop without a great deal of social control and without the cooperative team work of the whole group of leaders in the social sciences. The new frontier offers a challenge to agricultural economists as much of the subject matter of the zone is involved in agricultural economy. People in the field of agriculture can make a great contribution to its evolution and development. It should be approached by what Rex Tugwell several years ago called an experimental technique. The subsistence homestead community should not be over-sold as a panacea nor a utopia. Let us hope that it will offer in the future to a great group of people who seem to be stranded in the present industrial city or on hopeless submarginal land, the opportunity to have dignified, wholesome and well-rounded, abundant lives.

Milburn L. Wilson, "The Place of Subsistence Homesteads in Our National Economy," Speech delivered to the American Farm Association, Philadelphia, December 27, 1933.

PROGRESS AND CHANGE
E. B. White

In resenting progress and change, a man lays himself open to censure. . . . People who favor progress and improvements are apt to be people who have had a tough enough time without any extra inconvenience. Reactionaries who pout at innovations are apt to be well-heeled sentimentalists who had the breaks. Yet for all that, there is always a subtle danger in life's refinements, a dim degeneracy in progress. I have just been refining the room in which I sit, yet I sometimes doubt that a writer should refine or improve his workroom by so much as a dictionary: one thing leads to another and the first thing you know he has a stuffed chair and is fast asleep in it. Half a man's life is devoted to what he calls improvements, yet the original had some quality which is lost in the process. There was a fine natural spring of water on this place when I bought it. Our drinking water had to be lugged in a pail, from a wet glade of alder and tamarack. I visited the spring often in those first years, and had friends there—a frog, a woodcock, and an eel which had churned its way all the way up through the pasture creek to enjoy the luxury of pure water. In the normal course of development, the spring was rocked up, fitted with a concrete curb, a copper pipe, and an electric pump. I have visited it only once or twice since. This year my only gesture was the purely perfunctory one of sending a sample to the state bureau of health for analysis. I felt cheap, as though I were smelling an old friend's breath.

E. B. White, "Progress and Change," in *One Man's Meat* (New York: Harper Brothers, 1944), p. 35.

Free America

Herbert Agar

The collapse of the government-sponsored homesteading program was a great disappointment to those agrarian idealists who shared its objectives. During the 1930s the crisis of the Depression had brought together a coalition of groups advocating what they called distributism or decentralism. They included the Nashville Agrarians, Ralph Borsodi and his followers, the Catholic Rural Life movement, which sought to revitalize rural life and thereby revitalize spiritual and family values, and the consumer cooperative movement, led by Bertram Fowler, who saw in cooperation the means of enhancing mutualism and diminishing the competitive and enslaving effects of the consumer culture. These groups initially supported the New Deal's efforts to revive Jeffersonian values, but by 1937 they had decided that private initiatives were necessary. Government, despite its good intentions, nevertheless tended to promote greater centralization and less freedom. These neo-Jeffersonians wanted to help generate a modern version of republican simplicity that would ensure maximum individual property ownership and initiative. To help do so they founded a journal in 1937 called *Free America*. It was edited by the prominent journalist and historian, Herbert Agar (1897–1980). For the next ten years *Free America* served as a vital organ of decentralist simplicity.

For those concerned with the continuing appeal of this kind of modern version of Jeffersonian simplicity and self-reliance, the pages of *Free America* provide a necessary starting point. For ten years, spanning part of the Great Depression and World War II, *Free America* united home-steaders, cooperativists, and decentralists into a coherent movement. Its contents included philosophical essays and "how-to" articles. But its message clashed with the expectations of most middle-class Americans. While they might admire nostalgically the political independence and economic self-sufficiency of their ancestors, few were willing to abandon the consumer culture—even during the Depression. The prevailing American dream of the 1930s and 1940s—and since—was a return to full employment and carefree consumption.

In his first editorials Agar outlined the background and principles of the "distributist" or decentralist movement.

Free America hopes to express the reborn desire of our people to save democracy. During the past few years groups of citizens have sought to go to the root of the modern failure of democracy. The period of reform (when we tried to save democracy by adopting the short ballot and the direct primary) is giving way to a more revolutionary period. We are beginning to see that democracy presupposes a certain quality of life, a certain set of values, and that democratic institutions are of no importance unless they are used by people who cherish these values.

The first step in the new defense of democracy is to understand what democracy means, not in terms of a set of laws but in terms of a set of principles. The second step, when we are clear in our minds, will be to insist that society be organized in such a way as to support these principles.

The various groups which have been trying to face our basic problem have for the most part been working in isolation. Each was confident of being on the right track, but unhopeful of gaining a hearing for ideas that seemed to go against the current of the day. Lately, the isolated groups have begun to recognize that they are not so isolated as they seemed, that they stand for a set of ideas which make a wide appeal to Americans. Out of that recognition has come an attempt to form a loose alliance for our common war. Out of that alliance has come *Free America*. . . .

The reason for insisting on a wide distribution of property has been put as briefly as possible by John Adams, one of the makers of America. The maxim of politics, said Adams, is that power follows property. If, therefore, we want a nation in which power is widespread (a self-governing Republic, for example), we must see to it that property is widespread. . . .

Democracy (as a hope and as a half-realized fact) came into our world with the growth of widespread ownership. Wherever democracy has weakened in the modern world, the property-system has weakened first.

In America we have seen widespread property give way to concentrated control in private hands. And we have seen democracy give way to the plutocracy against which our people are now in revolt.

There may be many methods of recreating, in terms of modern society, the moral and economic benefits of a property-system. The Co-operatives, for example, offer a method of which our forefathers knew nothing. *Free America* is not dogmatic about methods. It is founded, in fact, in order to promote the search for the most useful methods. But it is dogmatic in the statement that those moral and economic benefits must be restored. For without them there can be no democracy. . . .

We do not pretend that *Free America* is prepared to offer a blueprint for the revolution that is needed if American democracy is to endure. We do pretend to know the principles on which a democratic society must be built. And we do intend to push forward with the task of discovering how those principles must be applied, and to insist that it is the duty of statesmanship to adapt our economic and political and social institutions to the American ideal rather than sacrifice that ideal to the economic flux. On that point, at least, we dare to be intransigent. . . .

. . . .

It is likely that a disproportionate part of the discussion in *Free America* will stress the economic and political rather than the moral aspect of distributism. This is because there are points in the economic and political phases of the doctrine which are controversial, whereas its moral basis is self-evident. In each of the three roots of the modern phase of the movement in this country—the Catholic Agrarian Movement, the Borsodi Homestead Movement, and the Southern Agrarian Movement—the original impulse was moral and spiritual. Each represented a revolt against materialism, both in thought and practice, and a reassertion of the belief that spiritual motivation was ultimately

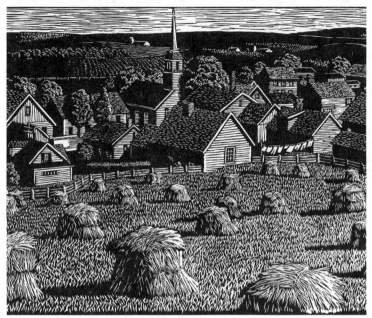

Leroy Sauer, *Small Town*, 1943.

stronger in man than economic motivation. At the outset the leaders of at least one of these movements believed themselves to be preaching a doctrine of inefficiency, and they were ridiculed accordingly. In the last four or five years research and the newer mechanics have shown them that they are in fact preaching a doctrine whose application is more efficient, more economical, than that of collectivism over most of the fields of human activity. The distributist argument, accordingly, now talks clothed in economic and mechanical arguments. But the core and axiom of it is still the moral and spiritual importance of the individual.

In outline, then, the distributist argument now proceeds through the three following propositions, in this order:

1. The moral proposition that the purpose of humanity is the realization of the free and responsibile individual human being. (This distinguished from the totalitarian assumption that the purpose of humanity is the perfect hive or state.)

2. The economic proposition that the individual can remain free and responsible only when he is secured against want, and that he

is best secured against want by the effective ownership of so much of the means of production as will enable him, with reasonable industry, to supply his own needs. (This distinguished from the collectivist assumption that the individual is best secured against want as a participant in the collective ownership of the means of production by all the citizens.)

3. The political proposition that the individual can remain morally free and responsible and economically secure in the ownership of his share in the means of production only if he also has a share in the determination of the policies of his government—democracy. (This distinguished from the centralist assumption that the individual can be secured against want and so in spiritual independence only when regimented under some kind of absolute dictatorship.)

. . . .

We like life in the country, plus all modern conveniences, and we want everybody who is anxious to lead that good life to be able to do so, whether he is a farmer, a railroad conductor, a jeweler, a lawyer, a miner, or a worker in a pin factory. . . . All we ask is that he and his family be secured in the ownership of so much of the means of production—we are here talking about land, the best of all means—as will insure them, with moderate industry, plenty of food, shelter, and clothing in no matter how severe an emergency. This, to begin with, will give them a chance to be healthy, responsible citizens, alive physically, mentally, morally, and spiritually. As part of this we should like them to enjoy such sentimental advantages as the possession of a cow or a couple of goats, the sight of a few real trees and hills and a real sky, a proximity to neighbors averaging perhaps a hundred yards instead of a hundred inches, and a necessary interest in community life as carried on by free human beings. We assume without argument that they will be within one to twenty miles of the best possible educational advantages, theatres, music auditoriums, museums, athletic fields, playgrounds, zoos, and the other advantages of present city life, to be reached by bus, subway, or private motor as quickly as they can now be reached in New York. Agronomy?— horrible word, isn't it?—worse, if that is possible, than "distributism." But on some of these heavy, awkward words it may yet be possible to build a civilization.

Herbert Agar, "Free America," *Free America* 1 (January 1937):1-2, 14-15; 1 (March 1937):3; 1 (June 1937):4-5.

Catholic Simplicity

Peter Maurin

One of the leading spokesmen for the Catholic Rural Life
Movement during the 1930s was Peter Maurin. A Catholic
John Woolman, Maurin migrated to America from France
in the 1920s. A determined social activist, he collaborated
with Dorothy Day in founding *The Catholic Worker*
newspaper in New York City in 1933. They promoted
hospitality houses for the poor and homeless as well as
round-table discussions of social and religious issues. But
one of Maurin's most persistent editorial messages was the
need for Catholics to promote a "green revolution," a
return to the land and to the organic sense of community
and faith that was their medieval heritage. Through
homesteading, truck farming, and crafts, people would
renew their sense of vocational pride and self-reliance. The
sense of alienation and uprootedness that characterized the
urban and rural proletariat would thereby be alleviated. In
the midwest Fathers Luigi Ligutti and John C. Rawe put
into practice this Catholic rural ideal. They helped organize
a successful homestead community under the auspices of
the Divison for Subsistence Homesteads. But they realized
with Maurin that any widespread back-to-the-land movement must ultimately result from private rather than
public initiatives. So they contributed to *Free America* in
the hope of stimulating a grassroots Catholic commitment
to renewed rural living.

BETTER AND BETTER OFF

The world would be better off
if people tried to become better.
And people would become better
if they stopped trying to become better off.

For when everybody tries to become better off,
nobody is better off.
But when everybody tries to become better,
everybody is better off.
Everybody would be rich
if nobody tried to become richer.
And nobody would be poor
if everybody tried to be the poorest.
And everybody would be what he ought
   to be
if everybody tried to be
what he wants the other fellow to be.

Christianity has nothing to do
with either modern capitalism
or modern Communism,
for Christianity has
a capitalism of its own
and a communism of its own.
Modern capitalism is based on property
   without responsibility,
while Christian capitalism
is based on property with responsibility.
Modern Communism
is based on poverty through force
while Christian communism
is based on poverty through choice.
For a Christian, voluntary poverty is
   the ideal
as exemplified by St. Francis of Assisi,
while private property
is not an absolute right, but a gift
which as such can not be wasted,
but must be administered
for the benefit of God's children.

ECONOMIC ECONOMY

In the Middle Ages
they had a doctrine,
the doctrine
of the Common Good.
In the Middle Ages
they had an economy
which was economical.
Their economy
was based on the idea
that God wants us
to be our brothers' keepers.
They believed
in the right to work
for the worker.
They believed
in being fair
to the worker
as well as the consumer.
They believed
in doing their work
the best they knew how
for the service
of God and men.

CULTIVATION

(inspired by Herbert Agar)

. . . Two rooms and kitchenette
is not the right place
for the home.

The right place for the home
is a homestead.

Peter Maurin, *Easy Essays* (Academy Guild Press, 1961), pp. 37–39,
132–33; Marc Ellis, *Peter Maurin: Prophet in the Twentieth Century*
(New York: Paulist Press, 1981), p. 129.

Simplicity for Urbanites
Lewis Mumford

Though *Free America* focused on the need to generate a
back-to-the-land movement and thereby encourage more
widespread ownership of property and greater self-reliance,
some of its supporters stressed the need to revitalize urban
life. Lewis Mumford, the distinguished cultural historian,
social philosopher, and urban planner, pointed out in a
letter to the editors of *Free America* that most Americans
could not voluntarily take up self-sustaining homesteading.
He therefore called for an equal emphasis on imaginative
city planning. Mumford had earlier been involved with the
development of a planned "garden city" at Radburn, New
Jersey, and during the 1930s he supported the Resettlement Administration's efforts to construct new planned
"greenbelt communities." Such communities, Mumford
persuasively argued, offered an alternative to the city-
country dichotomy that had for so long shaped the outlook
of those promoting the simple life. Life in such planned
communities would be an ideal combination of the best of
city and country living. People would enjoy a genuine sense
of organic community life. Greenbelt communities would
offer a richly integrated and cooperative social experience
stressing rewarding relationships among people, enriching
contact with nature, meaningful work experiences, and
creative leisure.

TO THE EDITORS:

I seriously think that it is a fundamental mistake to make the
notion of domestic production and partial industrial and

agricultural self-sufficiency the only possible pattern for future economic change or for urban planning. Unlike those who see the whole problem of the present situation from the metropolitan angle, I do not deny either the possibility or the use of such a mode of living: so far from denying it, I have followed it for three years, at least to the extent of running a garden that keeps us provided with vegetables the better part of the year, from June to the end of November, and even, by canning and preserving, through part of the winter months. But it does not seem to me that this pattern of life is necessarily the only valid one; indeed, my own needs and those of my family are now sending me back to New York again for the winter months; and though I value the balance that rural occupations give, and I believe that they must be worked into all city living, it seems to me that the sort of integration that has been achieved in Radburn and Greenbelt is also worth working for. I think there is a temptation to criticize the government projects a little too easily simply because they are governmentally sponsored and collectively organized, because you regard the individual holding of property an ideal or at least highly creditable mold: but on that point I can't agree with you; for your aim does not seem to me to apply to all the needs and opportunities of modern civilization.

In other words you have a far greater bias against collective undertakings than I have against your individualist program. Even under the most socialized system of production I would grant the partial validity of your scheme, provided that it didn't carry with it the right to exploit the labors of others: but you are inclined to say the absolute No against anything that rivals the household economy you think most valuable. I don't think the apartment is or can be the only type of urban home; but I would not rule it out altogether, as you appear to do—forgetting the existence of bachelors, of childless people, of people who have entered old age, and again of those whose work may temporarily sequester them from active participation in rural industry and rural life.

It is because I accept so much of your intuitions about the central importance of country living, because we join together at so many points in a program of decentralization, that I regret the one-sided and therefore, in appearance, fanatical emphasis that *Free America* gives to its proposals. It is high time that the balance was restored between city and country; it is high time that we nurtured people at home in both territories, people capable of living balanced lives; it is high time, too, that places like Radburn and Greenbelt overcame the unconscious suburban bias that has vitiated their design, or kept it at least from being as rigorous as it should be. . . . But all this does not mean that collective planning and government aid are inevitably uneconomic or that they are to be disparaged because they go along another line than your own.

I have put forward my criticisms without reserve because I feel that this kind of honesty is essential between men of good will whose differences are all of a rational and discussable nature, and therefore need not be approached in the timid, gingerly fashion that is common among those less sure of their own feelings or those of their opponents.

Lewis Mumford

Lewis Mumford, Letter to the Editors, *Free America* 3 (October 1938):16.

Greenbelt Simplicity

As Lewis Mumford indicated, the "greenbelt" or "garden" cities proposed by the New Deal were intended to bridge the gap between city and country living. Rexford Tugwell, head of the Resettlement Administration, announced in 1936 a grandiose plan to construct a network of 3000 federally-financed and -designed greenbelt communities. As the following early promotional pamphlet indicates, the greenbelt program was intended to be much more than simply a public housing project. Like Milburn Wilson and other idealistic New Dealers, Tugwell hoped to reverse the demographic and sociological trends of the previous hundred years and in the process help solve the chronic problem of urban unemployment and over-crowdedness.

The greenbelt cities would combine the best features of town and country, farm and factory, and thereby establish a habitat in equilibrium with nature and civilization. Such communities would be limited in both spatial and population size, surrounded by a greenbelt of farmland and forests, and interspersed with human-scale manufacturing enterprises designed to provide satisfying work and a basic sufficiency for the community, thus differentiating them from traditional suburbs. Common greens, open courtyards, bicycle and pedestrian paths, playgrounds and parks, trees and gardens, would all help naturalize the townscape, as well as help overcome the alienation endemic to city living. The greenbelt idea would also improve the life of farmers by bringing markets closer to them as well as making available new social and cultural opportunities.

It was a tantalizing scheme. But Tugwell's reach exceeded his grasp—and his budget. By 1937 only three greenbelt cities were under construction—Greenbelt, Maryland; Greenhills, Ohio; and Greendale, Wisconsin. Although these experiments in planned community living attracted international attention and acclaim, many Americans criticized them as being socialistic and expensive. By the late 1930s, as the nation began to prepare itself for a possible war, appropriations for the greenbelt program were sharply reduced. The first three communities were thus the last three constructed—and even they were never completed according to the original plans.

The Suburban Resettlement Division of the Resettlement Administration is engaged in building several rural-industrial communities on the outskirts of badly crowded cities. These projects are intended to give permanent, valuable assets to the Nation in return for money spent on relief. Eventually each town will provide low-rental homes for 3,000 to 5,000 families, although only from 750 to 1,300 dwellings will be constructed at first.

In the strictest sense, the Resettlement Administration is not in the housing field at all. True enough, it is building houses, but its considerations go beyond that fact—important as that fact is—that millions of Americans need new homes if a minimum standard of decency is to be attained. What the Resettlement Administration is trying to do is to put houses and land and people together in such a way that the props under our economic and social structure will be permanently strengthened.

That is, of course, a huge task, but the RA is beginning modestly. Its suburban projects are being carried out only on a demonstration basis and are few in number. Yet if these communities are successful, they should prove invaluable as examples to local governments and private industry, and have a profound effect on the future.

TESTED BY EXPERIENCE

The fact is that nearly all of the principles upon which these communities are founded have already been tested and found worthy. The idea of the greenbelt town was first worked out in 1898 by a young Englishman, Ebenezer Howard, one of the pioneers of modern city planning. He pictured a union of city and country life in which every foot of land was planned to eliminate waste and to provide its inhabitants with pleasant and spacious living. Towns built to his model—such as Welwyn and Letchworth—have been operating successfully in England for the last twenty years. His ideas have had a deep influence on the better housing projects of Sweden, Holland, and Germany. The development of similar communities to house American families with modest incomes was urgently recommended in 1931 by the President's Conference on Home Building and Home Ownership. Many of Howard's principles have been partially carried out in Radburn, N.J., America's first scientifically planned garden town.

The significance of a greenbelt town extends far beyond its own boundaries. Every growing metropolis should—if it is wisely planned—develop a chain of similar suburban communities around its borders. They would offer an opportunity for orderly, efficient expansion. Their greenbelts, linked together, would form continuous permanent open spaces around the city, protecting it and each suburb from overcrowding and sprawling, haphazard suburban developments and encroaching industries.

BLENDING TOWN AND COUNTRY

The new communities will be "greenbelt" towns, so-called because each of them will be surrounded by a broad girdle of park and farm land. A greenbelt town is simply a community built on raw land, in which every acre is put to its best use, and in which the traditional dividing lines between town and country are broken down. To the city worker, it offers a home in healthful country surroundings, yet within easy reach of his job. To the small farmer living in the greenbelt area, it offers better facilities and a steady market within a few hundred yards of his own fields. For both of them, it combines the conveniences and cultural opportunities of a city with many advantages of life on the land. Such a union of town and country has been made possible by technology, transportation improvements, and a host of other factors. We need only to make use of the tools which are lying at our hand.

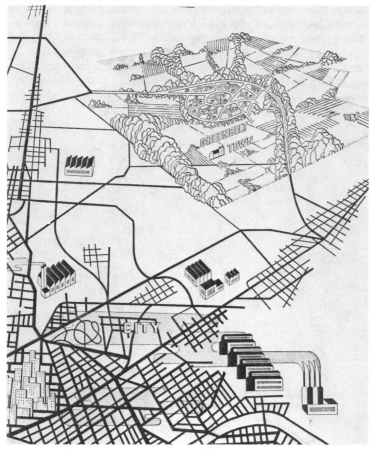

A Resettlement Administration drawing of an idyllic "Greenbelt Town" contrasted with the unplanned sprawl of a city.

THE GREENBELT

Within such a site every acre is assigned to its own place and function in an expertly designed plan. Around the town's edge is the greenbelt, the distinctive feature of all the RA's suburban communities. The girdle of permanent open space is intended to protect the town forever from overcrowding and undesirable building on neighboring land. In addition, it offers special opportunities for both recreation and gardening. Part of the area is reserved for parks and playgrounds. Other tracts are set aside as gardens, for families which wish to supplement their incomes by raising their own fruit and vegetables. Still other sections are allotted to full-time farmers, who can bring their produce to market simply by crossing their own fields. All the sites have ample land for the future expansion and growth of the community.

Resettlement Administration, *The Greenbelt Community* (Washington, D.C.: Government Printing Office, 1936), pp. 1–5.

Simplicity Amid Abundance

8

During the quarter century after the end of World War II, the corporate and consumer cultures dominated the contours of American domestic life, and the utopian efforts of the New Dealers to create a government-sponsored revival of republican simplicity came to a grinding halt. Economists, government officials, marketing specialists, and advertisers repeatedly stressed that the nation's well-being required that the public abandon traditional notions of frugality and embrace a regimen of rising expectations and continuous consumption. As President Eisenhower pleaded during a press conference in the mid-1950s, "Buy anything."

This sanctification of an undiscriminating consumerism reflected the unprecedented abundance of the era. The material standard of living rose dramatically, leisure time increased, and cultural opportunities were enhanced. But affluence brought heightened anxieties as well. Social critics such as Lewis Mumford and Joseph Wood Krutch argued that a good society could not be defined primarily by the quantity of its goods or by the height of its skyscrapers. Despite money's real benefits in broadening one's opportunities for self culture, it too often was addictive and debasing. Compulsive getting and spending was imposing severe psychological strains. The increasing domination of huge corporations made many jobs seem less fulfilling. Relationships grew more impersonal and bureaucratic, and work itself seemed more hurried and unsatisfying. Employees increasingly yearned for the weekends when they could again enjoy life. Indeed, the incidence of stress, anxiety, and depression in America tended to rise with the level of affluence.

Such unsettling developments, however, were largely ignored during the good times of the Eisenhower and Kennedy years. But beginning around 1965 the country was jolted by a series of shocks—racial violence, antiwar protests, and the youth revolt. By the late 1960s observers were describing the emergence of a "counter culture," a small but highly visible group of young Americans who explicitly rejected the values of corporate and suburban life. Usually from middle-class backgrounds, these so-called "hippies" sharply criticized the nervous materialism and social conservatism of their elders and sought to develop instead their own autonomous existence in a transcendent world of drugs, love, and community.

There were many motives activating these radical new transcendentalists. Some were adolescent and self-serving in their rebelliousness, others were profoundly sincere. Like earlier romantics, the hippies called for a new sensibility that would affirm the mystical and intuitive aspects of life and reject the bourgeois preoccupations of the age. A pervasive emphasis among those associated with the counter culture was the desire to move beyond the treadmill of the consumer culture and create a simpler way of life that would prize human relationships, sensual freedom, individual introspection, and spontaneous joy. In search of such a liberated life, many of these flower children flocked to congenial urban neighborhoods such as the Haight-Ashbury district in San Francisco. Others preferred rural living on homesteads or in communal settlements with colorful names such as Morningstar, Drop City, Dawn, and Hog Farm.

Though many were blissfully unaware of the past, these youthful rural settlers were linked to a rich tradition of back-to-nature simplicity. The West Coast poet Gary Snyder alerted the alienated young to the mystical simplicity so prevalent in Oriental religion and primitive cultures. Others found in Thoreau a congenial model for the good life, and *Walden* was a common reference work in many hippie communities. Equally influential was *Living the Good Life*, by Scott and Helen Nearing, the prominent socialist homesteaders. But unlike these successful practitioners of rural self-reliance, many of the young rebels were woefully unprepared for the requirements of living on the land.

Indeed, most hippie settlements in the countryside, like Brook Farm and Fruitlands before them, lasted only a few months or years at most. Many of the transcendental pioneers rejected the compulsive consumerism of their parents only to replace it with a sensory hedonism promoted by such tie-dyed philosophers as Timothy Leary and Charles Reich. They and other self-appointed "gurus" of the counter culture denigrated hard work and celebrated sexual promiscuity and the use of mind-altering drugs. This was a fatal prescription for those trying to survive in crowded urban settlements or in the countryside. Initially determined to separate themselves from a corrupt capitalist society, many of them were soon utterly dependent on that society for their existence. As their experiments in alternative ways of living failed, they lined up at government offices in order to collect welfare checks, food stamps, and unemployment compensation. The few communes such as The Farm in Tennessee and Twin Oaks in Virginia that survived did so because they had charismatic leadership, adopted strict regulations, and recognized the need for organized work and individual self restraint.

The naivete and eccentricity of many of the hippies make them easy targets for caricature. The counter culture did attract its share of zanies and crazies. But highlighting the excesses of the movement does an injustice to the problems they were confronting and the ideals they were espousing. Though strewn with comic aspects, their efforts to develop a way of life that transcended conventional materialism represented a profound statement about the superficiality of the much-heralded postwar American way of life. The actions of the youth culture provoked both outrage and reflection, and in the process helped transform the cultural agenda.

Thoreau on Madison Avenue

Joseph Wood Krutch

Joseph Wood Krutch (1893–1970), writer, editor, naturalist, and conservationist, was an eloquent analyst of the tension between modern technology and the spiritual and physical environment. He was also an impassioned defender of simplicity as an elevating way of life. "If you drive a car at seventy miles an hour," he once wrote, "you can't reflect or think about anything, you can't do anything but keep the monster under control. I'm afraid this is the metaphor of our society as a whole." Krutch published an excellent biography of Thoreau in 1948, and his enthusiasm for the enduring wisdom of his subject was infectious. In 1955 Krutch read an account of an advertising conference which provoked him to write the following imaginary interview.

Not long ago the shade of Henry David Thoreau visited me at midnight, as it occasionally does. As usual I broke the silence, but our conversation seems to me worth reporting.

ME: Well, Henry, this is an important day for you.

HENRY: I never knew a day that wasn't.

ME: The same old Henry, I see. I really should have anticipated that one. But I had something less transcendental in mind. I mean that it was just one hundred years ago that *Walden* was published.

HENRY: It was also just a hundred years ago today that I met in a bean field the plumpest woodchuck I ever saw. I didn't eat him, but I thought to myself that if I did eat meat I would want it to be some such savage meat as that.

ME (Dryly): I have read your *Journal*. But you were a writer after all. You did hope for some readers—for rather more than it seemed likely you would ever get. How do you like being the author of an accepted classic?

HENRY: A classic is a work which everyone acknowledges the obligation to read and nobody thinks it necessary to take seriously. The New Testament is generally regarded as the most indispensable of classics. It is read every Sunday in churches and, occasionally, even in private. But if it were once actually heard by any congregation not a stone would be left standing of that church—or of any other.

ME: Oh! Come, come. It is generally admitted that your influence has been tremendous. Your writings are said to have been accepted as Bibles by many modern reformers, including the founders of the British Labor Party.

HENRY: And I have just reminded you how much influence Bibles really have. Where today are men any less exclusively concerned with getting and spending? What else does what they call "a higher standard of living" amount to? What necessities of the soul that money can't buy are they trying to attain? Where have they learned that what mankind needs to know is not how to be rich, but how to live well in poverty?

ME: Perhaps all that will come in time. One must begin somewhere.

HENRY: What I do know is that one must not begin at the wrong end. One should put first things first.

ME: What is the right end? Where should they begin?

HENRY: Simplify. Simplify. Wise individuals have done that from time to time. But what society has ever voluntarily taken one step in that direction? More things for more people is the noblest ideal any modern reformer has ever been able to think of. He supposes the curse will no longer be a curse if only everybody is cursed with it. But that is not what is implied in *Walden*—or in a much older book. Who can truly say that he was ever "influenced" by either my life or my writings if he still believes that the need of mankind is for still more things? In my day the mass of men led lives of quiet desperation. The lives of such men are less quiet in 1954, but they are no less desperate. And this is what you call Progress. The mud-turtles in Massachusetts have not changed. But they are no worse than they were when I admired them for their persistence in the ways that mud-turtles had found best for their kind. Would I could say the same for those men who are now said to live in New England.

ME: But, Henry, our society could not possibly simplify—even if it wanted to, which it certainly doesn't. That agricultural economy which was one of the few things in Concord village you approved of could not serve the needs of one-third the population of the United States—to say nothing of those in distant parts who now depend upon us for so many things. Not all the machines yet invented are more than barely sufficient to keep abreast of the needs of a constantly growing population.

HENRY: And neither will all those you may manage to invent

in the future do more. It is for want of a Man that there are so many men.

ME: You can hardly be serious. You are extravagant.

HENRY: It is because I am serious that I always try, in vain, to be extravagant. No extravagance can be adequate to the plight of man. His potentialities are so great that no one can imagine them; his actuality is something that makes angels weep and sent even me to mud-turtles and woodchucks for fellowship. How can such facts be moderately stated?

ME: It is not your judgment upon us that I question so much as the practicality of your proposals for improving our condition. Do you think that letting most men die of want would produce a Man? Do you hold even ordinary lives that cheap?

HENRY: Not so cheap as your world holds them. Does not that world show plainly enough that it regards them as freely expendable? Has it not improved the methods of mass destruction even more spectacularly than it has improved the methods of agriculture? Does it not act as though it had come finally to the conclusion that it is simpler to slaughter populations than it is to feed them?

ME: Perhaps, perhaps. At least it is a platitude to say so.

HENRY: That honesty is the best policy is a platitude also. And none the worse for that.

ME: I suppose so. But I still don't see how we could possibly simplify. It has become too difficult. We have gone too far.

HENRY: It will not get any easier. Is having gone too far a good reason for going further? Or is that an act of desperation? It is not the part of wisdom to do desperate things.

ME: Not all men today feel desperate or even pessimistic. The future looks very bright to some. Only the other day some representative of a highly optimistic group sent me through the mail a whole sheaf of optimistic pronouncements by a very successful citizen.

HENRY: And in what calling or profession was this optimist so highly successful?

ME: Advertising.

HENRY: Indeed. And what Gospel, what Good News, does he bring us? I can hardly imagine that he is a prophet of simplicity. Or is it some necessities of the soul that he is advertising just now?

ME: No—not exactly. Or perhaps I had better say not at all. In fact, I don't think he would agree with any of your premises or your proposals. He sees the future as bright chiefly because men in his profession have learned how to persuade people to want more

George Tooker, *The Subway.*

and more things—even things they would never have dreamed of wanting before.

HENRY: And he thinks that will make them happier?

ME: I am afraid, Henry, that you do not understand the modern world. You see . . .

HENRY: Are you so sure that it understands itself? But go on.

ME: Thank you. The truth of the matter is that in your day nobody understood the role played in a modern economy by Consumption as the underlying cause of Prosperity. As a matter of fact, in your world it did not play this role. At that time it was not yet possible to produce enough to meet the needs of your fellow citizens. Therefore, it was a virtue in the individual to use no more of anything than he needed and not to think that he needed anything he did not. But technology has changed all that. If everybody did not demand that Higher Standard of Living which advertising has taught us all to insist upon, we should soon plunge into the deepest Depression our world has ever known. To supply it with only what you would call necessities would not keep one-tenth of the workers busy half the time. To use up what they are making in increasing quantities is a necessity which even the advertising man finds it difficult to persuade us to meet. The first duty of a Good Citizen in our republic is to be a Good Consumer. Sometimes we call a man who doesn't vote a bad citizen. But society can get along passably well even if a third of the people don't vote; but if a third of them stopped buying what you call superfluities catastrophe would be upon us. Simplify indeed! To a modern economist it is perfectly evident that unless we keep on complicating more and more exuberantly the whole of our world will come tumbling down.

HENRY: What I call Economy I understand well enough. It means the way in which men get a living, how they are fed and clothed and sheltered. But when you change Economy to Economics—another one of those modern words with a paralysis in its tail—it seems to be a very different matter. Somehow the right of men to food and clothing has got itself transformed into their duty to use up as much food and clothing as possible.

ME: That to begin with. But it is only a beginning. It is also their duty to buy hundreds of things never heard of in your day and then to buy new ones before the old have worn out. Only a society which operates on this principle can be healthy today.

HENRY: And does your very successful optimist say this in so many words? I should like very much to know what words he finds to say such things with.

ME: (Extracting from my pocket a report on some of the pronouncements made in Salt Lake City last June 27 at the Fifty-first Annual Convention of the Advertising Association of the West): Well, the most general statement was made by the director of advertising for a California public service corporation: "We of the advertising world are custodians of the indispensable key to the mass selling that must accompany production."

HENRY: The words are English but it doesn't sound like English to me. But please go on. There is nothing I ever valued more than getting new thoughts.

ME: I think a few sentences by the chairman of the board of a large New York advertising agency will make it all clearer. "Perhaps the most dynamic and unique contribution of American economy to the world is ... that in a society which emphasizes psychological obsolescence rather than the physical wearing out of products, we have helped to achieve the most productive economy in human history."

HENRY: Give me a moment to translate that. I understand that we are going to be told what America's greatest contribution to the world really is. But I am not sure that I understand what that emphasis on "psychological obsolescence" rather than "physical wearing" really means. Can it really mean what I think it does? Does it really mean that our most valuable contribution to the world is our method of persuading men to throw things away while they are still just as good as they ever were? And is this "most productive economy in human history" something to boast about principally because it provides us with things to throw away and could not produce so much unless we did throw them away?

ME: Well, if you want to put it that way. It means, for instance, that the ordinary housewife must buy another vacuum cleaner just to keep the production of vacuum cleaners at a high level. It also means that the better class of citizen must buy a new automobile every year because the changed chromium ornaments make it obvious that last year's model is "psychologically obsolescent."

HENRY: And you say that all this wasting is necessary to our prosperity? I should think it would keep everybody's nose to the grindstone a good deal more constantly than is necessary.

ME: But when you work hard to buy things you don't need and thereby keep other people working hard to make them we don't call that "keeping noses to the grindstone." We call it "maintaining employment at a high level." Let me go on. As the gentleman I have just been quoting goes on to say, advertising has been "a constructive and facilitative force. . . . By creating a psychological desire to own—as opposed to that of necessity—advertising has increased the number of jobs available; raised the standard of living by reducing selling costs; increased company profits as well as company security." By way of a gloss the editor of this report adds: "Of some 500 classified psychological wants only ninety-six are necessary. . . . New markets—newlyweds, the bumper crop of babies, etc.—are constantly developing. To tap these markets desires must be created. And advertising is the means." As you see, an annual bumper crop of babies is necessary because every newborn child is potentially a consumer—of what goods and what future, God only knows.

HENRY: And this gentleman is convinced that desires ought to be created and that "the psychological desire to own" should be fostered. Mankind is not yet sufficiently devoted to material things! Upon such treasures it should be encouraged to set more irrevocably its heart. . . . Does not anyone rebel against the trick that has been played upon them?

ME: A few individuals rebel. But I am not sure I admire them. They may be artists or thinkers or whatnot. But they are not good citizens. They are not Efficient Consumers. And in this age the efficient consumer is what we need most. We already make more of everything than we can really use up. Getting rid of the stuff is our problem.

HENRY: I see. I do indeed.

ME: And what, may I ask, do you intend to do about it?

HENRY: I don't need to do anything about it. Where I now

IN SEARCH OF THE SIMPLE LIFE

dwell there is no obsolescence, either physical or psychological. And the psychological desire to own seems to have been left somewhere behind by all those I have had occasion to talk with. But I know what I would do if I were alive in your world.

ME: Which is?

HENRY: I refused to live in the bustling nineteenth century. I said that I would stand, or sit, quietly while it passed by. I would refuse even more firmly to live in the still more bustling twentieth.

ME: You would not mind being called a bad citizen? You would refuse to contribute to Progress?

HENRY: I refused in my own day, and I was called a bad citizen for doing so. "Skulker" was, I think, the word Mr. Stevenson, the romancer and essayist, chose. But according to you I am a classic now.

ME: Would not a rebel be better advised if he worked instead for that better world in which leisure rather than a superfluity of goods had become the consequence of mechanization?

HENRY: I once knew a would-be poet who proposed to get rich so that he could devote his time to poetry. He should have gone up to the garret immediately.

ME: Really, Henry, you dodge the question. Why, if everybody . . .

HENRY: They won't.

Joseph Wood Krutch, *If You Don't Mind My Saying So* (New York: William Sloane, 1964), pp. 215–23.

DEATH OF A SALESMAN
Arthur Miller

BIFF: Well, I spent six or seven years after high school trying to work myself up. Shipping clerk, salesman, business of one kind or another. And it's a measly kind of existence. To get on that subway on the hot mornings in summer. To devote your whole life to keeping stock, or making phone calls, or selling or buying. To suffer fifty weeks of the year for the sake of a two-week vacation, when all you really desire is to be outdoors, with your shirt off. And always to get ahead of the next fella. And still—that's how you build a future. . . .

HAPPY: All I can do now is wait for the merchandise manager to die. And suppose I get to be the merchandise manager? He's a good friend of mine, and he just built a terrific estate on Long Island. And he lived there about two months and sold it, and now he's building another one. He can't enjoy it once it's finished. And I know that's just what I would do. I don't know what the hell I'm workin' for. Sometimes I sit in my apartment—all alone. And I think of the rent I'm paying. And it's crazy. But then, it's what I always wanted. My own apartment, a car, and plenty of women. And still, goddammit, I'm lonely.

Arthur Miller, *Death of a Salesman* (1949; New York: Viking, 1978), pp. 22, 23.

264

The Conduct of Life

Lewis Mumford

Lewis Mumford has been one of the twentieth century's sanest spokesmen for simpler living. A spiritual descendant of Emerson and Thoreau, he has persistently criticized what he once called a "blankness, a sterility, a boredom, a despair" generated by modern urban industrial life. In *The Conduct of Life* (1951) he stressed that to restore meaning to the American experience required neither liberalism nor socialism nor any other program that focused primarily on changing the external social structure. Instead it required a personal transformation initiated by the individual. He also stressed the danger of those opposed to any form of technology and critical of all aspects of modernity. These "Terrible Simplifiers" would be willing to use coercion to make people revert to more traditional ways of living. Instead of such extreme approaches, he argued, those caught up in the consumer culture should strip away superfluities, try to make work more satisfying and less stifling, concentrate on developing more sincere personal and familial relations, and strive to reach the difficult synthesis of practicality and spirituality, mechanism and humanism, that idealists had for so long prescribed as the truly simple life.

But we shall not achieve a more adequate philosophy merely by rejecting wholesale our present way of life or by reverting to some simpler archaic scheme of life and thought. It is not enough to say, as Rousseau once did, that one only has to reverse all the current practices to be right. The cure for our over-concentration on the outer world is not a recoil into an equally sterile and shut-off inner world; the alternative to blindly conquering nature is not to neglect nature entirely and focus wholly on man. If our new philosophy is to be well grounded we shall not merely react against the "air-conditioned nightmare" of our present culture; we shall also carry into the future many of the elements of positive good that this culture actually embraces—its sense of impersonal truths that lie beyond mere wishful thinking, its technique for collective verification, its capacity for directed thought; indeed, we shall transfer its sense of order from the too-limited realm of science to life at large. . . .

To escape the Terrible Simplifiers one must recognize the actual danger of the condition through which they obtain their ascendence over the frustrated majority: for the condition these charlatans profess to correct is in fact a serious one. Instead of closing our eyes to its existence, we must turn to art and reason to effect a benign simplification, which will give back authority to the human person. Life belongs to the free-living and mobile creatures, not to the encrusted ones; and to restore the initiative to life and participate in its renewal, we must counterbalance every fresh complexity, every mechanical refinement, every increase in quantitative goods or quantitative knowledge, every advance in manipulative technique, every threat of superabundance or surfeit, with stricter habits of evaluation, rejection, choice. To achieve the capacity we must consciously resist every kind of automatism: buy nothing merely because it is advertised, use no invention merely because it has been put on the market, follow no practice merely because it is fashionable. We must approach every part of our lives with the spirit in which Thoreau undertook his housekeeping at Walden Pond: be ready, like him, even to throw out a simple stone, if it proves too much trouble to dust. Otherwise, the sheer quantitative increase in the data of scientific knowledge will produce ignorance: and the constant increase in goods will produce a poverty of life. . . .

Many effective kinds of simplification will perhaps be resisted at first on the ground that this means a "lowering of standards." But this overlooks the fact that many of our standards are themselves extraneous and purposeless. What is lowered from the standpoint of mechanical complexity or social prestige may be raised from the standpoint of the vital function served, as when the offices of friendship themselves replace, as Emerson advocated in his essay on household economy, elaborate preparations of food and service, of napery and silver.

Consider the kind of frugal peasant living that Rousseau first advocated, when he chose to live in a simple cottage, instead of in the mansion of his patron, surrounded by "comforts": all this wipes away time-consuming rituals and costly temptations to indigestion. Or consider the gain in physical freedom modern woman made, when the corset and petticoats, the breast-deformers, pelvis-constrictors, backbone-curvers of the Victorian period gave way to the garb of the early 1920's, without girdle, brassiere, or even stocking supporters: a high point of freedom in clothes from which women sheepishly recoiled under the deft browbeating of manufacturers with something to sell.

Naturally the sort of simplification needed must itself conform to life-standards. Thoreau's over-simplification of his diet, for instance, probably undermined his constitution and gave encouragement to the tuberculosis from which he finally died. By now we know that a diet consisting of a single kind of food is not part of nature's economy: the amino acids appear to nourish the body only when various ones are present in different kinds of food: so that the lesson of life is not to confuse simplicity with monotony. So, too, a tap of running water, fed by gravity from a distant spring, is in the long run a far more simple device, judged by the total man-hours used in production and service, than the daily fetching of water in a bucket: as the bucket, in turn, is more simple than making even more frequent journeys to the spring to slake one's thirst directly. Simplicity does not avoid mechanical aids: it seeks only not to be victimized by them. That image should save us from the imbecile simplifiers, who reckon simplicity, not in terms of its total result on living, but in terms of immediate first costs or in a pious lack of visible apparatus.

Sporadically, during the last three centuries, many benign simplifications have in fact come to pass throughout Western civilization; though, as in the case of women's dress just noted, they have sometimes been followed by reactions that have left us as badly off as ever. Rousseau, coming after the Quakers, carried their simplification of manners through to diet, to child nurture, and to education; while Hahnemann began a similar change in medicine, a change followed through by Dr William Osler, under whom hundreds of spurious drugs and complicated prescriptions were discarded, in favor of the Hippocratic attention to diet and rest and natural restoratives. In handicraft and art and architecture the same general change was effected, first by William Morris, in his rule: "Possess nothing that you do not know to be useful or believe to be beautiful." Modern architecture, though it has often been distracted and perverted by technical over-elaboration, can justify its essential innovations as an attempt to simplify the background of living, so that the poorest member of our society will have as orderly and harmonious an environment as the richest: it has discarded complicated forms as a badge of class and conspicuous waste. Wherever the machine is intelligently adapted to human needs, it has the effect of simplifying the routine of life and releasing the human agent from slavish mechanical tasks. It is only where the person abdicates that mechanization presents a threat.

But in order to recover initiative for the person, we must go over our whole routine of life, as with a surgeon's knife, to eliminate every element of purposeless materialism, to cut every binding of too-neat red tape, to remove the fatty tissue that imposes extra burdens on our organs and slows down all our vital processes. Simplicity itself is not the aim of this effort: no, the purpose is to use simplicity to promote spontaneity and freedom, so that we may do justice to life's new occasions and singular moments. For what Ruskin said of the difference between a great painter, like Tintoretto, and a low painter, like Teniers, holds for every manifestation of life: the inferior painter, not recognizing the difference between high and low, between what is intensely moving and what is emotionally inert, gives every part of his painting the same refinement of finish, the same care of detail. The great painter, on the other hand, knows that life is too short to treat every part of it with equal care: so he concentrates on the passages of maximum significance and treats hastily, even contemptuously, the minor passages: his shortcuts and simplifications are an effort to give a better account of what matters. This reduction to essentials is the main art of life.

Withdrawal, detachment, simplification, reflection, liberation from automatism—these are all but preliminary steps in the rebuilding of the self and the renewal of the society of which we are a part. These initial acts may, and in fact must, be taken by each of us alone: but the purpose of our withdrawal, of our fasting and purgation, is to reawaken our appetite for life, to make us keen to discriminate between food and poison and ready to exercise choice. Once we have taken the preparatory steps, we must return to the group and re-unite ourselves with those who have been undergoing a like regeneration and are thereby capable of assuming responsibility and taking action. In relatively short order this fellowship may enfold men and women in every country, of every religious faith, of every cultural pattern.

Lewis Mumford, *The Conduct of Life* (New York: Harcourt Brace Jovanovich, 1951), pp. 17–18, 253, 270–74.

Why Tribe

Gary Snyder

Gary Snyder was an important inspiration, first to the Beat Generation of the 1950s and then to the counter culture of the 1960s. A mystical poet steeped in the study of Buddhism and Taoism, he found in Oriental religion and philosophy a reverence for nature and simplicity that complemented his own experience growing up on a struggling farm near Seattle during the Depression and then later working as a fire lookout in the cascades of the Pacific Northwest. "When I was young," he explained to an interviewer, "I had an immediate, intuitive deep sympathy with the natural world which was not taught me by anyone." Snyder also developed an intuitive resistance to mainstream American capitalism and its consumer culture. His grandfather had been an organizer for the Industrial Workers of the World (I.W.W.), and Snyder found great merit in that organization's motto—"forming a new society within the shell of the old"—because it stressed constructive rather than destructive social change.

Soon after graduating from Reed College in 1951 Snyder settled in San Francisco. There he spent four years enrolled in the Oriental language program at Berkeley. He also became good friends with Allen Ginsberg, Jack Kerouac, and the other Beats living in the Bay Area. In 1956 Snyder sailed for Japan, where for the next several years he studied Zen intensively and practiced meditation. These experiences among the Beats and the Oriental mystics led him to write the following prophetic essay describing the emergence of a new "tribal" sensibility in the West.

We use the term Tribe because it suggests the type of new society now emerging within the industrial nations. In America of course the word has associations with the American Indians, which we like. This new subculture is in fact more similar to that ancient and successful tribe, the European Gypsies—a group without nation or territory which maintains its own values, its language and religion, no matter what country it may be in.

The Tribe proposes a totally different style: based on community houses, villages and ashrams; tribe-run farms or workshops or companies; large open families; pilgrimages and wanderings from center to center. A synthesis of Gandhian "village anarchism" and I.W.W. syndicalism. Interesting visionary pamphlets along these lines were written several years ago by Gandhians Richard Gregg and Appa Patwardhan. The Tribe proposes personal responsibilities rather than abstract centralized government, taxes and advertising-agency-plus-Mafia type inter-national brainwashing corporations.

In the United States and Europe the Tribe has evolved gradually over the last fifty years—since the end of World War I—in response to the increasing insanity of the modern nations. As the number of alienated intellectuals, creative types and general social misfits grew, they came to recognize each other by various minute signals. Much of this energy was channeled into Com-munism in the thirties and early forties. All the anarchists and left-deviationists—and many Trotskyites—were tribesmen at heart. After World War II, another generation looked at Communist rhetoric with a fresh eye and saw that within the Communist governments (and states of mind) there are too many of the same things as are wrong with "capitalism"—too much anger and murder. The suspicion grew that perhaps the whole Western Tradition, of which Marxism is but a (Millennial Protestant) part, is off the track. This led many people to study other major civili-zations—India and China—to see what they could learn. . . .

We came, therefore, (and with many Western thinkers before us) to suspect that civilization may be overhauled. Before anyone says "This is ridiculous, we all know civilization is a necessary thing," let him read some cultural anthropology. Take a look at the lives of South African Bushmen, Micronesian navigators, the Indians of California; the researches of Claude Lévi-Strauss. Everything we have thought about man's welfare needs to be rethought. The tribe, it seems, is the newest development in the Great Subculture. We have almost unintentionally linked our-selves to a transmission of gnosis, a potential social order, and techniques of enlightenment, surviving from prehistoric times.

The most advanced developments of modern science and technology have come to support some of these views. Conse-quently the modern Tribesman, rather than being old-fashioned in his criticism of civilization, is the most relevant type in contemporary society. Nationalism, warfare, heavy industry and consumership, are already outdated and useless. The next great step of mankind is to step into the nature of his own mind—the real question is "just what is consciousness?"—and we must make the most intelligent and creative use of science in exploring these questions. The man of wide international experience, much learning and leisure—luxurious product of our long and sophisti-cated history—may with good reason wish to live simply, with few tools and minimal clothes, close to nature.

The Revolution has ceased to be an ideological concern. Instead, people are trying it out right now—communism in small communities, new family organization. A million people in America and another million in England and Europe. A vast underground in Russia, which will come out in the open four or five years hence, is now biding. How do they recognize each other? Not always by beards, long hair, bare feet or beads. The signal is a bright and tender look; calmness and gentleness, freshness and ease of manner. Men, women and children—all of whom together hope to follow the timeless path of love and wisdom, in affectionate company with the sky, winds, clouds, trees, waters, animals and grasses—this is the tribe.

Gary Snyder, *Earth House Hold* (New York: New Directions, 1957), pp. 113, 115–16.

Living the Good Life

Scott and Helen Nearing

At the same time that Gary Snyder was promoting a new "tribal" sensibility in the Pacific Northwest, an elderly couple across the continent was practicing and preaching their own alternative way of living. Much like the Borsodis, Scott and Helen Nearing left New York and started a new life of self-sufficient homesteading during the interwar years. But where Ralph Borsodi was a decentralist libertarian, Scott Nearing (1883–1983) was a Tolstoyan socialist. As a young economics professor he was dismissed from two universities during World War I because of his outspoken pacifism and his social activism. Nearing joined the Communist Party in 1927, only to be defrocked three years later for not following the Party line. Thus by 1932 Nearing found himself blacklisted from teaching and struggling to make a living in the midst of the Depression. So he and Helen Knothe, a musician and vegetarian, decided to take control of their own fate. They purchased a dilapidated farm in Vermont, and through sheer grit and inventiveness, they carved out a successful version of homesteading simplicity. Twenty years later, as the area around their Vermont farm began to be developed into a ski resort, they relocated to the seashore near Harborside, Maine, where they repeated their experiment in good living.

In 1954 the Nearings published *Living the Good Life*, an account of their Vermont experience. The book reveals how, unlike so many other utopian romantics, before and since, the Nearings were able to combine the practical and the visionary. These gritty, self-reliant socialists worked hard, disdained frivolous activities, planned carefully, kept systematic records, and adopted efficient production methods. The book attracted little attention in the 1950s, but when it was reprinted in paperback in 1970 it became a best-seller. Soon the Nearings were besieged with visitors who flocked to their Maine homestead in search of guidance and inspiration.

We were in the country. We had land. We had all the wood we could use, for the cutting. We had an adequate supply of food from the gardens. We had time, a purpose, energy, enough ingenuity and imagination, a tiny cash income from maple and little cash money on hand.

We were on a run-down, run-out farm. We were living in a poorly built wooden house through which the winter winds swept like water through a sieve. We owned a timber tract that would come into its own only in twenty to thirty years. We owned the place next door, another run-down farm, equipped with wretched buildings. Our soil was swampy, rough and rocky, mostly covered with second growth, but there was a small amount of good timber left on it. Our gardens were promising, but the main garden was too low and wet to be really productive.

We were in good health. We were solvent in that we had no debts. We were fairly hopeful of the future, but inexperienced in the ways of subsistence living and somewhat uncertain as to how we should proceed. After due consideration and in the spirit of the times, we drew up a ten year plan.

This plan was not made out of whole cloth, all at once. It was modified by experience, as we went along. It was flexible, but in principle and usually in practice we stuck to it. Suppose we set down the main points which the plan covered when we outlined it in the middle 1930's.

1. We wish to set up a semi-self contained household unit, based largely on a use economy, and, as far as possible, independent of the price-profit economy which surrounds us. . . .

We would attempt to carry on this self-subsistent economy by the following steps: (1) Raising as much of our own food as local soil and climatic conditions would permit. (2) Bartering our products for those which we could not or did not produce. (3) Using wood for fuel and cutting it ourselves. (4) Putting up our own buildings with stone and wood from the place, doing the work ourselves. (5) Making such implements as sleds, drays, stone-boats, gravel screen, ladders. (6) Holding down to the barest minimum the number of implements, tools, gadgets and machines which we might buy from the assembly lines of big business. (7) If we had to have such machines for a few hours or days in a year (plough, tractor, rototiller, bull-dozer, chainsaw), we would rent or trade them from local people instead of buying and owning them.

2. We have no intention of making money, nor do we seek wages or profits. Rather we aim to earn a livelihood, as far as possible on a use economy basis. When enough bread labor has been performed to secure the year's living, we will stop earning until the next crop season. . . .

3. All of our operations will be kept on a cash and carry basis. No bank loans. No slavery to interest on mortgages, notes and I.O.U's.

Under any economy, people who rent out money live on easy street. Whether as individuals or banking establishments, they lend money, take security and live on a rich harvest of interest and the proceeds of forced sales. The money lenders are able to enjoy comfort and luxury, without doing any productive labor. It is the borrowing producers who pay the interest or lose their property. Farmers and home owners by the thousands lost everything they had during the Great Depression because they could not meet interest payments. We decided to buy for cash or not at all.

4. We will make our cash crop from maple syrup and will work out a cooperative arrangement wherever possible. . . .

Again and again people have asked us: "Why did you escape to this idyllic spot? Why not stay in the noise, dirt and turmoil of one of the great urban centers, sharing the misery and anguish of your fellow humans?" We recognize the relevance of this question. Indeed, it extends to the social foundations upon which those not satisfied with western civilization must strive to build an alternative culture pattern. We would go further and agree that this question reaches beyond sociology into the realm of ethics. In several respects, it is the question of questions. Like any basic social or ethical issue, it cannot be answered easily, nor can it be met with a categorical reply. Any attempt at an inclusive answer must contain exceptions and limitations.

Helen and Scott Nearing in their Harborside, Maine, home.

Suppose we begin our answer to this perennial question by admitting that in a remote Green Mountain valley one is not in daily contact with the labor struggle, nor is he subject to the pressures of those who live, work, travel and recreate in New York, Chicago or San Francisco. The life in Vermont is different in texture from that of a metropolis. Is it "better" or "worse?" That depends upon the way in which the words are used. For us the life in Vermont was definitely better because it permitted frequent contacts with nature, because it afforded an opportunity to master and direct nature forces, because manual skills were still practiced and because the routine of living was less exacting. Instead of spending early and late hours in dirty, noisy, subway or train, we stayed on our own grounds week in and week out. Travelling to and from work, for us, meant walking two hundred yards from kitchen to saphouse. If snow was deep, the trip might require snowshoes or skis, but that was an advantage because it called for another skill.

This answer does not meet fully our central question: "Why should you avail yourself of these many advantages when fellow humans are deprived of them in city slums?" If we were compelled to answer this question categorically, we would say that under any and all conditions one is responsible for living as well as possible within the complex of circumstances which constitutes the day-to-day environment. Where there is a choice, with the evidence all recorded and the circumstances all considered, one chooses the better part rather than the worse.

Living is a business in which we all engage. In the course of the day, there are certain things we must do,—for example, breathe. There are also things we may do or may decide not to do,—such as, stay home and bake a cake, or go out and visit a friend. The center of life routine is surrounded by a circumference of choice. There is the vocation which provides livelihood, and the avocations which thrive on leisure and surplus energy.

A professional actor or musician must live close enough to his job to get there every working day. A poet or painter has a wider range from which to choose his living place. Under what obligation are these individuals to stay in the congested centers of population?

We would put the matter affirmatively. Since congestion is a social disadvantage, these individuals are in duty bound to avoid congested areas unless for some reason business or duty calls them there. If they go into the centers of population, instead of improving matters they make congestion worse.

We may state the issue in another way,—whatever the nature of one's beliefs, one's personal conduct may either follow the belief pattern or diverge from it. In so far as it diverges, it helps produce unwanted results. At the same time, it splits practice away from theory and divides the personality against itself. The most harmonious life is one in which theory and practice are unified.

From this it follows that each moment, hour, day, week and year should be treated as an occasion,—another opportunity to live as well as possible, in accordance with the old saying "Tomorrow is a new day" or the new Mexican greeting "Siempre mejor" (always better) in place of the conventional "Buenos dias" (good day). With body in health, emotions in balance, mind in tune and vision fixed on a better life and a better world, life, individually and collectively, is already better.

On this point we differ emphatically with many of our friends and acquaintances who say, in effect, "Never mind how we live today; we are in this dog-eat-dog social system and we may as well get what we can out of it. But tomorrow, in a wiser, more social and more humane world, we will live more rationally, more economically, more efficiently, more socially." Such talk is nonsense. As we live in the present, so is our future shaped, channeled and largely determined.

Apply this thinking to our problem of living in the Green Mountains and believing in and working for a cooperative, peaceful, social order. Our life in Vermont may be justified, or can justify itself,—(1) as an instance and an example of sane living in an insane world; (2) as a means of contacting nature, a contact in some ways more important than contacting society; (3) as a desirable, limited alternative to one segment of the existing social order; (4) as a refuge for political deviants; (5) as a milieu in which heretofore active people can spend their riper years (in accordance with the Eastern conception of life stages: the sage or anchorite following the stage of householder); (6) as an opportunity for the sage or mature person to follow his profession and avocations.

Action has its advocates. Contemplation also has it adherents. The former tends to be exterior, peripheral or centrifugal; while the latter, by comparison, more inner, central and vital.

Perhaps we can summarize our point of view in this way. We are opposed to the theories of a competitive, acquisitive, aggressive, war-making social order, which butchers for food and murders for sport and for power. The closer we have to come to this social order the more completely are we a part of it. Since we reject it in theory, we should, as far as possible, reject it also in practice. On no other basis can theory and practice be unified. At the same time, and to the utmost extent, we should live as decently, kindly, justly, orderly and efficiently as possible. Human beings, under any set of circumstances, can behave well or badly. Whatever the circumstances, it is better to love, create and construct than to hate, undermine and destroy, or, what may be even worse at times, ignore and *laissez passer*. We believed that we could make our contribution to the good life more effectively in a pre-industrial, rural community than in one of the great urban centers.

During several decades we have been in close contact with like-minded men and women all through the United States who have tried the rural alternative and with others who have tried the urban alternative. We feel that both groups have made and are making a contribution. We still feel, however, as we did in 1932, that the rural alternative (the "small community" of Arthur E. Morgan, Baker Brownell and Ralph Borsodi) offers greater individual and collective constructive possibilities than the urban.

We are far from assuming that the ruralists will be able to set up a social communal alternative to capitalist urbanism. In the face of centuries of experience we did not assume that in 1932. We are surer now than we were then that these communities are confined rigidly to the few, rarely endowed and super-normally equipped men and women who are willing and able to live as altruists after being trained, conditioned and coerced by an acquisitive, competitive, ego-centric social system.

What we did feel and what we still assert is that it is worthwhile for the individual who is rejected by a disintegrating urban community to formulate a theory of conduct and to put into practise a program of action which will enable him or her to live as decently as possible under existing circumstances.

Viewed in a long perspective, our Vermont project was a personal stop-gap, an emergency expedient. But in the short view it was a way of preserving self-respect and of demonstrating to the few who were willing to observe, listen and participate, that life in a dying acquisitive culture can be individually and socially purposeful, creative, constructive and deeply rewarding, provided that economic solvency and psychological balance are preserved.

Scott and Helen Nearing, *Living the Good Life: How to Live Sanely and Simply in a Troubled World* (1954; New York: Schocken Books, 1970), pp. 21-27, 181-85.

We Learn By Doing

Patsy Sun

Unlike the Nearings, many of the alienated young people who set out on their own during the 1960s and early 1970s to lead simple lives in the country were indulgent, naive, and immature. Yet others displayed courage, determination, and a refreshing introspection about the meaning of the good life. In this selection, Patsy (Richardson) Sun describes how she and a dozen or so other aspiring communalists established Freefolk, a small farm community in northern Minnesota. They tried to predict pitfalls and problem areas. But Freefolk collapsed after only a little over a year. Its quick demise was typical of most such experiments. Yet as Patsy Sun illustrates, their experience was not wasted. They learned much about themselves and about their version of the simple life.

The night we first got here, hitching in from the closest bus depot in late November last year . . . it was snowing and there were no lights on, and the driver of the car who had gone out of his way to drive us out to the farm asked for the tenth time, "You sure this is the place?" He couldn't believe we had come all the way from Connecticut with almost all our worldly goods on our backs to move to a place we'd never been to, live with people we didn't know, by god, weren't even related to! We fumbled in the dark to light the kerosene lamp, and there were all the remembered smells of wood smoke and linoleum and maybe sauerkraut fermenting. I think Bob built up the fire, and I got out my guitar, and we waited for a while, looking at the pictures on the wall, checking the place out the way you do when the host is out of the room. Then they came in, Ferdi and Rebecca and little Geordie, these pacifist anarchist types we'd come to live with on a hunch or a hope.

We stood around looking at each other, feeling shy. I remember Rebecca asked in one sentence whether we were organic gardeners, nudists, and anarchists. . . . It was a funny way to begin a community, if that's when it happened, standing round the stove looking at each other, without any outlined programs or objectives, not even knowing each other or what we meant by community. And I think that it is a good thing we didn't write it down, but mostly let what happened happen.

For over a year now we've called ourselves freefolk, being freer than some and wanting to be more free. And people come and go and stay longer than they planned or come back, or maybe leave to search further. We'd like more people to share this life with us, who think their dreams might sit well with ours, people who are seriously interested in community as a way of life. There are no other membership requirements. We like visitors, too, or people who want to stay a short while to learn more about homesteading and community living, but we like them best when they write to us first to let us know they will be passing by and see if it is a good time to drop in. Living out here in the north woods your mind gets blown easily if you see too many strangers all moving in on you at once. When our numbers doubled in a few days this summer we panicked, thinking of other communities that had been swollen and burst by a sudden overwhelming population explosion. There were ten or twelve of us here then, I think, and we decided that what we wanted was a small close community of twelve or fifteen adults. It was a hard decision to make for people who wanted to share their possessions, their land, and their lives, to start writing letters, "Listen man, it is really great to hear you are interested in community, but we are swamped with visitors . . . and could you come in the fall." It was painful, and I'd write these complex replies trying to explain, and that is what we decided. We weren't going to throw anybody out, we'd just try to explain, kindly but firmly, how we felt . . . and so far it's worked. Someday, perhaps, after we have really established a community here, we will split and divide—mushroom and spread—right now we're growing too hard to think of it.

It was about that time we started having meetings when new people arrived to talk about their hopes and plans, to share our feelings and to explain what we were and what we wanted to be. It is sort of an artificial custom, and it has never come quite naturally, but for us it was a necessary way to avoid misunderstandings and let us all know what was happening.

We talked about drugs, too, and where we all were with them. Too many places had been busted. At other communities we knew of, heads got paranoid, avoided local residents, only wanted hip people around. For us, part of the whole scene was a kind of witness to the life we believed in. We didn't want to start excluding straight visitors or playing cops and robbers (who's the narc?). There were a lot of other drug communities around: we wanted to try something different. So the word spread, and we helped it, "They don't have any rules there, but don't bring drugs."

One of the first things people ask us is "So how do you get along with your neighbors; do you get a lot of static?" and they are always surprised when we say, "Great, it is one of the best things about living here." A community surrounding our community has developed, partly because we are living in an area where money is scarce. The divergence in ways of life isn't that great. Bartering, trading, exchanging labor is a frequent occasion. We are able to help some of our neighbors, and they often help us, giving us the skim milk they would otherwise throw out, teaching us stuff you won't find in books. Another major reason we have a good thing going with our neighbors, besides the fact that we really dig people and try to make friends, is that the community has grown slowly, giving people a chance to get used to us, to know that we are friendly, "hardworking, honest folk, even if they do look a bit weird." Rebecca and Ferdi were here alone for two years before anyone came to join them, which was too hard on them to be recommended as a really good idea, but there is no doubt that it has helped our local relationships. This doesn't mean that there aren't rumors—but there are enough people who know and like us to offset them.

There are eight of us here now, counting the kids (and kids do count, making more noise and taking up more room than the rest of us). Deena came here with her twin babies Josh and Amy, one and a half, looking for a place to grow roots. She lives upstairs in the loft room. Bob and I have built a cabin down in the woods under the fir trees. Ferdi, Rebecca and Geordie sleep in the cabin across from the pump house. The community room, a lean-to on the barn, is where we all eat, sing, read, and bounce the babies.

All of us are city people; we learn by doing. With a book in one hand, seeds in the other, and a kind of optimism, we grow most of our own food. We have no electricity, no telephone, no running water, no tractor. We do have a car and a truck that runs sometimes, but not so many bills and as little dependency on the industrial-technocracy as we can now manage. We dig living this way—but it's more than that. For me, it seems like the whole industrial thing is based on exploitation. Exploitation of earth and trees and water, or animals and people and nations. It is something I don't want to be a part of, not raping the land or taking slaves either, even willing ones (to stand on an assembly line screwing on bolts is a job I couldn't bear for a week). Maybe technology could be used well, but it isn't now—and it is more than that.

For it seems machines separate me from a part of life I don't want to be separated from. I like to pump my water, to know that the power comes out of my own body. I like to drag wood in from the forest and to cut it by hand with a two-man saw, because it keeps me in touch with what I think is basic: food, warmth, water. So we live here, and we don't go to war or pay federal taxes. We encourage other people not to either. When the spirit moves us, we crank out leaflets, speak at meetings, or leave cryptic notes on the bulletin boards at the nearby state college. What all that means is we groove on people getting free. For every day is a kind of demonstration of what we believe.

A couple poses in front of their teepee in the Morning Star commune near Occidental, California.

Freefolk community may not be intentional, but it is on purpose. Each of us comes here, no matter how long he stays, for his own reasons; a lot of them are the same, but some things are more important for some people. For us at this point, this is a satisfying way of life, but it is more than an end in itself; it is a means toward a gentle revolution where people drop out of the system and take responsibility over their own lives. We want to create a place where work is fun and meaningful, where children can grow straight and beautiful according to their natural inclinations. A place where people have a chance to discover who they are and what they really want, where each man deals with his neighbor sensitively and compassionately, where laws and prisons and armies are not needed. We don't have any group goals. We dream of having a school here, or a camp, or trying some street theatre, of bringing Kountry Kulture to our local township meeting house.

It is hard to talk about community. There are so many things that don't make sense unless you have tried it. It is hard to talk about Freefolk because it is something different to everyone, so much of it, smells and sights and sounds. Whatever you say comes out sounding like not quite the truth. We haven't created a utopia here, I can say that. There are a lot of hassles. People who want to escape hassles should forget community. You get hurt a lot. And there is always the question whether the hurt is worth the good times, or whether you're learning anything from it. For me, I guess so far it has been worth it. Every hassle is so basic it becomes a discovery in human need, your own and your friends'. Often I don't feel myself growing on beyond the insight, but maybe, I think, the insight itself is a kind of growth.

Harder than the hassles with each other are the hassles with yourself, wondering if this is, after all, where you should be, discovering that the world you wanted to create doesn't come all that easy, not even when people want it to. There is bitterness and maybe yelling. Sometimes there is silence which can be the worst of all, or hate; but more loving, I think, because we have the trees and the sunset fields to run in. Whatever mess our lives are in, the mess is at least our own mess and when we sing "Love means each other everyday," we know where that's at.

Patsy (Richardson) Sun, "We Learn by Doing," in *The New Communes*, ed. Ron Roberts (Englewood Cliffs, N.J.: Prentice-Hall, 1971), pp. 130–34.

A Desperate Poignancy
Angela Carter

Angela Carter, a British journalist and novelist, traveled to the United States in the late 1960s. While in America she visited several urban and rural communes. Her account is quite critical—perhaps unfairly so—but she does isolate several of the obvious weaknesses in the hippie version of simple living.

Dawn was breaking over the flat, boring countryside between Los Angeles and San Francisco when I reached my destination. I stayed in a suburb of Berkeley opposite a hot-dog stand which advertised its presence by means of the leering plaster head of a dachshund sporting a chef's cap.

In the shadow of this obscene beast, my host sat in an unlikely little old clapboard house which looked as though it had been knocked together out of gingerbread. He studied astrology, leafed through the Apocrypha and did yoga exercises while his wife gardened organically in the backyard. Sometimes, husband and wife colored coloring books together. They ate a good deal of wheat germ in their food, one way or another, lots of nut butter and loaf after loaf of terribly brown bread. For a while they had run a rock band but some of the other musicians sacramentally consumed acid, mescalin and other hallucinogens during rehearsals and found it difficult to concentrate.

After a while, I grew tired of the city and went to stay in a log cabin in a forest by the ocean. There was a polluted well, six cats and a Siberian husky pup with worms and diarrhea. The owners of the cabin were city people who had left San Francisco after a black man had been murdered in the street outside their apartment. Although the wooden walls boxed up the heat, the family sat in the cabin all day and played Bob Dylan records. Because the well was not only polluted but also about to run dry, every so often somebody went to get fresh water from a nearby spring. Everybody fished the midges and dead leaves out of it and exclaimed how good it tasted. Milk and eggs were obtained from a hippie farm. The farm buildings had been effortfully reconstructed from an original blueprint in a picture book of the last century. Behind the high, wooden gate, fastened with a wooden latch, there was a barn, a duck pond and a flurry of squawking chickens. A cow with a crumpled horn and a bell round its neck browsed in a very green field. It was the prettiest toy farm I have ever seen.

Little homesteads were scattered throughout the forest. Nobody ever locked their doors. The menfolk went diving in wet suits for fish and abalone, which they traded for vegetables and meat. They were talking of going down to Arizona and trading abalone shells with the Indians for turquoise. I thought that after 200 years of exploitation by the white man, the Indians might approach this offer with some suspicion, but they told me the Indians would immediately respect their obvious sincerity. Meanwhile the women stayed at home, baked wholemeal bread in wood stoves and reared innumerable children with names like Aragorn, Raven and Caspar. A strict monogamy appeared to be the general rule.

In these picturesque but primitive conditions, it was obvious that only those with the qualities that make a good boy scout would survive for any length of time. So it seemed only fitting that, one evening, I should find myself at a campfire where they barbecued a goat and a fish called a wolf-eel.

As we sat round the fire that evening, the handcrafted marijuana pipe went round. People picked banjos and guitars. The moon rose over the redwoods while the women exchanged recipes for blueberry muffins and hash brownies, a favorite sweetmeat in those parts. Everyone talked about how much money they saved by being dropouts and raising their own goats.

There seemed to me a desperate poignancy about this Thoreau-like attempt to pursue a simple life. They have reached Candide's conclusion and decided to concentrate on cultivating their garden, but have managed to evade the overtones of irony in the rest of the story. I suppose, historically, America missed out on the Enlightenment. Sociologically, the hippie sub-culture, which is, rather, a loose network of interlocking sub-cultures, is almost as complex a phenomenon as the society which produced it. A discontent with that society is often the only common area of agreement amongst a group which includes ex-academics, ex-Marxists, anarchists, mystics, criminals and thugs. Yet one underlying theme is an actual horror of cities, as though the eternal verities lay only in drawing one's own water, hewing one's own wood and, in emergencies, consulting the I Ching, the Chinese fortune-telling manual, to find out what to do. A girl I met in San Francisco said: "Our commune is building a boat out of ferro-concrete and we're going to sail out to Tahiti out of disgust with civilization." This seemed a particularly poignant ambition because Gauguin went there 80 years ago for much the same reasons and all he found, even then, was a spoiled Eden inhabited by syphilitic noble savages.

The sub-culture may have reversed the obvious goals of American society and put personal values at the top of their list of necessities for the good life, but they still fall prey to the great American conviction that if you believe in an illusion passionately enough, it will come true. They exhibit a modest self-satisfaction, although their artforms—rock and the Art Nouveau writhings of psychedelic art—are at best wistfully derivative and at worst inane. Socially, however, all have reversed the trend of one-hundred years of European progress towards female emanipation and put their womenfolk squarely back where they belong: cooking on wood stoves and bearing children without the benefit of anaesthetics. They grope for images of an innocence which is not so much lost as only glimpsed vaguely, in fairy tales.

Interestingly enough, in view of the publicity which has been given to their appearance, a prime physical characteristic of the "beautiful people" of Northern California is their lack of charm. The rural hippies look like figures from Brueghel but the urban hippies look more like figures from Bosch. Many are ravaged by dirt-spread diseases and also by gonorrhea, hepatitis, measles, scabies and vermin. Perhaps lice in the hair, even more than flowers, proves to a middle-class American boy that he has transcended his socio-economic environment. America is still an aggressively asexual nation.

The hippies go along with this cultural pattern in their own way. All walk with the same abashed slouch. It seems possible they can only stomach sexual intercourse with one another whilst in drugged stupors. "Ah," said my host, "we've gone beyond all that. We don't bother about physical packaging anymore." But they didn't seem so much to have transcended packaging as to have gone in for a different style which still, like all American clothing, never even hints at the living, breathing, erotic, subversive flesh underneath. The hippies have gone a long way towards de-eroticizing sex itself. Perhaps this is the last baleful legacy of the Protestant ethic which they have taken with them, willy-nilly, to the woods.

As examples of the purely grotesque, however, there is very little to choose between an American "straight" in holiday attire—brutal crewcut, madras cotton bermuda shorts, tee shirt—and some limp rag doll from Haight Street. Both have a curious physical shamefacedness, as if ill at ease inside their skins.

The hippies react to the noncomprehension about them by cultivating paranoia. The end of the film *Easy Rider* is an example of a common paranoid fantasy in the subculture: set one's immediate social group or class anywhere and a red-neck will shoot you. And it is not an entirely groundless fear. But paranoia is an endemic American malady at the best of times, and a defensive fear of those outside the charmed circle of one's immediate social group is not a deviation from the norm at all.

Angela Carter, "A Desperate Poignancy," in *The Good Life*, ed. Jerry Richard (New York: New American Library, 1972), pp. 230–34.

SIMPLE LIVING AIN'T SO SIMPLE
Jubal

We all have an idea in our heads of what is meant by 'simple living.' To some of us it may mean a life in the country, away from the noise and pollution of the city, just 'getting away from it all.'

Simple living embodies the concept of getting closer to nature, of homesteading, of eating good organic foods, of getting along with less instead of more, of becoming less dependent upon others and more dependent upon self, of raising our own food, making our own clothes and our own entertainment.

To those who haven't yet tried 'simple living' it is often sort of a dream, a romantic notion, a romance with 'mother nature.' It means being your own boss and not out working for 'the man.' It means more time for doing what you want to do and less of doing what you have to do.

Unfortunately, the realities of 'simple living' are not as simple as the dream. Simplicity is generally defined as the absence of complexity, intricacy or artificiality. But anyone who has tried a life of self-sufficiency has soon learned that the amount of knowledge and skill, fortitude and hard work—combined with the ability to improvise—that are required sometimes make the simple life very complicated indeed. It is much simpler to turn a switch and have electricity, to set the thermostat and have heat, than it is to learn to light and care for a wood stove or an Aladdin lamp. It is much simpler to buy your food than it is to prepare the soil, tend the young seedlings, and then harvest and preserve the food. At almost every step, the newcomer to simple living finds that the new life style takes more hours and/or more skill and talent and knowledge than the old life required. . . .

We have neither been trained with the skills to take care of ourselves nor do we have the knowledge to do so. We don't even know where to go to get the necessary knowledge and skill that we would need to care for ourselves if the military-industrial complex suddenly ceased doing it.

We may or may not think that our state of dependency has been deliberately planned by those who stand to profit by it. Either way, the first step in getting out of the rut is to recognize that even a simpleton can survive in a plastic world but only a person of skill and knowledge can enjoy the wonders of simple living.

Jubal, "Simple Living Ain't So Simple," *Green Revolution* (November 1976):7–8.

Communal Simplicity

Keith Melville

The alternative ways of living promoted by the rebellious youth of the 1960s and early 1970s attracted not only journalistic attention but also serious study by sociologists, anthropologists, psychologists, and historians.

Courtesy of World Wide Photos

Members of the Brotherhood of the Spirit commune canning produce near Northfield, Massachusetts.

One of the best of the scholarly accounts was social scientist Keith Melville's *Communes in the Counter Culture.* His perspective is both sympathetic and critical, recognizing the seriousness of purpose and genuine concerns of the young rebels while at the same time impatient with their excesses and hypocrisies.

Aaron sat on his haunches, tracing patterns on the ground, occasionally rubbing his hands on bib overalls covered with dirt from the field where he had been working. Looking vacantly through a scraggly beard and shoulder length hair, he was remembering why he had come here. "I was living in Los Angeles, and every day I felt one step closer to cracking up and landing in a mental hospital, totally isolated from other people and their lives. Every time I turned on the tube, there was this very slick guy selling Miracle Formula 87 to save me from terminal halitosis. Like it was insane, it was a pressure cooker, and I had to get out. I racked my brains trying to figure out what I could do. I tried a shrink . . . no use, of course. Finally, I decided that I would have to live in the country and work closely with my brothers and sisters.

What was there to choose from in the city? City life offered me a trivial job I didn't want, a prison, or a mental hospital.

"I came here because I wanted to simplify my life as much as possible. It wasn't hard to drop out. I had a lot of things to get rid of—a car, a hi-fi, a million useless things. I mean, why did I need an electric toaster and a coffee maker all my own? So I got rid of it all. . . .

"I had done the political trip for a while, but I got to the point where I couldn't just advocate social change, I had to live it. Change isn't something up there, out there, and it isn't a power trip. It's in here." He thumped his chest twice, and little puffs of dust exploded from his coveralls. . . .

Aaron squinted in the direction of the lodge, where a dozen people were sitting, talking, doing nothing in particular. "This whole generation, all the people who are receiving these new energies and turning on, we don't want to be in the materialist bag anymore, and we don't want to get caught up in the nine-to-five career bag, the two-week vacation, barbecues-in-suburbia bag. We don't want these things because through successive incarnations we've been there. . . . If I was put on earth for anything, it was to love my brothers and sisters, and these other things just aren't important.

"It was my dream to belong to a tribe, where the energies flow among everyone, where people care for one another, where no one has to work, but everyone wants to do something because we're all mutually dependent for our survival and our happiness. So we got together here," and he waved his hand out over the garden and the mountains beyond, "and we've had a lot of problems and real conflicts, but we know the satisfactions of trying to work around them, of growing from them, the way you grow from a good marriage. And we're back to the land here, and like I get high just being close to the earth and trying to understand it.

"I think most people came here in the first place because it was a refuge. They weren't sure what to expect, but they had to escape. The new people come with their minds stamped with a thousand patterns that just don't make any sense here. But we're all learning new values, and we're learning how to live together. We still get hung up on a lot of bad trips. Everyone has his thing that's holding him back. But we're strong here because we know what we're trying to do. Like it's so obvious that civilization is doomed. I mean the whole thing's just going to self-destruct, and we don't want to go with it. The next step is community, and that's what we're trying to do.

"It's an entirely new evolutionary branch. The premise of all these places is that we love one another. And people have to experiment in order to figure out what that means. All the communes, all the families, are facets of the same thing, but no one knows exactly what that thing is, or what it should be, so we all go about it a little differently. . . . What we're really doing here is a pilot study of a life style for the near future. We're trying to slow down, to remember what this whole trip's about. We're simplifying, getting rid of all those things that just get in the way. We're retribalizing, and when we get it all together, the vibes are so high we know we're doing something right. And like so many people are getting turned on, it's the beginning of a whole new age."

. . . .

The essence of the counter culture's critique is that in a society so engorged with things people become an extension of, or at best servants to, their possessions. People define themselves in terms of their things, the cars they drive, the cigarettes they smoke. The rhythm of modern life imitates the rhythm of the productive process. As Thoreau put it, these lives of quiet desperation are "minced into hours and fretted by the ticking of the clock." The things that not long ago were clearly our servants have somehow gained the upper hand. This is the premonition of the late-night monster movies: The clever scientist is finally terrorized by his creation.

The solution? The simple life. Homesteading. A conscious program of trying to live with as few things as possible. Giving up electricity, the telephone, running water, washing machines. Getting close to the earth. Building houses out of mud or trees. Making homemade bread. Raising organic gardens. And all the while quoting Thoreau, chapter and verse: "It would be some advantage to live a primitive and frontier life, though in the midst of an outward civilization, if only to learn what are the gross necessaries of life. . . ."

In the midst of this campaign to regain the simple life, naturalness is one of the strongest themes. On most of the farms, voluntary primitivism means exactly that: There are no tractors; everything is done by hand, organically. Anything that's artificial is regarded with high suspicion. But having grown up in a world where so little was natural, it takes a while for some of the new recruits to sort out what is and what isn't. In one of the Taos communes, a girl was going on at length about how the group could make it without any power tools, without artificial fertilizers, without anything from the plastic world outside. A few minutes later, someone was leaving for a "milk run" to the nearest store (they didn't have any cows or goats) and asked her if she needed anything. She answered that she's been out of Breck hair rinse for a week and asked him to pick up a bottle.

For all these lapses, the emphasis on naturalness begins with a perception that is critically important, a newfound ecological consciousness, an awareness of the war that Western man has been waging against nature. At its fringes, this cult of naturalness has a way of shading off into absurdity. In Charles Reich's *The Greening of America*, the normal supermarket types of artificial peanut butter are portrayed as one of the major atrocities committed by the Corporate Conspiracy.

This emphasis on what is natural and the unwillingness to make any compromises with technology or the necessities of commerce create a serious problem. Very few of the communes have either craft industries or any other profit-making business. The garden is the center of most of the groups' economic life, providing much of the daily food supply. The economy is often supplemented by the use of food stamps and income from day labor in nearby jobs such as crop picking or fire fighting. Most of the group, however, are not economically self-sufficient. They have to depend on two sources of money that come in from outside: money taken from savings or sent by parents, and gifts and donations from visitors and new members. Twin Oaks, the Walden Two-oriented group in Virginia, is a notable exception. They have a thriving hammock-making industry and are planning an assortment of other small industries such as an electronic-parts business. But for most of the other groups, the commitment to a simple life in the country means farming, which is difficult and often boring. Nietzsche was not the only nineteenth-century writer to criticize the contemporary utopian colonies for their dullness, insipidness, and uneventfulness. Marx dismissed the whole thing as "rural idiocy." In his survey of the nineteenth-century American experiments, John Humphrey Noyes warned against farming for very practical reasons:

> We incline to think that this fondness for land, which has been the habit of socialists, had much to do with their failures. Farming is about the hardest and longest of all roads to fortune. . . . We should have advised the phalanxes

Members of the Farm, a thriving thousand-acre commune near Summertown, Tennessee, load sorghum for processing into molasses.

to limit their landholdings to a minimum and put their strength as soon as possible into some form of manufacture.

This is advice that the counter-culture communes are unlikely to follow. For all the ways in which these groups would like to be economically self-sufficient, to follow the Twin Oaks example and create small industries means to be implicated in the whole economic system. In this struggle between doctrinal purity and economic self-sufficiency, the first concern is more important, at least as long as most of the groups continue to receive subsidies from outside. . . .

Even if the dissident young have not as yet formulated an alternative to the complete submission to technology or the rejection of it, there is an essential wisdom in their critique. Having moved beyond the era of scarcity, the most important thing is not to allow the imperatives of technology to invade every aspect of our lives. What Kenneth Keniston called the "growing bankruptcy of technological values and visions" poses a huge problem for the young. Maybe it is only by choosing a life of voluntary primitivism—or, as Thoreau put it, learning what are the "gross necessaries of life"—that they can begin to define a new vision of a society that transcends technology.

Keith Melville, *Communes in the Counter Culture: Origins, Theories, Styles of Life* (New York: Morrow, 1972), pp. 11-13, 199-202, 204, 207.

Ecological Simplicity

9

During the 1970s the much-discussed youth revolt largely subsided. Most of the flower children abandoned their communal settlements and radical politics and re-entered the larger society. Yet many brought with them a continuing skepticism concerning the claims of the consumer culture and a growing anxiety about the degradation of the environment.

They were not alone in harboring such concerns. In late 1969 a *New York Times* survey of college campuses reported that students were quickly transferring their attention from the antiwar movement to the environmental movement. Many older Americans were likewise becoming increasingly concerned about the quality of the nation's air, water, and soil. Within a few years this ecological consciousness had mushroomed into a major national phenomenon cutting across political and generational lines. In the process it gave new urgency and credibility to the notion of simpler living and more conscientious patterns of consumption.

This ecologically-inspired simplicity drew much of its momentum from the crisis atmosphere of the mid-1970s. The apocalyptic warnings of naturalists and scientists such as Rachel Carson, Barry Commoner, Paul Ehrlich, Ivan Illich, Eugene Odum, and Garrett Hardin caused many Americans to question their tradition of indiscriminate consumption and their worship of unlimited economic growth as the measure of national well-being. The Arab oil embargo of 1973–74 and the ensuing inflationary spiral and recession gave added impetus to the cause of ecological simplicity. Most Americans were now forced to reduce their carefree consumption habits. As they had done during earlier crises such as wars and depressions, people started going without, sharing with others, and learning to become more self-reliant. Many resented and resisted such forced austerity, and corporate as well as government officials lamented what seemed to be a permanent restraint on the nation's heretofore freewheeling way of life.

But several observers saw in the growing crisis an opportunity to revive the republican simplicity of an earlier America. Wendell Berry, the Kentucky poet, novelist, farmer, and ecologist, hoped the environmental dilemma would help resurrect the old Jeffersonian idea of "an economy of necessities rather than an economy based on anxiety, fantasy, luxury, and idle-wishing." Others shared his dream of adapting republican simplicity to the contemporary American setting. Several observers pointed out that the oil embargo and its aftershocks were provoking forms of simpler living that promised to be more realistic and enduring than those adopted by the flower children. People were walking, car-pooling, or riding bicycles to work, conserving energy, installing woodstoves and solar heaters, recycling cans and bottles and garbage, reviving handicrafts, forming consumer cooperatives, planting vegetable gardens, and reassessing their patterns of living.

At the same time that the ecological crisis helped stimulate a revival of more temperate habits of living, it also provoked a renewed emphasis on spiritual simplicity. The deepening problem of global hunger also pricked the conscience of many Christians and Jews. In 1973 a group of religious retreat center directors met at the site of a restored Shaker village near Harrodsburg, Kentucky. Their discussions centered on the ecological crisis and the plight of the hungry millions around the world. In an attempt to address such concerns, the conferees drafted the Shakertown Pledge, a credo of pious simplicity for modern America which thereafter formed the basis for many congregational discussions of the relationship between the spiritual life and the material life.

These ecological and theological concerns soon began to bear fruit. Opinion polls and surveys in the mid-1970s reported dramatic shifts in American attitudes concerning getting and spending. Respondents increasingly stressed more concern about the quality of their lives than the quantity of their possessions. The analysis of a Lou Harris poll in

1977 noted that the "American people have begun to show a deep skepticism about the nation's capacity for unlimited economic growth, and they are wary of the benefits that growth is supposed to bring." Researchers Duane Elgin and Arnold Mitchell of the Stanford Research Institute concluded that as many as ten million Americans were consciously organizing their lives around the principle of voluntary simplicity.

Soon a whole new genre of publications appeared to address these developments. Magazines such as *Mother Earth News*, *The Whole Earth Catalog*, *Rain*, and *Organic Gardening* provided both philosphical support for the ideal of simple, more self-reliant living as well as practical advice. Best-selling books such as *Small Is Beautiful* (1973), by the British economist E. F. Schumacher, gave the concept even more visibility. President Jimmy Carter read Schumacher's book and found many of its themes compelling.

In his own attempt to mobilize the nation behind his energy program and in the process promote a solemn reassessment of American priorities, Carter drew explicitly upon the heritage of both pious and republican simplicity. He told the nation at his Inaugural: "We have learned that 'more' is not necessarily 'better,' that even our great nation has recognized limits." He also followed Jefferson's precedent in trying to project a plain republicanism from the White House. Carter repeatedly drew genuine sustenance from his small-town agrarian background and his Christian piety. And for a while the public seemed to embrace his moral leadership.

A Conservation Ethic

Aldo Leopold

The saintly naturalist Aldo Leopold (1887–1948) spent his career warning Americans of the consequences of their short-sighted attitude toward their physical environment.

Born in Iowa, he attended Yale's Sheffield Scientific School and the School of Forestry before joining the U.S. Forest Service in 1910. After eighteen years of distinguished service, he left the government and became a private consultant and writer. In 1933 he published his classic textbook, *Game Management*, and thereafter he served as a professor at the University of Wisconsin until his death.

Leopold was distinctive for the philosophical perspective he brought to his vocation. He was especially preoccupied with developing a comprehensive vision of the relationship between humans, animals, plants, and the land. Americans, he charged, had come to view the land as a commodity to be exploited rather than as a perishable gift from God. And such a myopic utilitarianism would ultimately lead to cultural suicide. But few listened to such warnings in the 1940s or 1950s. During the early 1970s, however, Leopold's writings were reprinted and his posthumous plea for a "land ethic" and an "ecological conscience" was finally taken seriously. Here, in an entry from his journal, he reflects on the dilemma facing conservationists in trying to educate a public addicted to waste and exploitation of the physical environment.

We shall never achieve harmony with land, any more than we shall achieve justice or liberty for people. In these higher aspirations the important thing is not to achieve, but to strive. It is only in mechanical enterprises that we can expect that early or complete fruition of effort which we call 'success.'

The problem, then, is how to bring about a striving for harmony with land among a people many of whom have forgotten there is any such thing as land, among whom education and culture have become almost synonymous with landlessness. This is the problem of 'conservation education.'

When we say 'striving,' we admit at the outset that the thing we need must grow from within. No striving for an idea was ever injected wholly from without.

When we say 'striving,' I think we imply an effort of the mind as well as a disturbance of the emotions. It is inconceivable to me that we can adjust ourselves to the complexities of the land mechanism without an intense curiosity to understand its working and an habitual personal study of those workings. The urge to comprehend must precede the urge to reform.

When we say 'striving,' we likewise disqualify at least in part the two vehicles which conservation propagandists have most often used: fear and indignation. He who by a lifetime of observation and reflection has learned much about our maladjustments with land is entitled to fear, and would be something less than honest if he were not indignant. But for teaching the fresh mind, these are outmoded tools. They belong to history.

My own gropings come to a dead end when I try to appraise the profit motive. For a full generation the American conservation movement has been substituting the profit motive for the fear motive, yet it has failed to motivate. We can all see profit in conservation practice, but the profit accrues to society rather than to the individual. This, of course, explains the trend, at this moment, to wish the whole job on the government.

When one considers the prodigious achievements of the profit motive in wrecking land, one hesitates to reject it as a vehicle for restoring land. I incline to believe we have overestimated the scope of the profit motive. Is it profitable for the individual to build a beautiful home? To give his children a higher education? No, it is seldom profitable, yet we do both. These are, in fact, ethical and aesthetic premises which underlie the economic system. Once accepted, economic forces tend to align the smaller details for social organization into harmony with them.

No such ethical and aesthetic premise yet exists for the condition of the land these children must live in. Our children are our signature to the roster of history; our land is merely the place our money was made. There is as yet no social stigma in the possession of a gullied farm, a wrecked forest, or a polluted stream, provided the dividends suffice to send the youngsters to college. Whatever ails the land, the government will fix it.

I think we have here the root of the problem. What conservation education must build is an ethical underpinning for land economics and a universal curiosity to understand the land mechanism. Conservation may then follow.

Aldo Leopold, *Round River* (New York: Oxford University Press, 1953), pp. 155–57.

Think Little

Wendell Berry

Wendell Berry is a poet, novelist, essayist, professor,
and farmer who lives with his family on a hillside farm near
Port Royal, Kentucky, only a few miles from where his
parents, grandparents, and great-grandparents also lived
and farmed. And it is this deeply-rooted sense of place and
love for the land that permeates his writing. Farming for
him is not just an exercise in literary romanticism or
bourgeois recreation; it is a way of life, a means of connec-
tedness with the soil and the past that cultivates his spirit
and nurtures his creativity. Berry is a conservator and
practitioner of the simple agrarian life—he celebrates the
fulfillment of hard work and the advantages of tradition.
He plows with a team of horses rather than a tractor.

Like Jefferson, Thoreau, Burroughs, and others before
him, Berry interprets the modern malaise as being caused
primarily by the estrangement of people from the land. An
outspoken critic of agribusiness and an impassioned
spokesmen for environmental concerns, Berry has inspired
many by his writing and by his way of life. Here, while
recognizing the power of the corporate culture in shaping
American perceptions and the benefits of collective action
in resisting such institutionalized hedonism, he nevertheless challenges his readers to accept individual responsibility for the ecological crisis and to take constructive
action on their own.

For most of the history of this country our motto, implied or
spoken, has been Think Big. I have come to believe that a better
motto, and an essential one now, is Think Little. That implies the
necessary change of thinking and feeling, and suggests the necessary work. Thinking Big has led us to the two biggest and cheapest
political dodges of our time: plan-making and law-making. The
lotus-eaters of this era are in Washington, D.C., Thinking Big.
Somebody comes up with a problem, and somebody in the government comes up with a plan or a law. The result, mostly, has been

the persistence of the problem, and the enlargement and enrichment of the government.

But the discipline of thought is not generalization; it is detail, and it is personal behavior. While the government is "studying" and funding and organizing its Big Thought, nothing is being done. But the citizen who is willing to Think Little, and, accepting the discipline of that, to go ahead on his own, is already solving the problem. A man who is trying to live as a neighbor to his neighbors will have a lively and practical understanding of the work of peace and brotherhood, and let there be no mistake about it—he is *doing* that work. A couple who make a good marriage, and raise healthy, morally competent children, are serving the world's future more directly and surely than any political leader, though they never utter a public word. A good farmer who is dealing with the problem of soil erosion on an acre of ground has a sounder grasp of that problem and *cares* more about it and is probably doing more to solve it than any bureaucrat who is talking about it in general. A man who is willing to undertake the discipline and the difficulty of mending his own ways is worth more to the conservation movement than a hundred who are insisting merely that the government and the industries mend *their* ways.

If you are concerned about the proliferation of trash, then by all means start an organization in your community to do something about it. But before—*and while*—you organize, pick up some cans and bottles yourself. That way, at least, you will assure yourself and others that you mean what you say. If you are concerned about air pollution, help push for government controls, but drive your car less, use less fuel in your home. If you are worried about the damming of wilderness rivers, join the Sierra Club, write to the government, but turn off the lights you're not using, don't install an air conditioner, don't be a sucker for electrical gadgets, don't waste water. In other words, if you are fearful of the destruction of the environment, then learn to quit being an environmental parasite. We all are, in one way or another, and the remedies are not always obvious, though they certainly will always be difficult. They require a new kind of life—harder, more laborious, poorer in luxuries and gadgets, but also, I am certain, richer in meaning and more abundant in real pleasure. To have a healthy environment, we will all have to give up things we like; we may even have to give up things we have come to think of as necessities. But to be fearful of the disease and yet unwilling to pay for the cure is not just to be hypocritical; it is to be doomed. If you talk a good line without being changed by what you say, then you are not just hypocritical and doomed; you have become an agent of the disease. Consider, for an example, President Nixon, who advertises his grave concern about the destruction of the environment, and who turns up the air conditioner to make it cool enough to build a fire.

Odd as I am sure it will appear to some, I can think of no better form of personal involvement in the cure of the environment than that of gardening. A person who is growing a garden, if he is growing it organically, is improving a piece of the world. He is producing something to eat, which makes him somewhat independent of the grocery business, but he is also enlarging, for himself, the meaning of food and the pleasure of eating. The food he grows will be fresher, more nutritious, less contaminated by poisons and preservatives and dyes than what he can buy at a store. He is reducing the trash problem; a garden is not a disposable container, and it will digest and re-use its own wastes. If he enjoys working in his garden, then he is less dependent on an automobile or a merchant for his pleasure. He is involving himself directly in the work of feeding people.

If you think I'm wandering off the subject, let me remind you that most of the vegetables necessary for a family of four can be grown on a plot of forty by sixty feet. I think we might see in this an economic potential of considerable importance, since we now appear to be facing the possibility of widespread famine. How much food could be grown in the dooryards of cities and suburbs? How much could be grown along the extravagant right-of-ways of the interstate system? Or how much could be grown, by the intensive practices and economics of the small farm, on so-called marginal lands? Louis Bromfield liked to point out that the people of France survived crisis after crisis because they were a nation of gardeners, who in times of want turned with great skill to their own small plots of ground. And F. H. King, an agriculture professor who travelled extensively in the Orient in 1907, talked to a Chinese farmer who supported a family of twelve, "one donkey, one cow . . . and two pigs on 2.5 acres of cultivated land"—and who did this, moreover, by agricultural methods that were sound enough organically to have maintained his land in prime fertility through several thousand years of such use. These are possibilities that are readily apparent and attractive to minds that are prepared to Think Little. To Big Thinkers—the bureaucrats and businessmen of agriculture—they are quite simply invisible. But intensive, organic agriculture kept the farms of the Orient thriving for thousands of years, whereas extensive—which is to say, exploitive or extractive—agriculture has critically reduced the fertility of American farmlands in a few centuries or even a few decades.

A person who undertakes to grow a garden at home, by practices that will preserve rather than exploit the economy of the soil, has set his mind decisively against what is wrong with us. He is helping himself in a way that dignifies him and that is rich in meaning and pleasure. But he is doing something else that is more important: he is making vital contact with the soil and the weather on which his life depends. He will no longer look upon rain as an impediment of traffic, or upon the sun as a holiday decoration. And his sense of man's dependence on the world will have grown precise enough, one would hope, to be clarifying and useful.

What I am saying is that if we apply our minds directly and competently to the needs of the earth, then we will have begun to make fundamental and necessary changes in our minds. We will begin to understand and to mistrust *and to change* our wasteful economy, which markets not just the produce of the earth, but also the earth's ability to produce. We will see that beauty and utility are alike dependent upon the health of the world. But we will also see through the fads and the fashions of protest. We will see that war and oppression and pollution are not separate issues, but are aspects of the same issue. Amid the outcries for the liberation of this group or that, we will know that no person is free except in the freedom of other persons, and that man's only real freedom is to know and faithfully occupy his place—a much humbler place than we have been taught to think—in the order of creation.

But the change of mind I am talking about involves not just a change of knowledge, but also a change of attitude toward our esential ignorance, a change in our bearing in the face of mystery. The principle of ecology, if we will take it to heart, should keep us aware that our lives depend upon other lives and upon processes and energies in an interlocking system that, though we can destroy it, we can neither fully understand nor fully control. And our great dangerousness is that, locked in our selfish and myopic economics, we have been willing to change or destroy far beyond our power to understand. We are not humble enough or reverent enough.

Wendell Berry, *A Continuous Harmony, Essays Cultural and Agricultural* (New York: Harcourt Brace Jovanovich, 1972), pp. 80–85.

THE PEACE OF WILD THINGS

Wendell Berry

> When despair for the world grows in me
> and I wake in the night at the least sound

in fear of what my life and my children's lives may be,
I go and lie down where the wood drake
rests in his beauty on the water,
   and the great heron feeds.
I come into the peace of wild things
who do not tax their lives with forethought
of grief. I come into the presence of still water.
And I feel above me the day-blind stars
waiting with their light. For a time
I rest in the grace of the world, and am free.

The Collected Poems of Wendell Berry (Berkeley: North Point Press, 1984), p. 69.

New Values

Tom Bender

One of the many new periodicals promoting ecological simplicity during the 1970s was *Rain*, a magazine published in Portland, Oregon. Tom Bender, then an editor of *Rain*, wrote a lengthy essay in 1975 in which he reflected upon the meaning and rewards of a life devoted to ecological simplicity. Unlike Wendell Berry, however, his perspective is not rooted in agrarianism but rather in the everyday reality of suburban and urban life. His comprehensive essay touches upon virtually every rationale for ecological simplicity. Bender is currently an architect, living with his family along the Oregon coast.

There is no longer any doubt that our age of affluence based upon depletion of our planet's non-renewable energy and material resources is at an end and that MAJOR changes must be made in every aspect of our lives. We have allowed our populations to rise above what can be sustained without massive injections of rapidly depleting fossil fuel energy. Our country, in particular, has used up much of its own non-renewable material and energy resources and has come to depend upon consumption of the resources of other countries at a prodigious rate. Americans currently consume more than a third of the entire world's production of oil, and must import nearly 100% of many "essential" materials. Such patterns and levels of resource use cannot be continued either physically or politically, as other countries require more of their own resources and realize the absurdity of allowing us to consume their irreplaceable source of wealth merely to support an unnecessarily wasteful way of life. . . .

Our ability to develop a culture that can endure beyond our own lifetimes depends upon our coming to a new understanding of what is desirable for a harmonious and sustainable relationship with the systems that support our lives.

STEWARDSHIP, NOT PROGRESS

We have valued progress highly during our period of growth, as we have known that changes were unavoidable, and have needed an orientation that could help us adjust to and assist those changes. Progress assumes that the future will be better—which at the same time creates dissatisfaction with the present and tells us that NOW isn't as good. As a result, we are prompted to work harder to get what the future can offer, but lose our ability to enjoy what we now have. We also lose a sense that we ourselves, and what we have and do, are really good. We expect the rewards from what we do to come in the future rather than from the doing of it, and then become frustrated when most of those dreams cannot be attained. The "future" always continues to lie in the future. Progress is really a euphemism for always believing that what we value and seek today is better than what we valued before or what anyone else has ever sought or valued.

Stewardship, in contrast to progress, elicits attentive care and concern for the present—for understanding its nature and for best developing, nurturing and protecting its possibilities. Such actions unavoidably insure the best possible future as a byproduct of enjoyment and satisfaction from the present. . . .

AUSTERITY, NOT AFFLUENCE

Austerity is a principle which does not exclude all enjoyments, only those which are distracting from or destructive of personal relatedness. It is part of a more embracing virtue—friendship or joyfulness, and arises from an awareness that things or tools can destroy rather than enhance grace and joyfulness in personal relations. Affluence, in contrast, does not discriminate between what is wise and useful and what is merely possible. Affluence

A family copes with the gas shortage during 1974.

demands impossible endless growth, both because those things necessary for good relations are foregone for unnecessary things, and because many of those unnecessary things act to damage or destroy the good relations that we desire. . . .

BETTERMENT, NOT BIGGERMENT

Quantitative things, because of the ease of their measurement by external means, have been sought and relied upon as measures of success by our institutionally centered society. We are learning the hard lesson that quantity is no substitute for quality in our lives, that qualitative benefits cannot be externalized, and that a society that wishes betterness rather than moreness, and betterment rather than biggerment, must be organized to allow individuals the scope for determining and obtaining what they themselves consider better.

ENOUGHNESS, NOT MORENESS

We are learning that too much of a good thing is not a good thing, and that we would often be wiser to determine what is enough rather than how much is possible. When we can learn to be satisfied with the least necessary for happiness, we can lighten our demands on ourselves, on others, and on our surroundings, and make new things possible with what we have released from our covetousness. Our consumption ethic has prevented our thinking about enoughness, in part out of fear of unemployment problems arising from reducing our demands. Employment problems are only a result of choices of energy- vs. employment-intensive production processes and arbitrary choices we have made in the patterns of distributing the wealth of our society—both of which can be modified with little fundamental difficulty. Our major goal is to be happy with the least effort—with the least production of goods and services necessary and with the greatest opportunity to employ our time and skills for good rather than for survival. The fewer our wants, the greater our freedom from having to serve them.

WORK, NOT LEISURE

We have considered work to be a negative thing—that the sole function of work was to produce goods and services. To workers it has meant a loss of leisure, something to be minimized while still maintaining income. To the employer it is simply a cost of production, also to be minimized. Yet work is one of our greatest opportunities to contribute to the well-being of ourselves and our community—opportunity to utilize and develop our skills and abilities, opportunity to overcome our self-centeredness through joining with other people in common tasks, as well as opportunity to produce the goods and services needed for a dignified existence. Properly appreciated, work stands in the same relation to the higher faculties as food to the physical body. It nourishes and enlivens us and urges us to produce the best of which we are capable. It furnishes a medium through which to display our scale of values and develop our personality. To strive for leisure rather than work denies that work and leisure are complementary parts of the same living process and cannot be separated without destroying the joy of work and the bliss of leisure.

From this viewpoint, work is something essential to our well-being—something that can and ought to be meaningful, the organization of which in ways which are boring, stultifying or nerve-wracking is criminal. Opportunity for meaningful work rather than merely a share of the products of work, needs to be assured to every member of our society.

TOOLS, NOT MACHINES

We need to regain the ability to distinguish between technologies which aid and those which destroy our ability to seek the ends we wish. We need to discriminate between what are tools and what are machines. The choice of tools and what they do is at root both philosophical and spiritual. Every technology has its own nature and its own effect upon the world around it. Each arises from, and supports a particular view of our world.

A tool channels work and experiences through our facilities, allowing us to bring to bear upon them the full play of our nature—to learn from the work and to infuse it with our purposes and our dreams—and to give the fullest possible opportunity for our physical and mental faculties to experience, experiment and grow. A tool focuses work so that our energy and attention can be fully employed to our chosen purposes.

Our culture has valued devices that are labor saving and require little skill to operate. By those very measures, such devices are machines which rob us of our opportunity to act, experience and grow, and to fill our surroundings with the measure of our growth. We need skill-developing rather than labor-saving technologies.

INDEPENDENCE AND INTERDEPENDENCE

Many of the basic values upon which we have tried to build our society have become weakened through the ways they have been interpreted and face the prospect of further weakening through the pressures inevitable in adapting our society to new conditions.

Independence cannot be maintained when we are dependent upon other people or other nations—as long as we are forced to work on others' terms, to consume certain kinds of education to qualify for work, to use automobiles because that kind of transportation system has made even walking dangerous or physically impossible; as long as we are dependent upon fossil fuels to operate our society; as long as we must depend upon resources other than ourselves and the renewable resources of our surroundings, we cannot be independent.

We have also discovered through the power that our wealth has given us that slavery is as enslaving for the master as for the mastered—by becoming DEPENDENT upon the abilities of the slave, whether the slave is a human, animal, institutional or energy slave, we forego developing our own capabilities to be self-sufficient.

In another sense total independence is never possible, for that means total power, which inevitably collides with the wants and power of others. We are also, in reality, dependent upon the natural systems that convert the sun's energy into the food upon which we live. Totally independent individuals may have freedom from organization, but have no special value, no special mission, no special contribution and no necessary role in the energy flows and relationships of a society that permits greater things than are attainable as individuals. Such freedom results in little respect or value for the individual. Our success and survival on this planet also must recognize the total interdependence that exists between us and the health, disease, wealth, happiness, anger and frustrations of the others with whom we share this planet.

Two things are important. We must have the CAPABILITY for self-sufficiency—in order to have options, alternatives, self-confidence and knowledge of how things are related and thereby be able to lighten our demands on others. We must also have the ABILITY to contribute our special skills to the development of interdependent relationships which can benefit all. Trade, as giving of surplus, of what is not necessary, is the only viable resolution of the interrelated problems of independence, interdependence and slavery.

As we begin to actually make changes, the things we come to find of value are almost the opposite of what we value today. What contributes to stability and soundness and to valued relationships is exactly what prevents and hinders disruption, change and growth—which have been both necessary and desired under the conditions we have until recently experienced. Meaningful work, localized economies, diversity and richness of employment and community, and controllable, clever, human-centered technologies will become important. Common sense and intuition will be recognized again as more valuable than armies of computers. Community will become more important than individualism and our present actions seen as unsupportably selfish. Strong roots and relationships will become more important than mobility. Buildings and equipment with long life and lower total costs rather than low initial costs will be favored. Cooperation will be seen as more positive, wiser and less costly than competition. Skill-using will replace labor saving. We will soon discover that all our present sciences and principles are not unbiased, but are built upon values promoting growth rather than stability, and will need to be modified when quantitative growth is no longer possible.

Tom Bender, *Sharing Smaller Pies* (Portland, n.p., 1975), pp. 1, 12–20.

THROWING AWAY THE MAIL

Wendell Berry

> Nothing is simple,
> not even simplification.
> Thus, throwing away
> the mail, I exchange
> the complexity of duty
> for the simplicity of guilt.

The Collected Poems of Wendell Berry (Berkeley: North Point Press, 1984), p. 215.

Why Voluntary Simplicity Won't Destroy Us
Karl Hess

The growing appeal for simpler living during the 1970s provoked many derisive and many sensible criticisms. Perhaps the most frequent objection was that, if everyone reduced their consumptive habits, the economy would be devastated, unemployment would soar, and social misery would be rampant. Karl Hess addressed this and other objections in the following essay. In his own career Hess has revealed how the appeal of simple living cuts across traditional political and ideological lines. After serving as a speechwriter for Barry Goldwater and Gerald Ford, Hess grew increasingly disenchanted with the compromises and hypocrisies of political conservatism. His own conservatism is rooted in the libertarian-decentralist tradition, and he became an outspoken critic of the Vietnam War as well as the growth of big government. During the 1970s Hess promoted a revival of local self-reliance through mutual aid, appropriate technology, and simpler habits of living.

What will happen to the economy if everyone starts moving toward a life of greater simplicity and increased self-reliance?

Bankers, politicians, businessmen, economists, statesmen, and a number of sensible and common-sense people think it will go straight to hell. We live in a complex world, they say. We live in a technological age, they say. We live in a world of rising expectations, they say. We must expand our economy if for no other reason than to help the poor, here and abroad, they say. It is only natural that we grow more complex, they say. It's like a law of nature, they say. You can't go backwards, they say. If it weren't for elaborate and elaborated demand, they say, there wouldn't be enough jobs to go around, and unemployment already is a ghastly, growing curse upon us.

Fortunately, there isn't a significant word of truth in anything they say. What they say should be taken seriously only if one can imagine a growing change in the way we live without a change in anything else. Unlikely, eh?

Let's start with jobs. The common argument about jobs is that they can be "created" only with the investments of going business, usually the biggest. Wrong. Jobs are created, also, whenever anyone enters into a fairly regular agreement with anyone else to provide goods or services in return for something of value.

Such jobs, incidentally, also create wealth—i.e., new things of value—rather than just swapping dollars as our Big Economy does.

The Big Economy is based upon the exchange of dollar bills or other instruments, upon credit. The dollars we exchange don't represent real wealth. They are not tokens of actual production or minerals or food. They are simply the issued paper of the central bank of the nation state—the Federal Reserve System.

One result of shifting the economy away from money that represents real production to dollars which are just government scrip has been the involvement of more and more of the economy in debt management rather than in production or the creation of value.

Big Business, for instance, has proven singularly un-innovative over the past several decades. Technology is developed in very small companies which are subsequently taken over by the big ones. The big ones deal not in bettered production and innovation but in acquisition, accumulation, hoarding on a massive scale. Banks finance their shenanigans along with other purely speculative things more than they finance genuinely new productive operations. And small businesses disappear into the abyss of this financial game playing. Actually, the more Big Business—the top two thousand corporations (out of several million) which account for somewhere around ninety percent of annual profits and hold about the same proportion of corporate wealth—destroys small business, the fewer jobs there are. The growth of the economy along its present lines does not mean more jobs except in the service industries, where jobs increase apace with population.

One of the major impacts simpler lifestyles and more self-reliance would have on the job situation is in agriculture. Our farm population, as everyone knows, shrinks daily under the impact of urbanization and agribusiness. Also, we move toward monocultural growing, or single-crop domination over vast areas. And we increase the use of pesticides, fertilizers and—most significantly—water for irrigation as this process continues. (Having just finished a fairly major research on water supply in America, I can say flatly that unless our agriculture changes drastically we are going to run out of water supplies all across the country. We won't run out altogether, of course, but we will have to start making very hard choices about how we use what's left—and what's left that is fit to use!)

A more self-reliant lifestyle should mean that communities, towns, counties—all local areas—would take a hard look at growing more and more, and ideally most, of their food within fifty miles of the point of consumption. Such decentralized agriculture—returning to more traditional diversity of crops; relying more on small, probably organic farms (which, incidentally, can be more nutrition efficient than big, chemical farms)—would create more opportunities for people to work on the land. Jobs would spring up everywhere as farms began springing up everywhere.

But, they say, Americans have become too sophisticated to go back to working on farms. Hah! What do city dwellers almost universally thirst for every weekend? A plot of land to tend. What do corporate vice-presidents do when they are sober? Tend gardens. And what sort of idiot supposition is it to believe that people, poor and battered in the cities, would be worse off independent and farming in the countryside?

Also, in manufacturing, if quality were ever to be emphasized above quantity, jobs would fountain up in a geyser of new prosperity.

The productive bonus of a simplified lifestyle—rejecting the profusion of trivial products which now account for the major space in most stores, such as supermarkets—is that it would focus more creative energy on the design and production of superb, rather than trivial products. Fine tools, instead of junk furniture. Wonderful, energy-light cooking devices instead of TV dinners. Constant local entertainments instead of Charlie's Angels. And so forth. Anyone who cannot envision a life of quality as superior to a life of sheer quantity will, of course, not opt for a simplified lifestyle. So? It shouldn't stop you. Your being simple, self-reliant or free does not shackle someone else.

Only the person prepared to say that we do and should live in a regimented society can say that people cannot turn back their clocks. In a free society they can turn at will. They simply can't force anyone else to do it also, or to pay for it or its consequences.

As for the complexity of demand being the key to a healthy society, as some say it is (thirty-four brands of equally innocuous deodorant being thought of as the epitome of "freedom of choice"), the proper answer is that choice to be free is not simply choice of things. It also involves the choice not to have things. Again, only advocates of a regimented society can make arguments in which freedom of choice is the freedom to choose only what the established authority offers.

Incidentally, my own vision of a simpler life does not happen to be a wholly primitive life in the sense of foregoing knowledge, foregoing tools, etc. I share, rather, the vision of a young physicist who wrote of being able to imagine a time when he could join with friends to do high energy, theoretical research as a co-operative venture; then ride his horse from the lab to a shared community work activity where he and they could produce community wealth (food, objects, art, etc.); and then go to a cabin in the woods where he could read philosophy by the light of a kerosene lamp. He was simply envisioning a society in which the way people live would blend into their own landscapes, becoming a true and shared culture, rather than an imposed and onerous life of necessity. I do not, in other words, feel that human beings will ever be content, or should be content, with the ultimately simplified life of a grazing animal. Simplicity for humans is not the same as simplicity for antelopes. On the other hand the sheer and mad complexity-for-complexity's sake of today's social organizations, with their wildly

Committed to a more self-reliant way of living, a couple near Plainfield, Vermont, stand outside their wood-heated and windmill-powered home.

artificial and contrived hierarchies, is not a fit human environment either.

The argument that a simplified, self-reliant economy might hurt our ability to help the poor here and abroad is based on the unreal assumption that we are helping them anyway. Today, what we call help—which takes the form of molding the developing peoples in our image and creating economies designed to service our own unwieldy one—simply diverts the poor of the third world from the necessary tasks of securing their own agricultural base and developing, in the texture of their own cultures, appropriate technologies and social agreements. What we are doing now is summed up best by our help in such areas as the Sahel where, by introducing the people to the wonders of modern, monocultural agribusiness, we managed recently to produce the spectacle of thousands of people dying in the agonies of starvation while huge amounts of crops were shipped from the same area to export markets in Europe.

It's the same with the poor in our cities and rural areas. Land—basic agricultural opportunity—would serve as a better base for the liberation of most current ghetto "prisoners" than any amount of continued welfare.

When it comes to technology, should that be of any interest—and it is to me—then rest assured that a simplified and self-reliant lifestyle will not hurt it. At least it will not hurt the development of the sort of technology which is non-lethal, resource conserving or re-using, capable of being understood and operated by people generally (if they try) and not shielded by artificial complexity or secrecy, and also scaled so that it becomes a tool of the person or persons using it and not a user of them.

Such technology is developing quite nicely among people who already are moving toward simpler life-styles and more self-reliant communities. . . .

Self-reliance, of course, means that people, individually and in volitional associations, communities, etc., depend largely upon their own energies, initiatives, and resources for the major portions of their needs. It may also mean that they accommodate needs to what they have and can do. At any rate, it surely means turning away from the compartmentalized, production-line, corporate, mystified sort of production that dominates us today. It does not say anything, in particular, about the tools we will use except that we will use them in a different way, a way that gives priority to personal involvement and responsibility, with less room to hide in fancy legal exclusions, like corporate law, or in privileged sanctuaries like universities.

As people become self-reliant they become, necessarily, more and not less productive in terms of their own needs. They, among other things, remove themselves as a burden on anyone else! At the very least they do that. How, then, do they hurt the economy? The only economy they could hurt would be the economy of non-producers, of people who expect to get by without being self-reliant.

Simplicity, on the other hand, means getting away from the duplicative, accumulative, massified forms of social and production arrangements which, today, are showing every sign of economic bad health: top-heavy and featherbedded managements; large amounts of resources siphoned off to absentee and non-productive interests; heavy drains to political influence; soaring debts; stagnating techniques of production as well as an increasing bias against innovation; a marketing philosophy that has shifted almost entirely to the merchandising of style rather than substance and toward creating new markets for trivia and tinsel novelty instead of competitively satisfying larger, more serious markets. Simplifying your life in the sense of getting away from that cannot hurt a real economy; it instead helps build one, while the old, sick mass economy putrifies around us.

That economy has killed itself. Worrying about it is to worry about the incurable. It may last, as a terminal patient, for years. If it does, the real economic vitality in the world will be found among the self-reliant and creative. They may weep for the old, but they cannot save it. They must build something new. And I believe they are. I believe we are.

Karl Hess, "Why Voluntary Simplicity Won't Destroy Us," *Alternative Celebrations* (1976): pp. 41-3.

THE WANT OF PEACE

Wendell Berry

> All goes back to the earth,
> and so I do not desire
> pride of excess or power,
> but the contentment made
> by men who have had little:
> the fisherman's silence
> receiving the river's grace,
> the gardener's musing on rows.
>
> I lack the peace of simple things.
> I am never wholly in place.
> I find no peace or grace.
> We sell the world to buy fire,
> our way lighted by burning men,
> and that has bent my mind
> and made me think of darkness
> and wish for the dumb life of roots.

The Collected Poems of Wendell Berry (Berkeley: North Point Press, 1984), p. 68.

Questions and Answers

Arthur Gish

Like Karl Hess, Art Gish (b. 1939), a Church of the Brethren theologian, social activist and writer, sought to address some of the most frequent objections to simpler living. The following questions and answers appeared in his book *Beyond the Rat Race*, published in 1973.

Isn't simplicity an escape? Doesn't it show an unwillingness to deal with the complexities of our modern world? Isn't simplicity a camouflage for irresponsibility and escapism?

It is true that this can be an escape. It can be a search for personal salvation without social involvement. One can get so caught up in growing one's own food and making one's own clothes that one never gets around to making any other contributions.

One can also call it irresponsible to delay living the good, simple life until tomorrow. The way we live now helps shape the future. The means determine the ends. We do not solve our problems by contributing to them and perpetuating them. It is a sad fact that most of us spend a major portion of our lives helping perpetuate the things we say we oppose. In the name of responsibility we continue our support of the old society.

We need a new understanding of responsibility to society. In a society gone mad we need the witness of a new kind of life. In the midst of the absurd, someone must begin to live with meaning and purpose. Instead of symbols like shallow movie stars, power hungry politicians, and greedy capitalists, we need the witness of a Francis of Assisi to call us to sanity. . . .

Simplicity is a break in the chain of complexity. Life does not need to become increasingly more complex. Mark Twain is supposed to have said, "Civilization is a limitless multiplication of unnecessary necessaries." He was right, but it need not be that way. Bondage to necessity can be broken. Necessity is only another word to justify our slavery.

The increasing complexities are not making people happier, more loving, or closer to each other. Our lives become shallow and meaningless through the over-abundance of opportunities and stimulation. Our learning more and more about less and less will produce greater and greater ignorance unless we begin to step aside for a new perspective. We use complexity as an excuse for not reaching conclusions and answers. Lowering the level of complexity will mean raising the level of vitality.

The way to master complexity is not through increasing complexity, but by finding simplicity in the midst of complexity. We need a new simplicity to unite our fragmented world. Simplicity is not an escape from responsibility, but a discovery of a new and deeper responsibility.

Doesn't simplicity mean that those who are living simply are benefiting at the expense of those who work hard within the system?

This question should cause deep humility on the part of those who would simplify. Yes, we are dependent upon all our brothers and sisters, in or out of the system.

That, however, is no argument against simplicity. Rather it is a reminder of how interdependent all of us are. To the extent we recognize our interdependence and share all we have with others we will simplify and move away from individualistic living.

This does not mean that simplicity would be impossible without some persons remaining in the old way of life to support those who choose to live more simply. With a new style of interdependence and sharing, greed and hoarding would not be necessary. Those who live simply and are dependent upon the old system, have not yet developed alternatives to it. One should attempt to be independent of the old system, but never cut oneself off from those still living within it. Being supported by those inside the system should not be a basis for living simply.

Some also object that one is enjoying the benefits of society without contributing to it (e.g., paying taxes). While one may not earn enough to pay much taxes, that in no way means that one is making no contribution to society. What our society needs most is not more money, but the contribution of moral energies. One's contribution can be in non-monetary ways. Those who live simply can and should serve human needs.

Isn't simplicity poor stewardship of time and talent?

It can be, but it need not be. Our first task is to be faithful. If we are faithful our talents can be put to much better use than when we compromise to be effective. Through singleness of purpose we can be most free to respond with our talents to needs. . . .

Simplicity does not mean becoming lazy and lethargic, but focusing activity in a new direction. It does not mean poor stewardship of talents, but putting talents into more positive and creative endeavors. Giving up our affluence may not solve all the ills of society, but not giving it up may well prevent us from solving many of them. Simplicity means liberation of our talents.

Some say one should earn as much as possible to be able to give more to worthy causes. This argument is also fallacious. Commitment is what is most needed. Many jobs compromise if not destroy that commitment. If the commitment is there, the money will come. Jesus made it very clear that the widow who gave the only penny she had gave much more than those who gave out of their abundance. Our total commitment is needed more than all our compromises. . . .

Aren't possessions important to the development of personality? Doesn't ownership help develop a sense of self-direction and self-control and give the person a feeling of security, independence, and responsibility? Doesn't ownership help develop character?

It is interesting to note that most of the great people of history lived with extreme simplicity. Consider Jesus, Buddha, Confucius, Kagawa, Socrates, Francis of Assisi, Gandhi and many inventors and artists. The more mature a personality becomes, the less significance possessions have. The essence of personality is in relationship with people and is expressed through love, friendship and creativity.

Things are a part of life and our relation to them is important. They affect our perspective, values, and relationships with people. Not to delight in things is to be ungrateful for the world God has given to us. But we must get beyond the commodity fetish that attaches the ego of each person to the possession and hoarding of things. We must move on to a position of true Christian responsibility for the production, distribution and consumption of things. . . .

Isn't poverty oppressive? Why should anyone romanticize it?

. . . Yes, forced poverty is a dehumanizing condition. Life can be so hard that it crushes the spirit and destroys creativity and initiative. We may not use a critique of affluence as a rationale for keeping the poor in poverty. It is sheer hypocrisy for the rich to talk to the poor of the spiritual blessings of poverty. No attempt is being made here to romanticize the lower classes and the poor. Rather, we are trying to be realistic about how affluence is based on the oppression of the poor.

The real problem of the poor is not poverty, but oppression, degradation, exploitation, and enslavement. Thus they need not just more material goods, but liberation from economic slavery and the birth of a new vision. The real problem is not the unequal distribution of material goods, but the system that perpetuates it. . . .

Voluntary poverty does not include the problems of forced poverty. Forced poverty creates resentment, frustration, and a desire for things. It is dehumanizing and oppressive. Voluntary poverty is founded on liberation, not enslavement. Voluntary poverty is an expression of joy. . . .

The good life is possible. The objections need not stop us.

Arthur G. Gish, *Beyond the Rat Race* (Scottsdale, Pa.: Herald Press, 1973, pp. 74–77, 79–81).

HOW SIMPLE?
Richard Gregg

If simplicity of living is a valid principle, there is one important precaution and condition of its application. I can explain it best by something which Mahatma Gandhi said to me. We were talking about simple living and I said that it was easy for me to give up most things but that I had a greedy mind and wanted to keep my many books. He said, "Then don't give them up. As long as you derive inner help and comfort from anything, you should keep it. If you were to give it up in a mood of self-sacrifice or out of a stern sense of duty, you would continue to want it back, and that unsatisfied want would make trouble for you. Only give up a thing when you want some other condition so much that the thing no longer has any attraction for you, or when it seems to interfere with that which is more greatly desired."

Richard Gregg, *The Value of Voluntary Simplicity* (Wallingford, Pa.: Pendle Hill, 1936), pp. 27–28.

The Christian Simple Life
Vernard Eller

The energy and ecological crises of the early 1970s helped generate a revival of interest in Christian simplicity. Religious periodicals devoted entire issues to the subject, and a spate of books discussing pious simplicity appeared.

In *The Simple Life,* Vernard Eller (b. 1927), a Church of the Brethren clergyman and theology professor, questioned whether such externally-imposed simplicity would survive the crisis atmosphere of the day. He stressed that Christians should not have to be compelled to simplicity by secular emergencies; they should adopt it as a natural expression of their faith.

Today an urgent new rationale for simple living has obtruded upon us. Unless we voluntarily discipline our present runaway rate of consumption, we shortly will bring disaster upon the race either through the contamination of our environment, through the depletion of essential natural resources or, most likely, through both at once.

Now the best analysis of the facts seems clearly to indicate that our description of the threat is accurate. The logic of what must be done is unimpeachable. Every rational consideration would indicate that this matter of survival should constitute the one most immediate and compelling motivation for simple living that could be offered.

Logically it should; practically, I am convinced that it does not. Why it does not is a little hard to say: partly, perhaps, because fear is not a motive to which people respond very well. Partly because men never have done too well at sacrificing present pleasure for the sake of any future advantage—the actuality of the accessible present too much overweighs the elusive possibilities of a remote future. And partly because of a weird perversity that moves men to act contrary to their own best interests just to prove that they don't have to be compelled by logic.

A contemporary social experience most strongly impels me to this conclusion. Established even more scientifically and certainly than the prediction of environmental disease and death is the diagnosis that smoking is a direct cause of individual disease and death. The threat in this instance not only is more certain, more closely linked to present activity, and more immediate and selective in its repercussions than is the environmental threat, but, as well, the removal of the smoking threat could be accomplished with very much less of personal sacrifice—merely through a giving up of the foul stuff. And yet people simply will not quit smoking. Now this perversity is at least somewhat understandable (and worthy of sympathy) in those who are caught in an addiction that will power is just incompetent to break. But the chilling thing is to watch our youth—the age group that is most knowledgeable about the effects of smoking, that is not impelled by the force of already established addiction, and that we have touted as having the superior moral sensitivity that is the hope of saving our environment—how chilling it is to watch them keep total cigarette sales climbing even while older smokers are quitting the habit at a rate that otherwise would bring them downward.

And what makes the situation even more difficult regarding the environmental crisis is that very many people will need to act before the action has any effect on the problem at all. Thus, if I look around and do not see that anyone else is hurting himself to save the situation, I draw the natural conclusion that it would be stupid for me to give up my piece of the pie to no purpose at all.

But if commanding self-interest can't lead us even to give up a noisome weed, what possible chance is there that, before we are forced to do so, it will lead us voluntarily to cut back on our oh-so-enjoyable consumption of "the necessities of life"?

And yet, in regard to our secular society, there is no alternative but to keep preaching the not-too-effective gospel of self-interest and to hope beyond hope that somehow people will wake up and do something. Christians, however, don't have to be stuck in this boat. They have a rationale for the simple life that is infinitely superior to mere self-interest. And even more to the point, they have a gospel that goes far beyond man's saving himself by pulling at his own ecological bootstraps: it includes a God who can and will straighten out perversities and give men what it takes to discipline their rate of consumption, first of all as a way of getting themselves correctly positioned to enjoy this God, and then—as an entirely free bonus—as an effective way of meeting the environmental crisis as well.

And if this is the way it is with the Christian doctrine of the simple life, how tragic it would be if we were to trade it in for the ecological doctrine of sheer self-interest. And yet this is precisely what is happening in our churches. I would wager that from our pulpits there are to be heard ten appeals to ecological threat for every appeal to Christian simplicity. Yet the ecologists themselves should be the first to applaud the fact that Jesus asks for loyalty to himself even before loyalty to the environment; his demand is the best possible guarantee that the environment will get what it needs.

Vernard Eller, *The Simple Life: The Christian Stance Toward Possessions* (Grand Rapids: Eerdmans, 1973). pp. 35–38.

THE SHAKERTOWN PLEDGE (1973)

Recognizing that the earth and the fulness thereof is a gift from our gracious God, and that we are called to cherish, nurture, and provide loving stewardship for the earth's resources,

And recognizing that life itself is a gift, and a call to responsibility, joy, and celebration,

I make the following declarations:

1. I declare myself to be a world citizen.

2. I commit myself to lead an ecologically sound life.

3. I commit myself to lead a life of creative simplicity and to share my personal wealth with the world's poor.

4. I commit myself to join with others in reshaping institutions in order to bring about a more just global society in which each person has full access to the needed resources for their physical, emotional, intellectual, and spiritual growth.

5. I commit myself to occupational accountability, and in so doing I will seek to avoid the creation of products which cause harm to others.

6. I affirm the gift of my body, and commit myself to its proper nourishment and physical well-being.

7. I commit myself to examine continually my relations with others, and to attempt to relate honestly, morally, and lovingly to those around me.

8. I commit myself to personal renewal through prayer, meditation, and study.

9. I commit myself to responsible participation in a community of faith.

Shakertown Pledge Group, *The Shakertown Pledge*, Simple Living Network, West 44th and York Avenue South, Minneapolis, Minnesota 55410.

The Erosion of Confidence

Jimmy Carter

President Jimmy Carter repeatedly called on the nation to view the energy crisis as the "moral equivalent of war," requiring individual sacrifice and a commitment to simpler living and felt spirituality. But Carter was unable to translate his vision into effective public policies. In fact he had difficulty convincing a majority of the public that there truly was an energy crisis. By July 1979 Carter was so discouraged at his inability to forge a national consensus around the energy issue that he secluded himself for two weeks at Camp David. There he invited representatives from nearly every aspect of American life—religion, labor,

business, minorities, education, government—to discuss
with him the "crisis of the America spirit" that he saw
enervating the national will. The result of that much
publicized personal retreat was a dramatic speech to the
nation from which the following selection was excerpted.

It was a unique address for a modern president to make.
Its tone was more that of a sermon, reminiscent of the
speeches of a John Winthrop, William Penn, Thomas
Jefferson, or Franklin Roosevelt. But Carter had concluded
that such a dose of old-fashioned candor and morality was
what the country needed to awaken it to the crisis. He
portrayed America as awash in a superficial materialism.
Yet he implied that this crisis of spirit was solely the result
of individual selfishness and secularism. He totally ignored
the fact that such social behavior was in large measure
promoted by an alluring consumer culture generated by
American's corporate economy.

But such a narrow diagnosis was not the reason why the
speech failed of its intended effect. Americans in 1979 were
not used to being so chastised by an elected official. Nor
were they ready to be weaned from their dependence on
the cult of more and more. In the end Carter failed to
communicate a sense of himself or of his social vision that
was sufficient to inspire assent or confidence among the
majority of Americans. His rejection of a limitless vision of
material happiness was too hard to swallow; postwar
Americans had become too committed to life in the fast
lane. Yet Carter, for all his defects as a political leader, did
express an eloquent moral vision reflecting his own ethical
and spiritual sensibilities.

It's clear that the true problems of our nation are much
deeper—deeper than gasoline lines or energy shortages. Deeper,
even, than inflation or recession. And I realize more than ever that
as President I need your help, so I decided to reach out and listen
to the voices of America. I invited to Camp David people from
every segment of our society: business and labor; teachers and
preachers; governors, mayors and private citizens.

And then I left Camp David to listen to other Americans. Men and women like you. It has been an extraordinary 10 days and I want to share with you what I heard. . . .

In a nation that was once proud of hard work, strong families, close-knit communities and our faith in God, too many of us now tend to worship self-indulgence and consumption. Human identity is no longer defined by what one does but by what one owns.

But we've discovered that owning things and consuming things does not satisfy our longing for meaning.

We have learned that piling up material goods cannot fill the emptiness of lives which have no confidence or purpose. The symptoms of this crisis of the American spirit are all around us. For the first time in the history of our country a majority of our people believe that the next five years will be worse than the past five years. Two-thirds of our people do not even vote. The productivity of American workers is actually dropping and the willingness of Americans to save for the future has fallen below that of all other people in the Western world. . . .

What can we do? First of all, we must face the truth and then we can change our course. We simply must have faith in each other. Faith in our ability to govern ourselves and faith in the future of this nation. Restoring that faith and that confidence to America is now the most important task we face.

It is a true challenge of this generation of Americans. One of the visitors to Camp David last week put it this way: We've got to stop crying and start sweating; stop talking and start walking; stop cursing and start praying. The strength we will need will not come from the White House but from every house in America.

We know the strength of America. We are strong. We can regain our unity. We can regain our confidence. We are the heirs of generations who survived threats much more powerful and awesome than those that challenge us now.

Our fathers and mothers were strong men and women who shaped the new society during the Great Depression, who fought world wars and who carved out a new charter of peace for the world. We ourselves are the same Americans who just ten years ago put a man on the moon. We are the generation that dedicated our society to the pursuit of human rights and equality.

And we are the generation that will win the war on the energy problem, and in that process rebuild the unity and confidence of America. We are at a turning point in our history. There are two paths to choose. One is the path I've warned about tonight—the path that leads to fragmentation and self-interest. Down that road lies a mistaken idea of freedom.

The right to grasp for ourselves some advantage over others. That path would be one of constant conflict between narrow interests ending in chaos and immobility. It is a certain route to failure.

All the traditions of our past, all the lessons of our heritage, all the promises of our future point to another path: the path of common purpose and the restoration of human values. That path leads to true freedom for our nation and ourselves. We can take the first steps down that path as we begin to solve our energy problem. Energy will be the immediate test of our ability to unite this nation.

And it can also be the standard around which we rally. On the battlefield of energy we can win for our nation a new confidence, and we can seize control again of our common destiny. . . .

We often think of conservation only in terms of sacrifice. In fact it is the most painless and immediate way of rebuilding our nation's strength. Every gallon of oil each one of us saves is a new form of production that gives us more freedom, more confidence, that much more control over our own lives so that solutions to our energy crisis can also help us to conquer the crisis of the spirit in our country. It can rekindle a sense of unity, our confidence in the future, and give our nation and all of us individually a new sense of purpose. . . .

Let us commit ourselves together to a rebirth of the American spirit. Working together with our common faith, we cannot fail.

Thank you and good night.

Jimmy Carter, "Energy Problems: The Erosion of Confidence," *Vital Speeches* XLV (15 August 1979): 642, 643.

Voluntary Simplicity

Duane Elgin

Though Jimmy Carter's attempt to generate a national commitment to simpler living failed, the ideal continued to inspire many Americans on an individual basis. During the late 1970s Duane Elgin, then a social analyst at the Stanford Research Institute, decided to learn more about the growing grassroots interest in voluntary simplicity as a way of life. To do so he and an associate, Arnold Mitchell, printed a questionnaire in *Co-Evolution Quarterly*, requesting readers to discuss their motives for and methods of simpler living. They were overwhelmed by the volume and seriousness of the responses. They heard from lawyers, teachers, social workers, students, government workers, firemen, carpenters, factory workers, retirees, and others from around the country, though most were from west of the Mississippi, where the bulk of *Co-Evolution Quarterly*'s subscribers reside. Most of the respondents were well-educated whites from affluent backgrounds. And most of them lived in suburbs or cities, not on farms or communes. The average length of time that respondents had been engaged in such voluntary simplicity was six years, thus attesting to the key role played by the energy and environmental crises in provoking interest in the phenomenon. These excerpts from the survey give a sense of the commitment and variety of those consciously trying to simplify their lives in contemporary America. Such actual "voices" provide the best testimony of its continuing satisfactions.

WHAT IS VOLUNTARY SIMPLICITY?

Voluntary simplicity has more to do with the state of mind than a person's physical surroundings and possessions.
(woman, twenty-three, single, small town, West)

As my spiritual growth expanded and developed, voluntary simplicity was a natural outgrowth. I came to realize the cost of material accumulation was too high and offered fewer and fewer real rewards, psychological and spiritual.
(man, twenty-six, single, small town, South)

Ecological consciousness is a corollary of human consciousness. If you do not respect the human rights of other people, you cannot respect the Earth. The desires for material simplicity and a human-scale environment are results of an ecological consciousness.
(man, twenty-six, single, small town, West)

Voluntary simplicity is not poverty, but searching for a new definition of quality—and buying only what is productively used.
(man, twenty-eight, married, rural, West)

We laugh that we are considered a "poverty" family as we consider our lives to be rich and full and completely rewarding—we are living in harmony with everything. I know for myself the source of "richness" or "poverty" comes from within me. . . .
(woman, forty-one, married, rural, West)

WHY CHOOSE VOLUNTARY SIMPLICITY?

I believe in the imminent need for the skills and resources I am developing now. I am not sure how it will come about, whether economic collapse, fuel exhaustion, or natural disaster, but whichever it is, I will need (and my family) all of whatever self-sufficiency I or we can develop.
(man, twenty-nine, rural, West)

I sincerely believe that voluntary simplicity is essential to the solution of global problems and environmental pollution, resource scarcity, socioeconomic inequities and existential/spiritual problems of alienation, anxiety, and lack of meaningful life-styles.
(man, thirty-two, married, suburb, South)

I have less and less to blame on other people. I am more self-reliant. I can both revel in the independence and be frustrated by my shortcomings—but I get to learn from my own mistakes. Each step is progress in independence; freedom is the goal.
(man, twenty-six, married, small town, East)

It was the injustice and not the lack of luxury during the Great Depression that disturbed me. I took up this way of life when I was seventeen. I remember choosing this simplicity—not poverty—because: 1) it seemed more just in the face of deprivation—better distribution of goods, 2) more honest—why take or have more than one needs? 3) much freer—why burden oneself with getting and caring for just "things" when time and energy could be spent in so many more interesting and higher pursuits? 4) but I wanted a simplicity that would include beauty

and creativity—art, music, literature, an aesthetic environment—
but simply.

(woman, sixty, married, suburb, West)

WHAT IS THE PATH TO VOLUNTARY SIMPLICITY?

Voluntary simplicity must evolve over a lifetime according to
the needs of an individual . . . the person must grow and be open to
new ideas—not jump on a bandwagon, but thoughtfully consider
ideas and see how they relate to themselves. . . .

(woman, twenty-one, single, small city, Midwest)

Voluntary simplicity began unfolding in my life as a process. It
was an inarticulate but seemingly sensible response to emerging
situations—and one response after another began to form a
pattern, which you identify as voluntary simplicity. Simplicity for
me was the result of a growing awareness plus a sense of social
responsibility.

(man, thirty-one, married, small town, West)

To me, voluntary simplicity as a life-style is not something you
take up in one moment, but occurs over a period of time due to:
1) consciousness raising; 2) peer group support; 3) background;
4) inner-growth interest, and many other factors—my whole-
hearted commitment to a certain spiritual path finds outer expression in a simple, gentle, humane life-style.

(woman, twenty-eight, single, suburb, West)

I quit my forty-hour-a-week slavery and got a twenty-hour-a-
week job that I love (working in a library). I started learning how to
grow food in the city and make compost. I became conscious of
what I was eating and how I was spending my money. I started
learning to sew, mend, and shop secondhand, and I've stopped
eating meat.

(woman, twenty-three, married, small city, West)

I recycle cans, bottles, and newspapers. We're very careful with
water. . . . I buy used and handmade things as much as
possible. . . . We've always been frugal in the way we f   ur
house. We've never bought on time, which means we

things. We wear other people's hand-me-downs and we buy used furniture when possible. . . . A large percentage of our spending goes for classes (music, dance, postgraduate courses for my credential), therapy, est, and other human potential experiences.

(woman, forty-seven, married, big city, west)

The greatest satisfaction derives from increasingly seeing the truth of one of the tenets of simplicity—my needs are always met, although my desires take a beating. . . . I begin to see that my satisfactions and dissatisfactions actually arise more from my attitude than circumstances. This for me is one of the most important aspects of voluntary simplicity . . . the state of consciousness associated with it.

(woman, thirty-two, single, city, midwest)

My life is less cluttered with "things" that control and befuddle me. Dissatisfactions? Only that it's sometimes the harder way to do something . . . I can't rely on fast food, fast service, fast buying. Everything takes longer—cooking, buying, fixing. But it's worth it—most times.

(woman, twenty-seven, married, rural)

A most satisfying life in that we have a very close family relationship (our children are grown). We see that the children have developed values which are simple and allow for coping flexibly with the changing world. Using our own ideas and hands to make our way in both professions and homelife is an exhilarating (and sometimes tiring) way to live.

(woman, forty-seven, married, suburb, west)

Duane Elgin, *Voluntary Simplicity: Toward a Way of Life That is Outwardly Simple, Inwardly Rich* (New York: Morrow, 1981), pp. 49, 52, 53, 58, 59, 82.

Epilogue

W ith the benefit of hindsight, we now know that Jimmy Carter as well as many other interpreters of the public mood during the 1970s greatly misread the willingness of Americans to end their addiction to the hedonistic imperatives of the consumer culture. One of the clearest messages of Ronald Reagan's victories in 1980 and again in 1984 was that the simple life had by no means driven the sumptuous life from the field of American aspirations. Throughout the 1970s Reagan steadfastly rejected the idea that the United States had entered an age of limits. Carter, he claimed, "mistook the malaise among his own advisers, and in the Washington liberal establishment in general, for a malady afflicting the nation as a whole." In his acceptance speech at the Republican convention in 1980, he stressed that economic expansion, not retrenchment and conservation, would be the theme of his Presidency.

Reagan lived up to his promise. With the waning of the energy crisis and the recovery of the economy, conspicuous materialism was suddenly in vogue again. A few months after the inauguration, *U. S. News and World Report* surveyed social life in a dozen major cities and announced that the old "less-is-more, down-with-materialism atmosphere that achieved a high art patina during the Carter years has been brushed aside by the new ruling class. A flaunt-it-if-you-have-it style is rippling in concentric circles across the land." A prominent sociologist, Amitai Etzioni, likewise reported: "We're beginning to see a turn from deliberate simplicity to a more elaborate lifestyle." Gucci quickly replaced L. L. Bean as the clothier of choice at the White House, and during the 1980s the ecological conscience has indeed yielded center stage to the entrepreneurial spirit. As publisher Malcolm Forbes recently exclaimed, "Capitalism is back in now." Where a decade ago the journalistic emphasis was on the popularity of organic gardening, VW Rabbits, solar energy, recycling, and cooperatives, the attention in recent years has focused on cuisinarts, Perrier, Hot Tubs, and BMWs.

At the end of 1984 *Newsweek* printed a special issue in which it declared 1984 to have been the "Year of the Yuppie." On the basis of interviews with about a dozen people, the editors asserted that a fundamental transformation was occurring in American values. This practice of announcing a social revolution on the basis of a few examples has been a regrettable tendency in American journalism for years. As early as the 1830s the perceptive French visitor Alexis de Tocqueville noted that American journalists tended to leap from the individual to the universal in one sentence. Yet such trendy journalism does garner attention and influence behavior.

Yuppie, of course, stands for young, upwardly-mobile, urban professional. *Newsweek's* cover story reported that the Yuppie philosophy of self-absorbed materialism and careerism had captured the imagination of the members of the "baby-boom generation." Aging hippies and former social activists of the 1960s who had earlier embraced the counter culture were now eagerly embracing the consumer culture. *Newsweek* and other journalistic accounts contend that Yuppies are convinced that an ever-increasing supply of money is the key to the good life. The managing editor of *Money* magazine, for instance, maintains that his survey research indicates that young adults are so preoccupied with money that it has "become the new sex." *Esquire's* editors reinforced this metaphor in a 1984 cover story entitled "Men and Their Money: The Passion of the Eighties." The feature opened by announcing that if "Freud were alive today, he wouldn't be writing about sex. He'd be writing about money." Indeed, this association between sex and money appeared in popular culture as well. The 1984 hit song "Material Girl," by the ironically named Madonna, included the chorus: "Don't you know that we are living in a material world, and I am a material girl." Later she adds: "They can beg and they can plead/But they can't see the light/cause the boy with the cold, hard cash is always Mr. Right."

And in this "material world" such traditional social priorities as marriage and children are often considered impediments. "Our marriages seem like mergers—our divorces like divestitures," explained one self-described Yuppie in *Newsweek*. Likewise, a female Yuppie (Yuppette?) gushed while fondling a bottle of imported wine, "I guess this is a substitute for children." Another person featured in *Newsweek* explained his recent divorce by pointing out that "my commitment to my job was greater than my commitment to the relationship. If it was a tossup between getting a deal done or coming home for supper, the deal got done." There is even a Yuppie religious orientation. *Newsweek* announced that the Yuppies had discovered "nothing less than a new plane of consciousness, a state of Transcendental Acquisition, in which the perfection of their possessions enables them to rise above the messy turmoil of their emotional lives."

Or so we are told. Such dramatic new social trends are the fodder of contemporary journalism. In their quest for eye-catching features, American newsweeklies have come to suffer from an excessive secretion of flimsy generalizations about American culture, and one should view their claims with much skepticism. Certainly there is some demographic and economic evidence to support the much-trumpeted shift in social values from the simplicity phenomenon of the 1970s to the Yuppie philosophy of the 1980s. And one can see such crass consumerism at work in many communities. Yet one suspects that the glossy accounts of such aggressive hedonism are more caricatures of social behavior than accurate portraits of contemporary American life. At least one hopes that is the case.

Likewise, reports of the death of simple living in the

Eighties are as exaggerated as those that proclaimed its triumph in the Seventies. Small is still beautiful; it's simply not chic anymore. Simplicity is not dead as an American dream or as an individual way of life. Though the ethic will never capture the sustained allegiance of the majority—at least it never has—it remains a guiding source of conduct for a significant number of Americans, as it has since colonial days. The simple life has always served as the nation's conscience, reminding us of what the pursuit of happiness should entail. Today it continues to represent a viable alternative to the consumer ethic and its pecuniary standards of value. Simple living, for all its difficulties, remains an animating path to a good life. It can be more than an anachronism, fad, or eccentricity. Simplicity in its essence demands neither an end to national economic growth nor a vow of abject poverty. It can be constructively practiced in cities and suburbs, townhouses and condominiums. As an ethic of self-conscious discrimination, its basic requirement is not a rural homestead or a hairshirt but a deliberate ordering of personal priorities so as to ensure that material desires do not smother or subvert "higher" activities. To those who still dream of a republic of virtue and a moral economy, the attractions of simplicity remain compelling, well beyond the capacity of a momentary shift in public mood or political fortunes to dislodge.

Throughout American history the simple life has displayed remarkable resilience. It will no doubt continue to do so. The Stanford Research Institute estimates that ten million Americans are today engaged in some form of simple living, determined to subordinate the material to the spiritual and ideal. In cities, suburbs, small towns, and farm communities, citizens are still consciously striving to make the good life mean more than mere goods. They engage in conscientious consumption, promote family nurture and the conservation of natural resources, seek greater self-reliance through home production and mutual aid, and share their abundance and their time with others less fortunate.

That such an ideal of simple living has survived at all in the face of the consumer culture's imperatives testifies to the ethic's intrinsic attraction. It can be a good life. True, as Thoreau recognized, simplicity appears utterly absurd to "those who find their encouragement and inspiration in precisely the present condition of things, and cherish it with the fondness and enthusiasm of lovers." Many Americans feel quite content with life in the fast lane, and they sneer at those who point out the dangers of such an existence. But not a few Americans continue to grow disenchanted with the hollow quest for more and more. A new study published by the Stanford Business School predicts that the 1990s will witness the "biggest wave of midcareer crises the nation has ever seen." Some overwrought Yuppies are already discovering that they cannot live by Brie alone, and they are flocking to therapists, counselors, and ministers. Stress management has become one of the nation's fastest growing industries.

It is in this context that the simple life retains its relevance even in the midst of renewed prosperity and the much ballyhooed appeal of the Yuppie way of life. Liberating oneself from the addiction of consumerism and careerism promotes an inner peace. Pressures are reduced and the pace of life returns to more reasonable levels. Simplifying one's life affords more opportunities for activities of intrinsic worth—family, faith, civic and social service, personal enlightenment. Simpler living also offers a more ecologically responsible way of living in today's complex, interdependent world.

The many voices, past and present, contained in this anthology demonstrate that the ideal of plain living and high thinking is part of our historical fabric, part of our common cultural soul, one of our most renewable and invigorating national resources. As Emerson once observed, "Life is a selection, no more." The enduring legacy of the simple life in American history is that we can all afford to select more wisely.

For, dear me, why abandon a belief
Merely because it ceases to be true.
Cling to it long enough, and not a doubt
It will turn true again, for so it goes.
Most of the change we see in life
Is due to truths being in and out of favor.

From Robert Frost, "The Black Cottage"

Courtesy of George Tice

The village of East Corinth, Vermont.

Select Bibliography

In addition to the sources from which selections were excerpted, the following selective bibliography is provided for those readers interested in learning more about the heritage of simple living.

Chapter One: Pious Simplicity

On the Puritan social ethic in America, see Richard L. Bushman, *From Puritan to Yankee: Character and the Social Order in Connecticut, 1690-1765* (New York: Norton, 1967); Stephen Foster, *Their Solitary Way: The Puritan Social Ethic in the First Century of Settlement in New England* (New Haven: Yale University Press, 1971); Philip J. Greven, *The Protestant Temperament: Patterns of Child-Rearing, Religious Experience, and the Self in Early America* (New York: New American Library, 1977); Robert S. Michaelson, "Change in the Puritan Concept of Calling or Vocation," *New England Quarterly* 26 (1953):315-36; Perry Miller, *Nature's Nation* (Cambridge, Mass.: Harvard University Press, 1967), pp. 14-49; Gary North, "The Puritan Experiment with Sumptuary Laws," *Freeman* 24 (June 1974):341-55; Darrett Rutman, *Winthrop's Boston: Portrait of a Puritan Town, 1630-1649* (Chapel Hill: University of North Carolina Press, 1965).

The literature on American Quakerism is also rich. The original writings of Woolman, Penn, and other Friends should be supplemented by Richard Bauman, *For the Reputation of Truth: Politics, Religion, and Conflict among the Pennsylvania Quakers, 1750-1800* (Baltimore: Johns Hopkins Press, 1971); Edward Beatty, *William Penn as Social Philosopher* (New York: Columbia University Press, 1939); Sydney James, *A People among Peoples: Quaker Benevolence in Eighteenth-Century America* (Cambridge, Mass.: Harvard University Press, 1963); Rufus Jones, *Quakerism and the Simple Life* (London: Headley Brothers, n.d.); Jack D. Marietta, "Wealth, War and Religion: The Perfecting of Quaker Asceticism, 1740-1783," *Church History* 43 (1974):230-41; Frederick B. Tolles, *Meeting House and Counting House: The Quaker Merchants of Colonial Philadelphia, 1682-1763* (New York: Norton, 1963).

Chapter Two: Pietistic Simplicity

There are many excellent studies of the various "plain sects." Some of the most perceptive include: Edward D. Andrews, *Work and Worship: The Economic Order of the Shakers* (Greenwich, Ct.: New York Graphic Society, 1974); Frederick Coad, *A History of the Brethren Movement* (Grand Rapids: Erdman's, 1968); Martha Denlinger, *Real People: Amish and Mennonites in*

Lancaster County (Scottdale, Pa.: Herald Press, 1975); Cornelius J. Dyck, *An Introduction to Mennonite History* (Scottdale, Pa.: Herald Press, 1967); Melvin Gingerich, *Mennonite Attire Through Four Centuries* (Breingsville, Pa.: The Pennsylvania German Society, 1970); John Hostetler, *Amish Society* (Baltimore: Johns Hopkins Press, 1964); F. L. Morse, *The Shakers and the World's People* (New York: Dodd, Mead, 1980); Mary L. Richmond, *Shaker Literature: A Bibliography* (Hanover, N.H.: University Press of New England, 1977); John Wenger, *The Mennonite Church in America* (Scottdale, Pa.: Herald Press, 1966); Robley E. Whitson, *The Shakers: Two Centuries of Spiritual Reflection* (New York: Paulist Press, 1983).

Chapter Three: Republican Simplicity

Some of the best studies of classical republican thought in early America include: Bernard Bailyn, *The Ideological Origins of the American Revolution* (Cambridge, Mass.: Harvard University Press, 1967); J. E. Crowley, *This Sheba Self: The Conceptualization of Economic Life in Eighteenth-Century America* (Baltimore: Johns Hopkins Press, 1974); Pauline Maier, *From Resistance to Revolution: Colonial Radicals and the Development of American Opposition to Britain, 1765-1776* (New York: Knopf, 1972); Drew McCoy, *The Elusive Republic: Political Economy in Jeffersonian America* (Chapel Hill: University of North Carolina Press, 1980); Edmund Morgan, "The Puritan Ethic and the American Revolution," *William and Mary Quarterly* 3rd. ser. 24 (1967):3-42; Robert Shalhope, "Toward a Republican Synthesis: The Emergence of an Understanding of Republicanism in American Historiography," *William and Mary Quarterly* 3rd ser. 29 (1972):49-80; Gordon S. Wood, *The Creation of the American Republic, 1776-1787* (Chapel Hill: University of North Carolina Press, 1969).

Those interested in learning more about individual Revolutionary figures should consult Pauline Maier, *The Old Revolutionaries: Political Lives in the Age of Samuel Adams* (New York: Knopf, 1980); John C. Miller, *Sam Adams: Pioneer of Propaganda* (Boston: Little, Brown, 1936); Peter Shaw, *The Character of John Adams* (Chapel Hill: University of North Carolina Press, 1976).

Chapter Four: Domestic Simplicity

Among the many excellent accounts of the "cult of domesticity" during the first half of the nineteenth century, see especially Ruth Bloch, "American Feminine Ideas in Transition," *Feminist Studies* 4 (1978):101-26; Nancy F. Cott, *The Bonds of Womanhood: "Woman's Sphere" in New England* (New Haven:

Yale University Press, 1977); Ann Douglas, *The Feminization of American Culture* (New York: Avon, 1977); Linda Kerber, *Women in the Republic: Intellect and Ideology in Revolutionary America* (Chapel Hill: University of North Carolina Press, 1980); Anne L. Kuhn, *The Mother's Role in Childhood Education: New England Concepts, 1830-1860* (New Haven: Yale University Press, 1947); Glenda Riley, "The Subtle Subversion: Changes in the Traditionalist Image of Women," *Historian* 22 (1970):210-17; Barbara Welter, "The Cult of True Womanhood: 1820-1860," *American Quarterly* 18 (1966):157-74.

Useful treatments of Andrew Jackson Downing's ideas are contained in Edward Halsey Foster, *The Civilized Wilderness: Backgrounds to American Romantic Literature, 1817-1860* (New York: Free Press, 1975), pp. 62-66, 90-99; Neil Harris, *The Artist in American Society: The Formative Years, 1790-1860* (New York: Braziller, 1966), pp. 208-16; John Ward, *Red, White and Blue: Men, Books, and Ideas in American Culture* (New York: Oxford University Press, 1969), pp. 170-81.

Chapter Five: Transcendental Simplicity

The best recent studies of Transcendentalism are Paul F. Boller, Jr., *American Transcendentalism, 1830-1860: An Intellectual Inquiry* (New York: G.P. Putnam's, 1974) and Anne Rose, *Transcendentalism as a Social Movement* (New Haven: Yale University Press, 1981). Two fine biographies of Emerson are Gay Wilson Allen, *Waldo Emerson: A Biography* (New York: Viking, 1981) and Ralph L. Rusk, *The Life of Ralph Waldo Emerson* (New York: Scribner's, 1949).

On Brook Farm see Georgiana Bruce Kirby, *Years of Experience, An Autobiographical Narrative* (Boston: G.P. Putnam's, 1887); John Van Der Zee Sears, *My Friends at Brook Farm* (New York: D. Fitzgerald, 1912); Lindsay Swift, *Brook Farm* (New York: Macmillan, 1900); Zoltan Haraszti, *The Idyll of Brook Farm* (Boston: The Public Library of Boston, 1937). The Fruitlands adventure is explored in Richard Francis, "Circumstances and Salvation: The Ideology of the Fruitlands Utopia," *American Quarterly* 25 (1973):202-34.

The best biographical studies of Thoreau remain Henry Seidel Canby, *Thoreau* (Boston: Houghton Mifflin, 1939) and Joseph Wood Krutch, *Henry David Thoreau* (New York: Sloane, 1948). Excellent interpretive essays of Thoreau are included in Walter Harding, ed., *Thoreau: A Century of Criticism* (Dallas: Southern Methodist University Press, 1954). On Thoreau's concept of simple living, see Leo Stoller, "Thoreau's Doctrine of Simplicity," *New England Quarterly* 29 (1956):443-61.

Chapter Six: Progressive Simplicity

For a summary analysis of the cult of simplicity during the Progressive era, see David E. Shi, *The Simple Life: Plain Living and High Thinking in American Culture* (New York: Oxford University Press, 1985), pp. 175-214. A provocative study of many of the themes relating to progressive simplicity is T. J. Jackson Lears, *No Place of Grace: Antimodernism and the Transformation of American Culture* (New York: Knopf, 1981).

Useful treatments of the Arts and Crafts movement include: Isabelle Anscombe and Charlotte Gere, *Arts and Crafts in Britain and America* (New York: Rizzoli, 1978); Robert Judson Clark, ed., *The Arts and Crafts in America, 1876-1916* (Princeton: Princeton University Press, 1972); Lionel Lambourne, *Utopian Craftsmen: The Arts and Crafts Movement from the Cotswalds to Chicago* (Salt Lake City: Peregrine Smith, 1980). Biographical studies of Gustav Stickley and his "Craftsman idea" are John C. Freeman, *The Forgotten Rebel: Gustav Stickley and His Craftsman Mission Furniture* (Watkins Glen, N.Y.: Century House, 1965) and Mary Ann Smith, *Gustav Stickley: The Craftsman* (Syracuse: Syracuse University Press, 1983).

The standard treatments of the back-to-nature phenomenon at the turn of the century are William L. Bowers, *The Country Life Movement in America, 1900-1920* (Port Washington, N.Y.: Kennikat, 1974); Roderick Nash, *Wilderness and the American Mind* (New Haven: Yale University Press, 1973), pp. 96-181; Peter Schmitt, *Back to Nature: The Arcadian Myth in Urban America* (New York: Oxford University Press, 1969). Edward Bok is profiled in David E. Shi, "Edward Bok and the Simple Life," *American Heritage* 36 (December 1984):100-09.

Chapter Seven: Simplicity Between the Wars

The best background study of *I'll Take My Stand* remains Virginia Rock, "The Meaning and Making of *I'll Take My Stand*," (Ph.D. diss., University of Minnesota, 1961). See also Robert Crunden, ed., *The Superfluous Men: Conservative Critics of American Culture, 1900-1945* (Austin: University of Texas Press, 1977) and *From Self to Society, 1919-1941* (Englewood Cliffs, N. J.: Prentice-Hall, 1972); Alexander Karanikas, *Tillers of a Myth: Southern Agrarians as Social and Literary Critics* (Madison: University of Wisconsin Press, 1969).

On Ralph Borsodi's life and career, see William E. Leverette, Jr. and David E. Shi, "Agrarianism for Commuters," *South Atlantic Quarterly* 79 (1980):204-18; William Issel, "Ralph Borsodi and the Agrarian Response to Urban America,"

Agricultural History 4 (1967):55-66. For additional information
concerning Herbert Agar and *Free America*, see William E.
Leverette. Jr. and David E. Shi, "Herbert Agar and *Free
America*: A Jeffersonian Alternative to the New Deal," *Journal
of American Studies* 16 (1982):189-206. The Catholic interest in
homesteading simplicity is discussed in Edward S. Shapiro,
"Catholic Agrarian Thought and the New Deal," *Catholic
Historical Review* 65 (1969):583-99. For a comprehensive study
of the New Deal homestead programs, see Paul Conkin,
Tomorrow a New World: The New Deal Community Program
(Ithaca, N.Y.: Cornell University Press, 1959). An interesting
evaluation of the homestead program is in Russell Lord and
Paul Johnstone, eds., *A Place on Earth: A Critical Appraisal of
Subsistence Homesteads* (Washington, D.C.: Government
Printing Office, 1942).

Chapter Eight: Simplicity and Abundance

Those interested in learning more about Lewis Mumford's life
and writings should consult Van Wyck Brooks, "Lewis
Mumford: American Prophet," *Harper's* 204 (June 1952):46-53;
Charles Glicksberg, "Lewis Mumford and the Organic
Synthesis," *Sewanee Review* 45 (1937):55-73.

The two most influential assessments of the "hippie"
phenomenon are Theodore Roszak, *The Making of a Counter
Culture: Reflections on the Technocratic Society and Its
Youthful Opposition* (Garden City, N. Y.: Doubleday, 1969) and
Charles Reich, *The Greening of America* (New York: Random
House, 1970). Informative studies of the communal movements
include: Marguerite Bouvard, *The Intentional Community
Movement: Building a New Moral World* (Port Washington,
N.Y.: Kennikat, 1975); Hugh Gardner, *The Children of
Prosperity: Thirteen Modern American Communes* (New York:
St. Martin's, 1978); Robert Houriet, *Getting Back Together*
(New York: Coward, McCann, and Geoghegan, 1971); Rosabeth
Moss Kanter, *Commitment and Community: Communes and
Utopias in Sociological Perspective* (Cambridge, Mass.: Harvard
University Press, 1972); Lawrence Veysey, *The Communal
Experience: Anarchist and Mystical Counter-Cultures in America*
(Chicago: University of Chicago Press, 1973); Benjamin Zablocki,
*Alienation and Charisma: A Study of Contemporary American
Communes* (New York: Free Press, 1980).

Chapter Nine: Ecological Simplicity

Excellent, though frequently conflicting, cultural analyses of the
1970s include: Peter N. Carroll, *It Seemed Like Nothing
Happened: The Tragedy and Promise of America in the 1970s*

(New York: Holt, Rinehart, 1983); Peter Clecak, *America's Quest for the Ideal Self: Dissent and Fulfillment in the 60s and 70s* (New York: Oxford University Press, 1983); Christopher Lasch, *The Culture of Narcissism: American Life in an Age of Diminishing Expectations* (New York: Norton, 1978); Theodore Roszak, *Where the Wasteland Ends* (New York: Doubleday, 1972); Daniel Yankelovitch, *New Rules: Searching for Self-Fulfillment in a World Turned Upside Down* (New York: Random House, 1981).

For a comprehensive analysis of the origins of the modern environmental consciousness, see Donald Fleming, "Roots of the New Conservation Movement," *Perspectives in American History* 6 (1972):7–94. Representative examples of the out-pouring of ecological studies during the 1970s include Wendell Berry, *The Unsettling of America: Culture and Agriculture* (San Francisco: Sierra Club Books, 1977); Barry Commoner, *The Closing Circle* (New York: Knopf, 1971); Warren Johnson, *Muddling Toward Frugality* (San Francsico: Sierra Club Books, 1977); William Ophuls, *Ecology and the Politics of Scarcity: Prologue to a Political Theory of the Steady State* (San Francisco: W. H. Freeman, 1977); Kirkpatrick Sale, *Human Scale* (New York: Coward, McCann, and Geoghegan, 1980).

Some of the many publications promoting a revival of Christian simplicity during the 1970s include: John Cooper, *Finding a Simpler Life* (Philadelphia: Pilgrim Press, 1974); Adam Finnerty, *No More Plastic Jesus: Global Justice and Christian Lifestyle* (Maryknoll, N.Y.: Orbis Books, 1977); Richard Foster, *The Freedom of Simplicity* (New York: Harper and Row, 1981); Andrew Greeley, *No Bigger than Necessary* (New York: New American Library, 1977); John Taylor, *Enough is Enough: A Biblical Call for Moderation in a Consumer-Oriented Society* (Minneapolis: Augsburg, 1977).

A number of articles appeared during the 1970s which both promoted and surveyed the growing interest in simpler habits of living. See Carter Henderson, "Living the Simple Life," *Human Resource Management* 16 (Fall 1977) and "The Frugality Phenomenon," *Bulletin of the Atomic Scientists* 34 (May 1978):24–27; Duane Elgin and Arnold Mitchell, "Voluntary Simplicity: Life-Style of the Future," *Futurist* 11 (1977):200–09; Laurance Rockefeller, "The Case for a Simpler Life-Style," *Reader's Digest* (February 1976):61–65.

Acknowledgments and
Permissions